ALFRED'S DYNASTY

ALFRED'S DYNASTY

HOW AN ANGLO-SAXON KING AND HIS FAMILY DEFEATED THE VIKINGS AND CREATED ENGLAND

W. B. BARTLETT

AMBERLEY

To Garth

My long-time friend and walking companion – with happy memories of exploring Portland with all its Viking connections

Illustrations, pp. 1 & 3: The Alfred Jewel, front and inscription. (*Dresses and Decorations of the Middle Ages*, Henry Shaw, 1843)

First published 2023

Amberley Publishing
The Hill, Stroud
Gloucestershire, GL5 4EP

www.amberley-books.com

British Library Cataloguing in Publication Data.
A catalogue record for this book is available from the British Library.

ISBN 978 1 3981 1041 0 (hardback)
ISBN 978 1 3981 1042 7 (ebook)

1 2 3 4 5 6 7 8 9 10

Typeset in 10.5pt on 13.5pt Sabon.
Typesetting by SJmagic DESIGN SERVICES, India.
Printed in the UK.

Contents

Acknowledgements

I would like to thank all those who have made this book possible. First of all, thanks to my research assistant (and more importantly my daughter) Deyna for her long-suffering patience and assistance in many vital tasks from its inception to its finalisation. Thank you, you have made my job much easier. Thanks also to Angela for viewing yet another fragmentary foundation of a Viking longhouse and saying with total conviction, 'Wow, that's amazing.' It has been fun travelling around the Viking world and seeing first-hand where some of the great events of Viking history took place. It has been an exciting journey so far from Norway, Denmark and Iceland, through Shetland, Lewis, Skye and Orkney and many places dotted across England. I look forward to many more visits to come.

Thanks also to Connor Stait and the team at Amberley for your professionalism and support throughout the process. It has been a pleasure working with you. Without you, none of this would be possible.

Wayne Bartlett
Shetland
June 2022

Author's Note

The *Anglo-Saxon Chronicles* should be considered as documents in the plural. Many historians take a different view but to my mind the different surviving versions have wide variations between them. Thinking of them in the plural acts as a reminder of these wide variations, even if there may have been one original common source. The abbreviation used throughout this book as *ASC* should be read as *Anglo-Saxon Chronicles* in the plural, not *Anglo-Saxon Chronicle* in the singular.

The Forgotten Dynasty

On 20 January 1936, George V, king of the United Kingdom and the Dominions and Emperor of India, died. His place was taken by his son and heir, who became Edward VIII (though he was never crowned as such). But there is something about this particular succession which reveals much about the way many perceive English and British history: Edward was not the eighth king of that name to rule England, only the eighth to do so since 1066. It is as if the Norman Conquest is some kind of Year Zero in English history. There is perhaps a broad recognition that for a few hundred years Britannia had formed a part of the Roman Empire, long before the Conquest, but it sometimes feels as if there was nothing much of note happening between the departure of the legions and the arrival of William the Conqueror in Pevensey Bay.

This is as far from the truth as it is possible to get. In the 650 years that elapsed between these two epochal events a new country was formed: England. It was in effect created in its current form by those who ruled it from the ninth century onwards. In fact, one constituent part of the ruling elite, the Angles, even gave their name to it.

There was one royal dynasty which more than any other was responsible for laying the foundations of modern England. This was the house of Wessex, which ruled in the ninth and tenth centuries. Theirs is a remarkable story, but the kings of this house are largely forgotten in the modern world. Not all of them perhaps – Alfred, the only English king to earn the epithet 'the Great', is certainly remembered, though possibly more for the doubtful anecdote about burning cakes in the Somerset Levels than his achievements. But other members of the dynasty have faded in the national memory. This is a pity given the scope of their collective achievements and the drama of their story. From around the year 800 – a hugely significant year as Charlemagne was crowned Holy Roman Emperor by Pope Leo III in Rome on Christmas Day – the dynasty gradually put in place the pieces which would eventually lead to the creation of England. Without them, the country that William conquered would have looked very different; indeed, it might not have been a lucrative prospect at all.

There was nothing predestined about this process. At the outset, the West Saxons were just one of a number of competing groups and their power was entirely regional, focused on a narrow strip of land around the Solent. Their territory gradually expanded, but it would be a long time before they were first among equals in what became England. In the centuries leading up to 800 the struggle for supremacy was mainly fought between Northumbria and Mercia, but that began to change with the arrival of the West Saxon king Ecgberht, who laid the foundations on which others like Alfred and Æthelstan later built.

To return to the original point, each of the three Anglo-Saxon kings called Edward have their own revealing stories. The first of them, known as 'Edward the Elder', was not king of what we know as England at all. He ruled over much of it, but not the northern lands of Northumbria.[1] The second, known as 'Edward the Martyr', was a teenager when he became king and was soon assassinated, possibly at the instigation of his stepmother, in a murderous succession dispute. The third, Edward 'the Confessor', spent his formative years in exile and only became king through a series of accidents that removed the ruling Anglo-Danish dynasty from the scene. The actions of this third Edward left a political vacuum that the Norman William could exploit.

For the first few hundred years, the Anglo-Saxons were busy fighting a host of enemies: Britons, Picts and Scots, not to mention each other. While that struggle persisted, around the year 800 a new enemy emerged. These were men from the North, who raided at first but later attempted to conquer. This foe proved to be the most dangerous of all, threatening to suffocate England at birth or perhaps even strangle it in the womb. Yet, in a twist of fate, this dangerous enemy would also play its part in the creation of England.

Many extraordinary men and women have a role in this tale. Kings, queens, nuns, monks, bishops, warriors and statesmen are all drawn into a story of colourful and dramatic events, with battles and assassinations, political posturing, plotting and manoeuvring, and major religious reforms. These episodes, and the people within them, helped shape England in a remarkable period which has almost been forgotten.

It deserves to be recalled. It is among the most significant epochs in English history, when a country was forged by possibly the greatest dynasty to ever hold the throne. Before them, all that existed was a patchwork of competing small kingdoms; when they were gone, they left behind a country that would play a major role in the history of not just Europe but the world. This is the story of that amazing transformation, and of the men and women who made it happen in the face of some of the most challenging conditions imaginable.

1

Beginnings

A dream came to me at deep midnight when humankind kept
their beds – the dream of dreams!
'The Dream of the Rood', Anglo-Saxon poem

The Coming of the 'English'

In the year 731, one of the most influential works of British history
was written. Its author, the Jarrow monk Bede – the 'Father of English
History' – entitled his great opus *A History of the English Church and
People*. Yet whilst he could write of an English people (the *Angelcynn* as
they were known in Old English), he could not yet write of one unified
English nation. In Bede's time what we might call the territory of the
English was divided into a number of smaller kingdoms. Bede's own
country in the north-east was Northumbria, which was historically
split into two. Deira was centred on York, whilst further north, around
Bamburgh and Lindisfarne, was Bernicia; it was at Bamburgh that
King Ida first founded the Northumbrian kingdom, by tradition in
the year 547. In the Midlands was Mercia, which would soon assume
a leading role in England, taking up the mantle from Northumbria.
In the south was Wessex, the land of the West Saxons, whose moment
in the sun had not yet arrived. These were not the only territories;
the land of the English was often regarded as a heptarchy, a land of
seven kingdoms (though at times there were more, with the lands of
the Hwicce in the west Midlands and Lindsey around Lincolnshire in
addition to these seven).[1]

But this broad categorisation is a great oversimplification, made with the benefit of centuries of hindsight at a time when the early Anglo-Saxon kingdoms of England were receding into memory. Contemporary chroniclers talk suggestively of many 'kings' being killed in battles fought in those early centuries, and it is likely there were many small, independent sub-kingdoms around that were eventually swallowed up by more powerful neighbours over an extended period. But as far as the simplifying concept of the heptarchy was concerned, in addition to Northumbria, Mercia and Wessex there were East Anglia, Essex, Kent and Sussex. Over time some of these smaller kingdoms would be absorbed by a hungry neighbour; some, like Kent, would move from one sphere of influence to another and then back again. Whatever else can be said about this period, these were not years of stability. This process also reminds us that it took a long time to create England, and furthermore that major kingdoms like Mercia, Northumbria and Wessex were constantly evolving before that moment was reached.

Bede wrote of Britain as a fertile land, rich in grain and timber and blessed with good pasturage. There were many land and sea birds, and rivers and springs of fresh water flowed freely. Even vines were plentiful, and the diet of the inhabitants was marked by good-quality salmon and eels whilst there were also shellfish in abundance. As far as minerals were concerned, copper, iron, lead and silver were present in good quantities. The northerly latitude of the region, Bede noted, made for long summer days and equally long winter nights. According to him, Britain was then divided into four peoples: Picts, Scots, Britons and Anglo-Saxons. Each had their own language, but learned men from each group spoke Latin.[2] This land offered great opportunities but, fragmented as it was, its potential had not yet been fulfilled. The Anglo-Saxons, who by Bede's time had come to dominate affairs in much of England (though on the fringes others continued to exert significance influence), had cultural similarities with each other although they did not always (or even often) see eye to eye.[3]

The history of Anglo-Saxon England up to Bede's time is a subject of ongoing debate and speculation amongst historians. The evidence on which to base a convincing story is scant, though not absent. It was Bede himself who wrote up what became the stock account of a key event in the making of England. He recorded how a British king, Vortigern, invited two Anglo-Saxon warlords over to protect his people from the aggressive Picts and Scots who laid waste to large parts of the country after the departure of the Roman legions in or around the year 410.[4] These warlords, Hengist and Horsa, quickly bit the hand that fed them.

Seeing the inherent weakness of the British, who had lost their fighting spirit and had come to rely on Rome to protect them, they invited more people to join them from their continental homelands.

And so the Jutes arrived to settle the Isle of Wight and the land opposite on the English mainland as well as Kent. The Saxons meanwhile established themselves in Essex, Sussex and Wessex, and the Angles settled in East Anglia, Mercia and Northumbria. As to where they came from, based on what Bede tells us it would seem that the Saxons, naturally enough, came from the region of Old Saxony in Germany, the Angles somewhere to the north of them (probably Schleswig-Holstein on the borders of Germany and Denmark), and then, further up still, came the Jutes, probably from Jutland in Denmark (although they seem to have been closely connected to the Angles). Even in their lands of origin they were close neighbours and shared cultural influences, though no doubt they were fiercely independent when occasion demanded. It is also worth noting that some of the Viking raiders who would so seriously threaten England's survival centuries later came from this region. There is also evidence, dating back as far as the Byzantine writer Procopius (active in the sixth century), that Frisians from the region of the Lower Rhine on the North Sea seaboard also settled in England.[5] The latter were certainly active in England (based on grave finds from Kent in particular), but for whatever reason their impact was less permanent, or perhaps more hidden, than that of the Angles, Saxons and Jutes. It seems probable that Frisians arrived later than these original waves of interlopers.

If interlopers they were. For in recent times historians and archaeologists have cast doubt on the theory of a wave of violent Anglo-Saxon invasions. Instead, they argue that there was a process of much more peaceful integration. They claim that finds suggest largely mixed or strongly indigenous populations, continuity in farming practices and maintenance of Roman roads. None of these features would have been likely to survive a cataclysmic breakdown of indigenous society in accord with the picture painted by Bede. Rather it is argued that any takeover was cultural in nature, as Britons searching for a new identity after the departure of the Romans voluntarily adopted continental trends and fashions. With the evidence inconclusive, the jury is out. But there is at least room to cast a little doubt on the conventional presentation of an Anglo-Saxon conquest.[6]

Why these incursions took place is not fully clear, but there are hints of a range of driving issues. A popular one is the domino effect of barbarian migrations into Europe pushing peoples like the Angles and Saxons westwards. There may also have been other contributory issues, such as a growing population that was increasingly difficult to sustain combined with rising sea levels on the North Sea coast reducing arable land. Keeping in mind perceived weaknesses in the defences of Britannia (weaknesses which were perceivable long before the Romans left – Saxon raids are likely to have started as far back as the late third century), the new arrivals may have been tempted to look for settlements beyond their continental homelands.

Another important factor to consider is that evidence suggests Saxons were already settled in England even before the Romans left. That they were raiding many decades before this time is evidenced by the construction of a series of coastal defences (of which Portchester near Portsmouth provides a magnificent surviving example) known collectively as the Saxon Shore forts. But these people were not just raiders. Several German tribes were recruited into the Roman army and appear to have set up home in Britannia. There is particularly strong evidence of German settlement during these years in the south-east of England and the east Midlands. This evidence (primarily archaeological in nature) points to the early presence of Angles, Saxons and Jutes amongst others included under the broad heading of 'German' tribes. The fact that many of these sites were on or near the seaboard is strongly suggestive of maritime peoples settling in England.[7]

A word of caution is necessary concerning the term 'Saxon', which appears to have become a shorthand for any type of Teutonic people affecting Britannia in one way or another. That the Saxons were a prominent group is beyond doubt. Their presence in Britain is proved by surviving pottery with distinct styles that can be matched to examples found in Saxon homelands in continental Europe. Yet there are also strong suspicions that anyone of a Teutonic origin may have been described generically as 'Saxon', even if they were Angles, Jutes or something else. The term 'Saxon' is employed by some as a derogatory epithet for people of a certain ethnic origin: the modern Scottish/Gaelic *sassenach*, which has in some contexts a derogatory implication, is a corruption of 'Saxon'. But this negative perception should not be overplayed. Later on, prominent individuals in so-called 'Angle' regions of England would refer to themselves as Saxons and it is unlikely that they would do so if the term had universally negative connotations. Although in broad and simplistic terms the south of England was Saxon (with Jutes largely disappearing into this generic category) and the north Angle (including East Anglia, Mercia and Northumbria), such distinctions ultimately became redundant even to the Anglo-Saxons themselves.

What these peoples did have in common was, at the start, their gods and their language (though with the coming of Christianity a new god took the place of the previous pagan collective). In the case of the gods there was not just Woden – the chief deity and renowned as a god of battle – but also Frig, the goddess of fertility, and Tiw, the god of war, from whom Tuesday takes its name. Then there was Thunor (the Anglo-Saxon equivalent of Thor), whose angry hammer was said to beat the skies during storms. They left their mark not only on the English names of the days of the week but also on the landscape in place names such as Wednesbury, Tysoe and Thunderfield. There was even the goddess Eostre, whose name survives in one of the most important Christian festivals of the year.

The Anglo-Saxons shared militaristic traditions, as well. This led to the emergence of a caste of strong warlords to whom warriors owed their allegiance. In this tradition a leader was expected to venture everything for his men and they in return would gladly give up their lives to defend him.[8] Strong bonds of loyalty formed between a warlord and his men (a phenomenon replicated in Viking society), leading to the development of warbands, which were hard to control. Later, when the concept of a conventional king started to develop in English society, there were power struggles between would-be monarchs and lords who continued to expect the undivided fealty of their people. These were not nation states in the modern sense, and this was a very different world than ours. But without the contribution of later Anglo-Saxon kings, matters might have taken a very different course in England than they ultimately did.

During the first post-Roman incursions there were horrific massacres of the Britons, so Bede tells us, and the British people were pushed out to the fringes of fen, forest and fell or even across the sea to Armorica (Brittany). But then a hero emerged, a Romano-British man called Ambrosius Aurelianus, who for a time stemmed the tide and won a great victory at the Battle of Badon Hill, temporarily halting the Anglo-Saxon advance.[9] The sixth-century historian Gildas – an important source for Bede – also mentions Ambrosius and Badon, though credit for victory there was ascribed by later observers to another man whose name has stood the test of time rather better, a warlord named Arthur. Gildas notes that by his time the cities of the old Roman Britain were now largely deserted.[10]

Bede postulates that the Anglo-Saxon advance had been irresistible. The suggestion that the Anglo-Saxons had effectively conquered England through a brutal and prolonged campaign of attrition was long held to be an undisputed fact. A classic of early twentieth-century history writing, Albany Major's *Early Wars of Wessex* (1913), gave the following explanation for how one of the kingdoms of England became Anglo-Saxon:

> The record is one of steady advance of a united and determined people in the face of an equally united and steady enemy, in a war carried on from generation to generation almost without intermission, until the last trace of British resistance in the furthest west was overcome, long after the midland kingdom had ceased to be harassed by wars with the Welsh.[11]

Major's account, which is eloquent and compelling even if many of its details have been refuted over the years, can be applied to describe what happened (or at least what was perceived to have happened) across the English political landscape as a whole. Yet the reality is we can only make informed guesses at what really occurred in these early years of post-Roman Britain. And we're not only in the dark as to *what* happened, but also *when* most of the famous events took place.[12] Yet if we are prepared to follow broad clues, we can have some modest success. For example, Gildas, who wrote his diatribe *De Excidio et Conquestu Britanniae* ('On the Ruin and Conquest of Britain') in the early decades of the sixth century, told how the people of Britannia appealed without success for help from Aetius, ruler of Roman Gaul. This must have happened between AD 446 and 453, for that is when Aetius reigned. If we accept Gildas's account (and there is little reason not to), the former Romano-Britons had effectively been abandoned by this point, leaving the door ajar for further Anglo-Saxon incursions.

Gildas's writings are as much moralistic sermon as they are history, but he nevertheless sheds a little light on the state of Britain in the early sixth century. He is a man with a message, and the message appears to be that post-Roman Britain is in a state of moral decline and something bad is about to happen as a result. He bemoans the fact that 'Britain has kings but they are tyrants', characterising these rulers as collectively unjust and sexually promiscuous creatures who constantly perjure themselves by breaking the solemn oaths that they so easily take. Badon Hill, Gildas conceded, had stalled the barbarian advance that had threatened to overwhelm England. When the Roman legions left, Vortigern had foolishly invited 'the fierce and impious Saxons, a race hateful to both God and men, to repel the invasions of the northern nations'. This interpretation presents the Anglo-Saxons as mercenaries hired to resist raids by Picts and Scots but ultimately they had proved a bigger threat than those they were hired to vanquish.[13] Yet, much as Gildas laments the state of affairs, like some Old Testament prophet giving dreadful prognostications of the future, even he is forced to write about 'the peace which, by the will of God, has been granted her [England] in these our times'.[14] Though he describes waves of warfare during the fifth century, they were in the past by the time he was writing. He is less disturbed by the state of political affairs during his life and more perturbed by the moral decline he perceives to have emerged after years of peace, which he feared could expose his country to a renewed threat of barbarian invasion.

From Paganism to Christianity

When Bede wrote in the early decades of the eighth century, it was less than a hundred years since the lands of the English had become largely Christianised. In the early part of his work Bede records the victories of Christian Britons against pagan Anglo-Saxons in the years after the Romans departed. He clearly recognised that Christianity predated more recent efforts by missionaries like Augustine, who arrived in 597, though he did not trust the Britons' new-found religious convictions. He complained that these earlier Christians were vulnerable to unorthodox beliefs such as the Pelagian heresy, which argued that men and women could find salvation by their own efforts without the help of God. Pope Gregory I despatched a delegation under Augustine to Kent and established (or, more accurately, re-established) the Christian religion in England. In fact, the conversion (or re-conversion) process was a pincer movement. Long before Augustine arrived, Celtic missionaries from Ireland had moved into Scotland and from there to the north of England. However, the Irish evangelical movement was quite different from the Roman Catholic one headed in the first instance by Augustine. The former was epitomised by individuality, in marked contrast to the latter with its strongly centralised operations and strict hierarchy of bishops to ensure orthodoxy and consistency.

In the north, the Angles established a kingdom called Bernicia. This was not without resistance from the Britons, led by men such as Urien of Rheged (in the Lake District) and Rhydderch of Strathclyde (in the region now straddling the western border between England and Scotland). Despite this resistance, in the reign of Æthelfrith (593–616), the Bernicians expanded at the expense of the indigenous inhabitants. During this period the Britons suffered a disastrous defeat at the hands of Æthelfrith's forces at Catterick. Aidan, king of Dalriada (a kingdom in the west of Scotland based on Dunadd in Argyll) was meanwhile defeated at 'Degsastan', the precise location of which is uncertain.[15] Bede seems to regard this battle, fought in 603, as a seminal event, from which the history of a unified kingdom of Deira and Bernicia – Northumbria – can be traced.[16] At Chester in around 615–16 Æthelfrith, the victor of Degsastan, crushed the men of Powys in a brutal victory and slaughtered many monks who were praying for a British triumph. Bede, no fan of 'Celtic' Christianity, considered this to be retribution for the monks' refusal to accept Roman practices as the only true way to Christ.

At this point there was no kingdom which consistently dominated England. At one stage, King Raedwald of East Anglia appeared to be the most influential man in the land; he is widely believed to be the leader immortalised for eternity in the amazing burial site at Sutton Hoo, and was described as *Bretwalda*, an appellation implying overlordship of the other kingdoms.[17] However, the actual power of the *Bretwalda* is a matter of debate. Some historians suggest that such a figure would have the power to extract tribute from other kingdoms in England, but evidence for early rulers does not always support this. In later years, however, those honoured as *Bretwalda* may have accreted more influence, and certainly some of the Northumbrian kings of the seventh century did appear to have a significant degree of 'real' as opposed to symbolic power. Quite why some of the powerful Mercian kings of the eighth century were not awarded the title when they also seemed to have some kind of superior role is not clear. It might simply reflect old-fashioned bias on the part of chroniclers.[18]

But then the battle for supremacy changed direction, with Mercia and Northumbria slugging it out. It was King Edwin of Northumbria who in effect succeeded Raedwald as the first amongst equals. This was ironic as Edwin had been forced into exile at Raedwald's court as a young man when his life was in danger back in Northumbria. While in the south he made contact with missionaries from the court of Kent (not many years after Augustine's mission there) and according to Bede was influenced by them so that when he later became king in Northumbria, he supported the Christian cause. He was also, like King Æthelberht in Kent, married to a Christian woman, and this may have played a part in his conversion.

Edwin's reign saw an unprecedented level of expansion. He captured the Isle of Man and Anglesey, and also defeated the West Saxons in battle – according to the *Anglo-Saxon Chronicles* (*ASC*), only Kent managed to evade his clutches.[19] This is probably an exaggeration, but overall it suggests that Edwin was a great power in relative terms. However, the Northumbrian king's reign was brutally cut short in 632 at the Battle of Hatfield when an army led by Cadwallon, ruler of the Welsh kingdom of Gwynedd, and Penda, the pagan leader of Mercia, decimated

Edwin's army, killing him and his son. The later Norman chronicler Henry of Huntingdon wrote of how 'the plain of Hethfeld [*sic*] reeked throughout with red streams of noble blood'.[20]

According to Bede, a reign of terror followed. As a Northumbrian, he was naturally biased against the enemies of his kingdom. However, reading his words over a millennium later, a genuine sense of horror comes through, and this may well have been a particularly brutal campaign even by the standards of the time. Penda, like many Anglo-Saxon rulers, traced his ancestry to the god Woden, and he would earn himself a terrifying reputation as a ferocious pagan warlord. As well as his invasion of Northumbria in alliance with the Christian Briton Cadwallon, Penda also overwhelmed East Anglia. In the meantime, two members of the dethroned royal family in Northumbria, Æthelfrith's sons Oswald and Oswiu, found sanctuary in the far north on the isle of Iona, home to Irish monks.[21]

Penda also had an interest in expanding in the south and forced the West Saxons to hand over territory in the Cotswolds. He worked closely with the Britons in Wales and forged a formidable alliance with Cadwallon. In fact, Bede reserved his greatest opprobrium for the latter, saying that the Christian Briton was worse than the pagan Mercian. To him, Cadwallon's actions bordered on the genocidal; he accused him of being 'set upon exterminating the entire English race in Britain, and spared neither women nor innocent children, putting them all to horrible deaths with ruthless savagery'. It sounds horrific, though Cadwallon's anti-English motivations are hard to reconcile with his alliance with the Mercian Penda. The name 'Penda' is an uncommon one, though, and members of his known family have names that are more Brythonic than Anglo-Saxon in character. Maybe Penda was not an Anglo-Saxon at all?

Oswald eventually picked up the shattered fragments of Northumbria left behind after Edwin's untimely death. He returned to Northumbria and killed Cadwallon in battle somewhere in the region of Hadrian's Wall. Northumbria was then expanded, especially in the north with the capture of Edinburgh, and the kingdom's borders were set as far as the banks of the Firth of Forth; indeed, in the subsequent reign of Oswiu even Stirling to the north was in Northumbrian hands. However, Oswald overstretched himself when he decided to launch a pre-emptive strike against the Welsh–Mercian alliance and on 5 August 643 he was killed in battle on the Welsh borders at a place known to the English as Maserfelth and to the Welsh as Cogwy. Tradition suggests that the site was called Oswald's Tree, the name changing over time to become Oswestry.[22]

Penda proved his viciousness by ordering that Oswald's hands and head be cut off and displayed on a stake, where they stayed for the next year. However, it is important to keep this brutality in perspective. Many centuries later, Christian kings would order that the bodies of prominent enemies be decapitated and quartered, and the various parts put on public display. Penda's 'crime' was to order the dismemberment of a future Christian saint. The pagan ruler of Mercia probably did not know (and maybe did not care) that by treating a Christian king in such a fashion he was establishing him as a martyr. Long into the future, when the political landscape of England looked very different, the martyr king would prove a rallying point for the English nation, his example a clarion call summoning England's warriors to fight to the death against a pagan enemy. Oswald's head was recovered and buried on Lindisfarne, but it was moved in 870, along with the body of St Cuthbert. Sharing a coffin, Oswald's head and Cuthbert's body ended up in Durham Cathedral, where they supposedly keep each other company to this day.

Penda seemed unstoppable. Another conflict broke out when Cenwalh of Wessex rejected the Mercian king's sister after marrying her, with the result that Penda displaced him, further spreading his influence. At the time of Penda's death, Mercia was still something of a patchwork. The territory he ruled was divided amongst several of his sons. But it was the foundation on which a strong and potentially dominant Mercia would be built over the next hundred years or so.

However, Mercian supremacy was not a given. In 655 or 656, Penda had gone to war once more with Northumbria, accompanied by Welshmen from Gwynedd and allies from East Anglia. He marched with confidence to the River Winwaed, generally believed to be in Yorkshire, on a fault-line between Northumbria and Mercia that was the site of regular battles between the two kingdoms. His army greatly outnumbered that of his opponent, the aforementioned Oswiu, who was faced by an alliance that included some of his own people. But then the men from Gwynedd deserted on the eve of battle. In the fight that followed, Oswiu emerged triumphant and Penda lost not only the war but his life as well. One modern historian remarked that Penda 'was the last of the fearsome pagan kind, and his death must mark the effective end of English paganism'.[23] The stock of the victor, meanwhile, soared. Oswiu united Northumbria, forced the Picts and Scots to the north onto the back foot, and went on the offensive to become overlord of Mercia. However, this was not a permanent state of affairs. Mercia launched a long, slow fightback, first under King Wulfhere (r. 659–675) and then his brother Æthelred (r. 675–704).

Oswiu made a major contribution to the establishment of Christianity in England. However, as churchmen from the south became acquainted with those coming down from the north, doctrinal differences as well as variations in approach created tension. There were debates around issues which seem abstract to the modern secular mind but were keenly felt then, not the least of which were disagreements about the correct date of Easter. It ultimately became clear that one strand needed to be chosen in preference to the other, a philosophical conflict which was finally arbitrated on in 664 at the Synod of Whitby (where Oswiu's kinswoman Hild would establish a highly influential religious foundation). Here, Oswiu opted for the Roman version of the faith at the expense of the Irish strand.

Oswiu's decision may have owed as much to pragmatism and a desire for status as it did to personal preference. The Northumbrian king had spent part of his youth on Iona with his older brother Oswald, and therefore might have been expected to opt for the Irish version of Christian practice, but he was also a man of vision. Much of Europe had already opted for the Roman approach, and by travelling down the same path Oswiu was considering the place of his kingdom in the wider world. There was also something compelling about the legacy of Rome, which seems to have had an impact on the thinking of so-called 'barbarian' peoples as they accrued military might and political power. More than one 'barbarian' leader chose to adopt Roman ways – the Franks copied many of their institutions and practices, as did others, arguably including the Anglo-Saxon kings in England.[24] They did not aspire to destroy Rome – rather they wished to develop a new version of it in their own lands. The legacy of Rome seemed to bestow legitimacy and a link to something long-established, glorious and stable.

From this perspective the adoption of Roman Catholicism in England made much political sense. It is instructive that after Augustine's forays into Kent in 597, Pope Gregory was soon after writing to Æthelberht as *rex anglorum*, reflecting a considerably heightened status. It seems possible that Oswiu was so entranced by the spell cast by Rome that he planned to travel there in his twilight years so that he could die in a holy place. He did not make it in the end, but more than one later Anglo-Saxon king did. The Anglo-Saxons were to achieve renown as staunch supporters of the papacy, and the English quarter in Rome was the destination for many pilgrims over the centuries. For those willing to look, glimpses of it can be seen today, such as the church known as Santo Spirito in Sassia.[25]

This was not the first intervention of Roman Catholicism in Northumbrian affairs. In the reign of Edwin, a papal delegation led by

Paulinus had achieved much success. However, the roots it put down were shallow. When Penda and Cadwallon came storming into Northumbria, Paulinus and the Christians with him had fled to Kent. When Oswald returned, he had brought with him a very different approach to the new religion. An enthusiastic Christian, he did much to strengthen the faith during his reign. He was integral to the conversion of King Cynegils of the West Saxons and sponsored him at his baptism. But he had been protected and brought up on Iona, and he never forgot the debt he owed those there. When he set up a monastery at Lindisfarne, which was to become a beacon in the north, he had asked Iona rather than Canterbury to provide its head, who took the form of the humble and inspirational Aidan. Now his brother and successor had opted to change tack as part of a wider trend across the kingdoms. It is notable that by 670 every reigning English king was a Christian.[26] When Theodore, the Byzantine/Greek archbishop of Canterbury, died twenty years later, he was the undisputed head of the church in England with fourteen bishops reporting to him, having also set up a school in which potential Anglo-Saxon priests could be educated. The religious infrastructure of the country was effectively a unified homogenous whole more than two hundred years before the political system caught up, making it an early and important factor in the birth of the nation.

It is difficult to understate the importance of this Christianisation in forging England. The authority of the Church brought a consolidating influence which helped to knit together the fabric of the emerging country. Things had changed forever, and this reality was brought home in 640 when Eorconberht of Kent in effect became the first English ruler to ban paganism in his kingdom.[27] When the Synod of Whitby met, there were still bumps in the road ahead; indeed, several kingdoms, including Sussex, accepted the new faith but subsequently rejected it for a time. Yet within half a century of Whitby, something extraordinary had happened. Rather than missionaries journeying to the Anglo-Saxon kingdoms to convert their people to Christianity, Anglo-Saxon missionaries were journeying to the continent to Christianise their pagan ancestors. Men such as Willibrord set out from great religious foundations like Ripon, set up by the strong and determined Wilfrid, who was a dominant figure in English Christianity at the close of the seventh century. They often gave up decades of their lives – and sometimes life itself – in their efforts.

Oswiu died in 671 and was succeeded by his son Ecgfrith. Ecgfrith was able to beat off a raid from Mercia early in his reign and in the main focused his attentions on the north rather than the south; border tensions between Picts, Scots, Britons from Strathclyde and the Northumbrians were a common feature of these turbulent years. However, there was about to be a change in direction. First Ecgfrith was defeated in 679 by Æthelred of Mercia, who took back lands in Lindsey that had been lost to Northumbria. Looking elsewhere for gains, Ecgfrith then launched an audacious raid across the sea into Meath in Ireland in 684. Such a foray suggests that Ecgfrith was a man of great ambition, but this was to be his undoing.

The following year he led his army north. This was, according to Bede, against the advice of his counsellors including Cuthbert, the bishop of Lindisfarne and a man destined to be Anglo-Saxon England's foremost saint. The preceding years had been challenging for Ecgfrith and he was determined to bring the troublesome Picts back into line. The Picts retreated before the Northumbrian king, but this was a ruse. Somewhere in the mountains, perhaps in Angus or Badenoch and Strathspey, and close to a lake at a place called Dun Nechtain (in Old English Nechtansmere), the Pictish trap was sprung. Ecgfrith's army was decimated and he himself was killed. The defeat marked the end of Northumbrian domination this far north, and perhaps it also signalled the end of any hopes of Northumbrian supremacy amongst the Anglo-Saxons. From this point on, their star was on the wane. By the ninth century, when the Vikings descended on England, Northumbria was ripe for the picking.

Despite their military losses, the artistic achievements of the Northumbrians, best evidenced by the magnificent illustrations in the *Lindisfarne Gospels*, were superb. The kingdom's reputation for learning was also outstanding. When Emperor Charlemagne (r. 768–814) was recruiting the best minds in Europe to serve at his court in Francia, top of the list of those who took up roles of importance was Alcuin, a renowned scholar from York.[28]

The Mercian Ascendancy

Perhaps it was thought that Penda's death would see a reverse in Mercian fortunes, but in reality the opposite proved to be the case. Penda's reign was a watershed moment. He fought a major battle on average once every three years when previously there had been one perhaps in every twenty years.[29] Before him the 'Mercians' were an abstract concept (and possibly not even that), a collection of loosely aligned interests rather than a people, but Penda cemented a stronger alliance. His successors would push the borders of Mercia further south, and one of them, Wulfhere, conquered Essex and attacked Hampshire, taking the Meon valley. This man stormed through the heart of Wessex and even captured the Isle of Wight, which was still defiantly pagan, in 661. Wessex did not reconquer it until 686, after which the West Saxon king, another man with a very Celtic name, Caedwalla, brutally imposed Christianity in a manner that presaged on a smaller scale Charlemagne's savage campaign against the pagan continental Saxons about a century later.

Mercia was aggressively expanding in a way that a nineteenth-century settler in America would appreciate – the very name 'Mercia' derives from *mierce*, frontier. The kingdom was at the centre of England, surrounded by potentially hostile polities: Northumbrians in the north, East Anglians in the east, West Saxons and Kentishmen to the south and Welsh to the west. Because of its position it also suffered economic disadvantages. It did not have direct access to coastal ports which oiled the wheels of commerce, nor was it blessed with natural resources. But it did have good internal lines of communication and an increasingly strong military machine, and it was these factors that lay behind Mercian expansion.[30]

At this stage England was a very fragmented region. A document known as the *Tribal Hidage*, prepared at an unknown date between the seventh and ninth centuries, lists thirty-five different kingdoms and sub-kingdoms ranging in size from Wessex with its 100,000 hides at one extreme to the lands of the Sweordada, Gifla, Hicca and Færpinga at the other with just 300 each. Of these smaller lands we know next to nothing. And even this underplays the divided nature of England at the time, for those lands listed in the *Tribal Hidage* do not include any in Northumbria.[31] The situation in Mercia in the early centuries of Anglo-Saxon settlement, with many small groupings independent of an overall overlord, may well represent the situation across England as a whole at the time.

In the early part of the Anglo-Saxon period the boundaries of the various kingdoms were in constant flux. This was true for all of them but perhaps for Mercia more than most. Its central position meant that it was well situated to expand in all directions, and some historians have even suggested that it may be helpful to think of a 'Central Mercia' and an 'Outer Mercia'. Central Mercia is the core, the seed from which the larger kingdom was propagated. This is a relatively constrained area in the Trent valley around Staffordshire and southern Derbyshire. Considerably larger, Outer Mercia encompassed all those other territories which were added over time, including much of the modern counties of Worcestershire, Herefordshire, Gloucestershire, Shropshire, Cheshire, Northamptonshire, Leicestershire and Lincolnshire. Present-day Oxfordshire and Berkshire were also in there, although the latter was subject to something of a tug-of-war with Wessex.[32]

The lands that Wulfhere took in Hampshire he gave to his godson, the king of Sussex, and Wessex itself was under threat on a longer-term basis. Wulfhere also took a wife from the royal house of Kent, a reminder that nation-building owed as much to marriage politics as it did to warfare. He also dominated Essex (though it was still ruled by a client king) and therefore indirectly became the first Mercian to have control of London. But he overstepped the mark and attacked Northumbria, by now under the rule of Ecgfrith, and lost. Wulfhere soon after succumbed to an unknown disease – a premature end as he was only in his thirties – and was replaced by his brother Æthelred, who defeated Ecgfrith at the battle of the Trent.

A treaty was agreed between Mercia and Northumbria, and the prolonged war between the two kingdoms was at last over. Æthelred, a true son of Penda, extended his territories, taking Lindsey and securing his southern borders in Gloucestershire and Wiltshire. He also maintained the good relations his father had enjoyed with the Welsh to his west. Æthelred reigned for nearly three decades and his end was a peaceful one. He did not die as a king but abdicated and lived out his last fourteen years as a monk at Bardney in Lincolnshire, where the relics of Oswald of Northumbria were buried (except for his head). His immediate successors made little impression – or so we judge from the lack of written records about them – but by 731, when Bede wrote his great work, the king of Mercia was Æthelbald, a man of considerable talent and achievement.

Æthelbald would later call himself 'king of all the southern English', a hint of pretensions to greater things. He certainly exerted a degree of dominance over Wessex, and in 733 he occupied Somerton, the place after which the modern county of Somerset took its name. Perhaps an even greater feather in his cap was his capture of London from the East Saxons. He then reversed former Mercian policy and attacked the Welsh, who had raided Mercia after Æthelred's abdication. Relationships with Northumbria, on the other hand, were largely peaceful during his reign, though this situation was encouraged by a remarkable alliance that he brokered with the Picts in the north, led by their king Oengus mac Fergus. With powerful neighbours on both sides, Northumbria naturally felt unable to risk aggressive action. During Æthelbald's forty-one-year reign, a great earthwork which became known as Wat's Dyke was erected on the border between Cheshire (recently acquired by Mercia) and Wales. For all his power, however, this did not make Æthelbald secure. In 757 he died, possibly killed by his own bodyguard or by enemies in battle at Seckington (the surviving records are not clear). There was a short but bitter civil war after his death, and the brief reign of one Beornred, before

Æthelbald's ultimate successor took power. This was Offa, one of the great rulers of Anglo-Saxon history.

Offa's reign had a profound effect not just on Mercia but on England, though the biased writers who put together the *ASC* in Wessex might not like to admit it. He was a man who could be generous with his patronage but who usually wanted something in return. When he granted land in a charter something was expected back, usually the construction of bridges or fortresses, or military service (the 'common burden' as these requirements were collectively known or, in the formal Latin of the day, the *trimoda necessitas*). It was a strategy that Wessex adopted soon after, and it would become a core tenet of kingship embraced by rulers such as Alfred the Great.

Offa did not miss an opportunity to extend his power. The peoples of the Hwicce and Lindsey, who had up until now had their own kings even though they were increasingly under pressure from Mercia, lost their rulers for good during Offa's reign. In 794, he ordered the beheading of King Æthelred of East Anglia, who had probably been trying to assert his independence. Sussex also effectively lost its independence, and Offa started to style himself as 'king of the English'. When Ecgberht II, king of Kent, issued charters in his own name, Offa cancelled them, asserting that Ecgberht was a client king and had no such authority. However, his position of dominance over Kent was not secure until 785, when he entered Canterbury in triumph nine years after being pushed back at a hard-fought battle at Otford. This was an important moment; Kent was closely linked to Francia and as such had a kind of cultural leadership in England.

Relationships with the Welsh deteriorated during Offa's reign. Several campaigns against them took place and the king famously ordered the construction of Offa's Dyke. At least that is what is generally believed, though there is limited evidence to prove that the work was constructed on his orders. The paucity of contemporary written records from Mercia are a real handicap here. Not until a century later when Asser, bishop of Sherborne, credited Offa with ordering its construction is any reference made to the mastermind behind the dyke's construction. Some historians are sceptical that Offa was behind such a massive project, seeing little need for him to undertake it, though they concede he might have added some additional elements to sections of the 'wall' that had already been erected in previous reigns.[33] If it was Offa's idea, at some 120 miles in length it was a major piece of construction which spoke volumes about the extent of his ambition. That ambition was also evidenced by his campaigns in the south of England, particularly against Sussex and Kent, which helped to cement his control of the increasingly important

London. He also upgraded his palace at Tamworth significantly and it appears to have become the nerve centre of his rule. This is a contrast from earlier periods in the Anglo-Saxon era, when itinerancy was the norm, and this change emulated the notion behind Charlemagne's palace in Aachen.[34] It was described in glowing terms: 'For its magnificence it was the wonder and marvel of the age.'[35]

Offa's ambitions went further than the secular though. In ecclesiastical terms, England was then divided into two with the south under the authority of the archbishop of Canterbury and the north under his counterpart in York. Offa argued for a third archbishopric in Mercia to be based at Lichfield and was ultimately successful, although the experiment only lasted for a few years and did not long survive his death.

Offa worried about his succession arrangements. The interregnum between one king and the next was a time of great danger in the Anglo-Saxon period. There was no predetermined passing of royal authority to the eldest son, and on many occasions this vacuum had led to vicious plotting and major instability. To guard against this, Offa had his son Ecgfrith ordained his successor whilst he was still alive. This was an unprecedented act in England, but similar steps had been taken in Carolingian Francia.

Offa's view of his own importance even led to him falling out with the great Charlemagne. The Mercian king came from an old and distinguished family – an ancestor of the same name had ruled in Schleswig before the Angles came to England – and he seems to have taken great pride in this fact. When Charlemagne proposed that one of his sons should marry a daughter of Offa, the Mercian king offended the emperor by responding that his son Ecgfrith should in return marry a daughter of Charlemagne. The two rulers had previously got on well, but a major rift now emerged. Charlemagne closed ports in Francia to English ships and Offa followed suit. The breach was eventually healed, but it showed that Offa was not a man to be crossed. At the same time, it also suggested that Offa gravely miscalculated in assuming that he was the equal of Charlemagne.

Offa's legacy in England was also economic. He significantly improved the quality of the silver penny, which was to remain the backbone of the English currency for hundreds of years thereafter (similar developments had been taking place in Francia throughout the eighth century), and recognised the opportunity for propaganda by becoming the first ruler to add his image to the coins. He also minted gold coins, perhaps to facilitate commerce with Arab traders, though these were naturally far less common than the silver penny.

Here the trend in England was mirroring developments on the continent. There had been something of an economic boom in Europe in the eighth century. After several hundred years of epidemics driving the population down, it had now rebounded. Even the climate was warming. There were still famines and outbreaks of pestilence hitting livestock particularly hard,[36] but these were occasional blips in a mainly upward trend. In the main, the economy strengthened and for some parts of Europe this was something of a golden age (though as would become apparent it also made for increasingly lucrative targets for piratical raiders). There is evidence of the wool trade taking root in England by the time of Offa's reign; it would of course become the mainstay of the English economy, though contemporary references are not altogether positive. In a letter to Offa, Charlemagne complained of the small size of woollen cloaks sent from England, protesting that they left him uncomfortable, especially when forced to attend to a call of nature in the outdoors.

Offa also drew up his own legal code, which Alfred later conceded put him amongst the foremost English legislators, though unfortunately no copy of Offa's code has survived the passage of time. Such developments remind us that the foundation of an English nation, although eventually brought about by the kings of Wessex, was not the achievement of one dynasty. Other kings such as Offa or some of the great rulers of Northumbria had also played their part, and not just as triumphant warriors. Germanic 'kings' of earlier times had been elected to lead armies in battle during military campaigns and were little more than warlords, but a king as a lawgiver was also a ruler in peacetime. It is true that such a man was expected to be a warrior and lead his men into battle, and to be a 'ring-giver', offering patronage and reward in return for the loyalty and service of his men. But much more was demanded of him. Men such as Offa not only shaped what became England, but helped to develop a completely different concept of what it meant to be a king.

Although Offa's achievements were clearly significant, some claimed they were built on shallow foundations. Whilst acknowledging Offa's many qualities, the Northumbrian commentator Alcuin, by now beavering away in Charlemagne's Francia, remarked after the king's death in 796 how quickly things had deteriorated. Coenwulf, by then king of Mercia (Ecgfrith, despite Offa's best efforts, would die having ruled for a mere five months), and Eardwulf of Northumbria were accused of being tyrants, not rulers, and the country as a whole was considered by Alcuin to be a place where 'faith is lapsing, truth is silent, ill will grows and pride increases'.[37] This contrasts markedly with a message that Alcuin had written to Offa during his reign when he described him – presumably with the sanction of Charlemagne – as 'the glory of Britain'.

Offa was a powerful king and many in England went in awe of him, but during his reign there were clear signs of trouble ahead from distant shores. Towards the end of his rule, Offa issued a grant to the Church in Kent exempting it from various obligations but notably retained their duty to support military activities 'against pagan seamen with migrant fleets'.[38] One would like more detail, but this is nevertheless a strong indication that pagan raiders were threatening England from the sea. Indeed, there was one much less ambiguous demonstration of their presence during Offa's reign. In 793, in an event that sent shock waves far and wide, the great monastic establishment of Lindisfarne was pillaged. Monks were slaughtered, precious items seized, and the buildings burned. The acrid smoke that hung heavy in the air above Cuthbert's famous beacon of learning as the plunder-laden ships sailed away was a terrifying signal that the Vikings had arrived. The raid became an iconic event. Less well known are reports that soon after another Viking raid on Northumbria at Monkwearmouth was intercepted and repelled. Some of the Viking leaders were killed and several ships were lost in a storm and the men on board drowned. A few were captured alive and beheaded on the beach.[39] But neither Offa in England nor Charlemagne in Francia had the capacity to deter the raiders completely, and this situation was going to get progressively worse in the succeeding decades.

Just the year after the raid on Lindisfarne a monk, possibly from Iona, wrote of *vastatio omnium insularum Britanniae a gentilibus* – 'the devastation of all the islands of Britain by the heathens'. It was a dark warning of things to come. With the benefit of hindsight, it would send a collective shiver down the spine of the peoples of these islands.

The Royal Family of Wessex

By the close of the eighth century, then, each region of England had seen its own specific course of development. In the north, Northumbria had been at one time a powerhouse though its fortunes were by now in marked decline. Mercia had fought toe to toe with its northern neighbour on several occasions and was now apparently the dominant power in England. Inevitably events in some of these kingdoms impacted on their near neighbours but each of them had their own unique story to tell. It was no different in the south of England where separate kingdoms such as Kent, Essex, Sussex and Wessex existed and attempted to forge their own destiny.

Kent for a time was an important kingdom and had its own unique story shaped in part by its close geographical proximity to the continent. Connections with the powerful Franks just across the narrow English Channel were particularly strong; when Augustine made his successful missionary overtures to Kent, its king, Æthelberht, was already married to a Frankish princess named Bertha. During the sixth and seventh centuries Frankish influence had become extremely strong in Kent.[40] Yet despite this, until Augustine's visit at the very end of the sixth century, Kent largely remained pagan even though the Franks had converted to Christianity much sooner. Even so, Kent's ultimate elevation as the effective headquarters of the English Church, with its archbishop ensconced in Canterbury, would make it a place of great symbolic significance whether or not its political power held.

Sussex, the 'land of the South Saxons', bounded on one side by the great forest of the Weald and on the other by the Channel, was – according to the *ASC* – the domain of a powerful late fifth-century ruler named Ælle. Based on archaeological evidence, Ælle's influence appears to have extended far across the south although the peak of Sussex's power appears to have come early in its history and it would later lose its status as an independent kingdom. The *ASC* relate that in 491 Ælle was responsible for the massacre of the Romano-British inhabitants of Andredesceaster (Pevensey). It appears that this helped to establish him as the pre-eminent ruler amongst the Anglo-Saxon (and Jute) inhabitants of the south of England, and indeed Bede names him as the first *Bretwalda*. The Weald – which in 892 was described as being 30 miles wide and 120 miles long – acted as a great natural barrier against other parts of England, though there were Roman roads through it and some historians believe that these were still serviceable even into Anglo-Saxon times.[41]

Most of the ruling dynasties in the kingdoms of England claimed their descent from the great god Woden (the Odin of the Vikings) and that of Wessex was no exception to this general rule.[42] Having a pagan god as the progenitor of a Christian dynasty later proved problematic for the West Saxon kings. The solution that was arrived at regarding this knotty problem was innovative if not entirely convincing to the sceptical modern mind. It was claimed that Woden was not a god but a mere mortal. Further, it was said that he was a grandson many times removed of a man named Sceaf. Sceaf, it was said, was the son of Noah. The inconvenient reality that Sceaf was not mentioned in the Bible was unconvincingly explained away with the suggestion that he was actually born on the Ark itself.[43] A story might begin life as a mere fabrication, but if it is told often enough to an audience that wants to believe it then it may eventually be regarded as something like the truth. This is particularly the case in a society that places high value on the contributions of poets, bards or *skalds*.

The more recent mortal who was credited with establishing the dynasty in Wessex from which later great kings like Alfred and Æthelstan would emerge has the suspiciously Celtic name of Cerdic. An early problem to face as far as he is concerned is that the *ASC* give two very different dates for his major contribution to the early years of the kingdom, 495 and 519.[44] Many modern historians now believe using the limited evidence available that the creation of Anglo-Saxon kingdoms in England should be placed in the sixth rather than the fifth century.[45]

Cerdic's son (or grandson – again, different versions of the *ASC* contradict each other on this point) Cynric won a battle against the Britons at Searoburh, which is probably near Old Sarum, just outside the later medieval city of Salisbury in Wiltshire. This allowed Cynric's people, the Gewisse, to expand further into fertile lands from their original foothold in Hampshire. Four years later a famous Saxon warrior, Ceawlin, fought in another victory at Barbury 'Castle' (actually a hill fort) near Swindon. This was the start of three decades of strong rule that was notable enough for Ceawlin to become the second *Bretwalda*. Ceawlin seems to have led his 'West Saxons' from the upper Thames valley to combine with the Gewisse and drive further Saxon expansion. Indeed, it has been suggested that the Gewisse was the name given to settlers from the upper Thames valley who moved west and took territories already occupied by other Saxons and Jutes. Eventually the name Gewisse disappeared altogether as the label 'West Saxon' came into use, which also subsumed the Jutes who had settled in the west of the region.[46]

Later genealogists would call Ceawlin a son of Cynric, also making him a direct descendant of Cerdic, but the truth of this is now largely unprovable. Ceawlin fought and defeated Æthelberht of Kent in 568, and in 577 he won a crushing triumph against the Britons at Dyrham just outside Bath. The victory allowed him to add Bath, Cirencester and Gloucester to his territories. This seemed to mark a decisive downturn in British fortunes and opened the way to further Anglo-Saxon expansion in the south. However, Ceawlin found that it was harder to hold territory than to win it and was driven out of some of his new lands in 592 after a vicious battle near the evocatively named 'Woden's barrow', a Neolithic barrow that is now called Adam's Grave in an interesting example of Christianisation. This may well have been a battle with other Anglo-Saxons. In any case, the ultimate winner was Æthelberht of Kent who was able to take advantage of the internecine squabbles to build his own power.

Whilst Northumbria and Mercia had slugged it out for supremacy in the seventh century and beyond, Wessex had been gradually expanding in the south-west. Generally speaking, Wessex had not achieved any kind of supremacy over the Anglo-Saxons to the north and indeed had sometimes been forced to concede power and lands to its rivals. However, it had steadily pushed its own boundaries further west. After an advance into Devon in 614, the ruling West Saxon dynasty was forced to focus its attention on the increasingly aggressive Mercians to the north. But in 658 the advance into Devon was resumed and an important victory was won at Peonnum, possibly Penselwood on the Somerset–Dorset border or Pinhoe near Exeter.[47] The victory opened up the rest of Devon to the West Saxons.

These triumphs, won by King Cenwalh, were followed up by his brother and successor Centwine. Sometime during the reign of the latter (which ended in 675), Dorset was added to Wessex's possessions. It had been protected for a time by its jagged Jurassic coast on one side and the defensive earthwork known as Bokerley Dyke on its north-easterly border, but with Wiltshire and Devon held by the West Saxons its capitulation was only a matter of time. Of the old British kingdom of Dumnonia only Cornwall remained, though that would continue for a while yet; indeed, some would say that the Celtic region of the far south-west has never been fully integrated into England.

At the beginning of the eighth century, a king called Ine emerged and added lustre to the kingdom of Wessex. He pushed into the eastern fringes of Cornwall but a serious defeat there in 722 blunted his advance. In 715 he also faced a serious threat from the Mercians; a battle that year seems to have been indecisive, but Ine was at least able to hang on to his territories in the south. He was a patron of the Church, and establishments at Sherborne, Malmesbury and especially Glastonbury benefited from his largesse. He is best remembered for his comprehensive set of laws which in many ways was ahead of its time, proving a source of reference and no little pride for future Anglo-Saxon generations. In 726, emulating other Anglo-Saxon kings in this period, Ine abdicated and retired to Rome to see out his last days.

Christianity had certainly taken hold and was about to spread beyond England to pagan parts of the continent, with many Anglo-Saxon missionaries joining the endeavour. Perhaps the most influential Anglo-Saxon missionary in the eighth century was Boniface (initially Wynfrith), who was born according to tradition in Crediton, Devon. This in itself is interesting as at the time of his birth Devon had not long been assimilated into Wessex. In 716, Boniface – who may have already been pencilled in for a high position in the Church – turned his back on the land of his birth and sailed for Frisia. When he arrived, he found that the region had just been taken over by a pagan ruler and was not ripe for a Christianising mission. Instead, he set out for Rome where he was given a commission to journey to central Europe on a mission to convert the pagans there (he was also given his new name, Boniface, by Pope Gregory II whilst there).

Boniface's courage was shown when he cut down a sacred oak dedicated to Thor and recycled its wood as part of a Christian church. These actions perhaps hinted at the reasons for his ultimate martyrdom when as an ageing bishop he was hacked apart by a pagan mob in 754. But his life and his death emphasised just how much Christianity had become engrained in Wessex specifically and Anglo-Saxon England more generally by this time. He was just one of many missionaries to the continent (though undoubtedly the best known and most influential). What is remarkable about this is that there was a regular flow of communications back to England from these missionaries, often to several different kings, defying assumptions of parochialism amongst its rulers and suggesting that long before England became a united polity some were already able to see a bigger picture.

As the century progressed, Wessex's position as an independent kingdom came increasingly under threat. Cynewulf became king of Wessex in 757 and reigned for nearly thirty years, and from time to time Offa tried to assert his superiority over Wessex by refusing to allow grants that Cynewulf had made without his permission. Yet this was not always the case; certainly some grants were issued by Cynewulf without Offa seemingly being involved. The impression one gets is that Offa believed himself to be the *primus inter pares* amongst the English kings and at times tried and failed to emphasise the point. But in 779 Cynewulf was defeated by Offa at Bensington in Oxfordshire and the position of Wessex looked increasingly precarious.

Cynewulf died in 786 in violent circumstances. He was visiting his mistress at Meretun (possibly Martin in Hampshire) when the house he was in was surrounded by over eighty men led by a rival claimant to the throne of Wessex. The house was attacked and nearly all the men inside, including Cynewulf, were slaughtered. Presumably due to the clandestine nature of his night-time visit there was only a small number of men guarding him. The next morning a group of Cynewulf's thegns arrived on the scene and, after a fight, gained a modicum of revenge by killing nearly all those involved in the assassination of the late king, including the rival claimant.[48]

With Cynewulf's death, the independence of Wessex was in great jeopardy. His successor, Beorhtric, was sponsored by Offa and indeed may well have been his puppet. He certainly became his son-in-law when he married Offa's daughter Eadburh, a woman who was so detested in Wessex that it prejudiced the West Saxons against the whole concept of queenship and for years after there was a reluctance on their part to honour a king's spouse with the title of queen. When Beorhtric died in 802, Eadburh left for exile on the continent where she is said to have lost her position as abbess of a convent due to her sexual promiscuity and died in poverty in Pavia.

At some time during these years, Ecgberht, a son of Eahlmund, king of Kent, made his way into exile in Francia. Relationships between Offa and Charlemagne became fraught at around this time, and it is tempting to speculate that the presence of Ecgberht at the emperor's court was a factor.[49] Ecgberht was seen as a threat to both Offa and Beorhtric, prompting him to flee to the continent. Offa's efforts to consecrate his son Ecgfrith as king at around this time – an unusual expedient – certainly suggest that the great king was much concerned by the succession. Sadly for Ecgfrith, this plan did not long survive Offa's demise, for he would reign for a mere 141 days before dying from an unnamed illness. Roger of Wendover says that father and son had already ruled jointly for eight years, but given what we know of Offa his son's role during that period was probably only symbolic.

As for Beorhtric, little remains of him in the historical record apart from two traumatic events. One was his death, which Alfred's biographer Asser credits to a botched attempt by Queen Eadburh to poison one of her husband's retainers. Having mistakenly supped from the poisoned goblet, Beorhtric died and was replaced by Ecgberht, that exile whom Offa had seemingly been determined to remove from the line of succession. The other event, however, proved more significant for the formation of England.

In 789, three ships from far across the seas – probably from Hordaland in Norway[50] – made landfall at Portland in Dorset. The most likely spot for the landing would seem to be Church Ope Cove, one of the few approachable spots on what is a very rugged coastline. There is a gently sloping if pebbly beach here, where a shallow-draft ship could be beached. Above the cove, the medieval Rufus Castle still stands sentinel. There is no mention of a raid, so perhaps this was an accidental landing or the ship needed mooring for repairs.

The king's reeve, Beaduheard, made his way down to the shore to find out what these interlopers were after. There was an altercation, tempers and voices were raised, and then the glint of axes could be seen as they smashed down hard into flesh and bone. The ships sailed off, but Beaduheard's sightless eyes would not see them go. He lay on the beach, his lifeblood ebbing away, staining the sands scarlet. Beaduheard's end was notable for he was the first known casualty of a Viking raid.

The chronicler Æthelweard, writing two centuries after Beorhtric's reign, describes Wessex under this 'pious' king as a peaceful, pastoral land where farmers were busy 'making furrows in the grimy earth in serene tranquillity' when the Vikings arrived. The chronicler noted that it was now 334 years since Hengist and Horsa had arrived in Britain to establish the first Saxon presence in the country. Now, heralded by the death of Beaduheard, a new invasion was about to begin, though it would be another fifty years before an all-out assault was launched.[51] The Viking menace had announced itself, and the portents for the future were ominous.

2

Ecgberht and Æthelwulf

He ruled it well for fifty winters, grew old and wise as
warden of the land...

Beowulf, Anglo-Saxon poem

Wessex Waxes, Mercia Wanes

In 802, Ecgberht became king of Wessex. Æthelweard noted that this was 'six thousand years except for five' since the beginning of the world and three centuries since Cerdic had become king of Wessex ten generations back.[1] Ecgberht's accession had been some years in the making. A story emerged that he had been a contender for the throne when Cynewulf was killed at Meretun back in 786 but that he had been unsuccessful in his bid. The story, if true, gives us an insight into his possible birthdate, which would have been at least as far back as 770 if he was to be a credible contender in 786.

Ecgbehrt's exile to Francia had allegedly come about at the instigation of Beorhtric but the timing is unclear. If he had been sent abroad during Offa's reign he could have been there for as long as thirteen years. Another version suggests that he been exiled in the reign of Coenwulf, Offa's ultimate successor, and may therefore have been abroad for as little as three years. Regardless of the truth concerning the duration of his exile, he was in Charlemagne's court long enough to marry Redburga, a Frank who was a relative of the emperor and possibly his illegitimate daughter – despite his reputation as a paragon of Christian rule, Charlemagne was renowned for his prolific sexual appetite both in and out of the marriage bed.[2] In fact, as early as the reign of his immediate successor, Louis the

Pious, accounts were written stating that Charlemagne was burning in purgatorial fire as punishment for his sexual misdemeanours. There are suggestions – unproven of course – that these transgressions included incest and necrophilia.[3]

The notion that Beorhtric was behind Ecgberht's exile does not entirely ring true, especially if it happened during Offa's reign. The young man would have been a useful bargaining chip for Offa, so why would he just let him leave? And there is no doubt who was the senior partner in the relationship between Offa and Beorhtric – the latter was in no position to force the former to do anything. Offa was renowned for his ruthlessness. Late on in his reign he ordered the execution of King Æthelberht of East Anglia. If the Mercian king had seen Ecgberht as any sort of threat, it would have been wise for the young man to take himself out of harm's way as quickly as possible. Where better than the court of the most powerful ruler in Europe and indeed the most powerful European since the end of the Roman Empire? It has even been suggested by some very well-respected historians that Ecgberht's presence at the court created friction between the emperor and Offa.[4]

Whilst he was in exile, Ecgberht may well have grown close with another man in the same position, Eadbert Præn, who hailed from Kent. Relationships between Mercia and Kent had been problematic in recent years. Kent had been dominated by Mercia for several decades but then in the mid-770s managed to break free for nearly a decade. It achieved temporary independence following the Battle of Otford in 776 and was then ruled without Mercian interference for a time by King Ecgberht II, from whom the future ruler of Wessex may have taken his name. In about 784 this man was succeeded by Eahlmund, the father of our Ecgberht. His reign did not appear to last long, as a year later Offa was issuing charters regarding Kent without reference to any local king. Now that Kent was dominated once more by Mercia, Ecgberht – the probable successor to the Kentish throne if it had remained independent – was a potentially dangerous rival to Offa.

All of this begs the question of how a man from Kent managed to become the king of Wessex in 802. It was said that Ecgberht (and by implication his father Ealhmund) was descended from the line of King Ine of Wessex, but this is viewed with scepticism by some historians who see it as an all too convenient justification for Ecgberht's succession.[5] It also appears unlikely that if Ealhmund was at heart a man of Wessex he would become the Kentish king. In addition, Ecgberht was a name that had been used by two Kentish kings, and in Anglo-Saxon times the ruling families of different kingdoms liked to name their offspring after powerful ancestors as a sign of status and ambition.

The issue of how Ecgberht became king of Wessex is a murky one, so some speculation is unavoidable. We can start by looking afresh at the murder of Beorhtric in 802. One of the favourite *topoi* (stereotypical motifs) of Anglo-Saxon chroniclers is that of the disloyal wife and queen, typically from a different kingdom than her husband, who arranges for him to be assassinated. A good example would be the seventh-century king Peada of Mercia (son of Penda), whose Northumbrian wife arranged for his elimination.[6] Closer to the time, Offa's wife Cynethryth was regarded by some chroniclers as the motivating force behind the murder of Æthelberht of East Anglia.[7] The image of the *femme fatale* was already well established, and scapegoating a powerful woman could be an effective way of distracting attention from the real culprit in such circumstances. In this respect, it is worth noting that the main beneficiary of Beorhtric's demise was Ecgberht. This would, in modern parlance, make him a 'person of interest' in an investigation into the late king's murder.

Not long after meeting Ecgberht, Offa's death had caused Eadbert Præn to return to Kent. He even became king for a short period, but then the Mercians moved to deal with him. His fate was brutal, if not unique for the time. He was blinded – a relatively common act that would debar anyone from a claim to regal power – and his hands were cut off as a punishment for 'theft'. There are also suggestions that this Eadbert was an ordained priest, which on its own should have been sufficient to make him ineligible for kingship.[8] Despite his appalling treatment, Eadbert survived and was later released by Coenwulf, who clearly felt he was no longer a threat. Eadbert probably lived out his shattered life as a monk.[9] But the fact that both Eadbert and Ecgberht made their moves after a time at Charlemagne's court might suggest that the emperor indirectly supported them in their respective enterprises.

The Mercian king was now Coenwulf. We know little about his pedigree, but it has been suggested that one ancestor was a man called Cenwalh. Someone of that name was king of Wessex back in Penda's time and he was married briefly to Penda's sister. Perhaps, then, Coenwulf had West Saxon blood in his veins. In any event, it seems that during his long reign, which lasted for a quarter of a century, Wessex and Mercia largely kept their distance from one another. Although details are sparse, it appears likely that the death of the mighty Offa left a vacuum in Mercia which in turn created a great deal of turmoil. Alarmed by the deaths of Offa, Æthelred of Northumbria and Ecgfrith of Mercia, Alcuin remarked, 'Times are dangerous in Britain. The death of kings is a sign of misery, and divisions a cause of bondage.'[10] Both the East Anglians and the people of Kent were soon in revolt against Mercia and Coenwulf was brutal in responding. He was therefore distracted and unwilling to take on Wessex. However, his heavy-handed approach meant that those on the receiving end might in the long term prefer Wessex to Mercia.

Although Ecgberht was not the founder of the West Saxon dynasty, he was the man who set it on the path to greatness. This was now a Christian world but there were complications. As a way of explaining a potentially embarrassing situation, commentators now averred that the pagan god Woden, from whom most Anglo-Saxon kings claimed descent, was in turn descended from Adam.[11] This was similar to the approach that later Icelandic saga writers employed to deal with the pagan Viking gods of the past, placing them in a Christian context. Ecgberht would be expected to act like a Christian king, particularly given his time at the court of Charlemagne where he was under the emperor's protection. Charlemagne was (very literally) a fierce defender of the faith and would have expected the new king of the West Saxons to be likewise.

We know little about the early years of Ecgberht's reign, but what is clear is that it got off to a spectacularly violent start. On the same day that Ecgberht became king of the West Saxons, an army of the Hwicce led by ealdorman Æthelmund crossed the upper Thames at Kempsford in Gloucestershire, clashing head-on with the men of Wiltshire led by ealdorman Weohstan. A brutal fight ensued, with both ealdormen killed, but at the battle's end the men of Wiltshire held the field. The timing is hardly likely to be coincidental; the Mercians probably raided in the hopes of destabilising the succession. If so the plan backfired, gifting Egcberht an inspiring early victory, albeit vicarious as he was not present. After this, there are no further records of any disputes between Mercia and Wessex until after the death of Coenwulf in 821. In Kent, Coenwulf had placed his brother Cuthred on the throne after his ruthless elimination of Eadbert Præn, making the territory little more than a satellite state of Mercia. When Cuthred died in 807, Coenwulf dropped all pretence and took the Kentish throne for himself.

Granted respite from Mercia, Ecgberht seems to have turned his attentions elsewhere. According to Henry of Huntingdon (and the *ASC*), in 815 he launched a campaign against the 'Welsh', who were powerless to resist him.[12] There is also a mention in the Welsh chronicles written by Caradoc of Llancarvan in the *Brut Y Tywysogion* ('The Chronicle of the Princes') of a campaign in 817 by the 'Saxons' into the mountains of Eryri and the taking of the kingdom of Rhufoniog.[13] These are two intriguing but unconnected references. The 815 campaign relates to the Britons of Cornwall, who were definitely within the sphere of influence of the West Saxons – the *Anglo-Saxon Chronicles* relate that he raided from east to west, perhaps in a very thorough *chevauchee*. Cornwall nevertheless remained a thorn in the flesh of Wessex, as would be evidenced on several different occasions in the succeeding decades. Rhufoniog and Eryri, on the other hand, were in the region of Snowdonia in Gwynedd, North Wales, and most definitely in the Mercian sphere of influence.

These passing references show that at the time the Anglo-Saxon kingdoms were still more concerned about their own internal affairs than any threat from Viking raids. Indeed, the *ASC* are extremely quiet about references to such raids during the first two decades of the ninth century. This does not mean that Viking activity was not going on elsewhere on the periphery of Britain, of course. Archaeological evidence increasingly suggests that there was a growing Viking presence in both the Northern and Western Isles of Scotland and in Ireland during this period. There is a considerable body of evidence emerging that raids during these years were extremely intense in these regions and that some form of permanent Viking settlement was even taking root. The relatively fractured situation in these areas helped to feed insecurity. For example, it has been suggested that in Ireland during the ninth century there were as many as 150 sub-kings. This did not make it easy to develop a coordinated and coherent response to Viking raids.

The death of Coenwulf in 821 ushered in a period of instability in Mercia. Indeed, with hindsight it is clear that this was a turning point in Mercian history. A king's death always meant instability in Anglo-Saxon times. This had been the case at the end of the seventh century in Northumbria, and it was about to happen again in Mercia. Coenwulf had reigned for a quarter of a century and had developed a reputation for ruthlessness. East Anglia stopped using its own coinage in around 800, suggesting a Mercian takeover to add to the reimposition of their rule in Kent. When the late Beorhtric had entered a formal alliance with Coenwulf in 799 the Mercian ruler had used the term 'emperor', showing an ambition to rule over all of the English. The later years of his reign had seen a rift with the church in Canterbury, a dangerous move on his part which he eventually rectified. Overall it had been a successful reign – in stark contrast to what was to come next.

Not long before, Coenwulf had launched extensive raids on Welsh territory encompassing Gwynedd in the north, Powys in the centre and Dyfed in the south-west. He died before he could complete a second expedition, but Welsh records suggest that the Mercians still stayed on the offensive. In 823 they state that 'the Saxons' destroyed the fortress at Deganwy on the River Conwy and captured Powys.[14] Coenwulf's brother Ceolwulf had taken over from him, but he only lasted until 823 before being deposed in favour of the middle-aged Beornwulf who, judging from his name, may have been descended from the eighth-century king

Beornred, who had been overthrown by Offa (different branches of the Mercian royal family liked to use similar names).[15]

Mercia and Wessex had largely kept at arm's length during the early decades of the ninth century, with the former focussing its expansionary efforts in the east and west rather than the south. However, Ecgberht had also been consolidating his power. The infrequent references to him in the *ASC* suggest that his reign so far had been steady rather than spectacular, but that was about to change. A major confrontation between Wessex and Mercia was not far off, possibly instigated by a battle between the men of Devon and the Cornish at Gafulford, which may have been in the west of Devonshire or the east of Cornwall. The Devonshire men were triumphant, and their actions showed how firmly they were now assimilated into Wessex. Whereas just a century and a half previously they had been part of the British kingdom of Dumnonia along with the Cornish, the two peoples now seemed to be implacable foes.

Perhaps Beornwulf sensed the need to make a pre-emptive strike against Ecgberht. He was a new king, in all probability a usurper, and needed to prove himself. He led his army into Wiltshire, the traditional frontier zone between the two kingdoms, to confront Ecgberht face to face. In 825 the two armies met at Ellendun, a location believed to be at Wroughton close to Swindon. Renowned historian Sir Frank Stenton called it 'one of the most decisive battles of Anglo-Saxon history' and suggests that it brought the supremacy of the Mercian kings to an end.[16] Henry of Huntingdon lays on gory details with relish: 'Ellendune's [*sic*] stream was tinged with blood, and was choked with the slain, and became foul with the carnage.' He describes a 'prodigious slaughter' on both sides, with Ecgberht emerging triumphant.[17]

The West Saxon triumph at Ellendun proved that power was shifting to Wessex. Lands in the south were now open to the advances of Ecgberht's armies, and the East Anglians felt emboldened to revolt against Mercian rule. Beornwulf was killed soon after while attempting to bring the East Anglians back into line. His place was taken by a man called Ludeca who met the same fate after barely a year. Very little is known of Ludeca, but a chance find of a stray coin from his reign in a Wiltshire field in 2016 showed that he controlled London in 826, a year after Ellendun.[18] The Mercian grip on power was slipping.

The year 825 was also significant for the monks on Iona as they were subjected to a further Viking attack, others having been recorded in 792, 802 and 806, the latter seeing eighty-six brethren slaughtered. The raid of 825 was particularly disturbing as the abbot, Blathmac, was killed when 'the violent cursed host came rushing through the open buildings, threatening cruel perils to the blessed men; and after slaying with mad savagery the rest of the associates, they approached the holy father, to compel him to give up the precious metals wherein lie the holy bones of St Columba'. But the monks had buried the sacred shrine and Blathmac would not reveal its location. His fate is graphically recorded in the following words: 'Therefore the pious sacrifice was torn limb from limb.' Blathmac became a martyr, an exemplar for hundreds of other unnamed men and women who would follow in his wake.[19]

The Vikings Return

Ecgberht was quick to take advantage of his triumph over the Mercians. Shortly afterwards he moved in on Kent, Sussex, Surrey and Essex, subsequently forming for the first time a coherent kingdom that covered the entire south of England. Astute enough to know that he couldn't keep this potentially fragile new polity together without help, he appointed his eldest son Æthelwulf as king of Kent. Soon after, East Anglia, seeking a powerful ally against Mercia, approached Ecgberht for assistance. He was very glad to oblige. East Anglia soon had a king called Æthelstan, appointed by Ecgberht. This man may well be a puppet king; it is telling that the name Æthelstan appears prominently in West Saxon royal dynastic history. There were even members of Ecgberht's own family with the name; a son of Æthelwulf bore it, though the date range means that the new king of East Anglia could not have been him. Even so, a possible direct blood connection to Ecgberht cannot be ruled out.

There is no such uncertainty over the identity of the new king of Kent. Æthelwulf was the son of Ecgberht and the little-known Frankish lady Redburga. He was in his mid-twenties and so had probably already cut his teeth as a warrior. Now he had the chance to prove himself as a ruler, with the added advantage that he could gain experience under the watchful – if slightly distant – eye of Ecgberht. Given Ecgberht's presumed connection with previous kings of Kent, it may even have felt like something of a homecoming. After all, Kent had been ruled by Mercians or Mercian puppets for several decades – the last such puppet, Baldred, had been sent packing by the West Saxons in alliance with the Kentishmen after a reign (according to Henry of Huntingdon)[20] of eighteen years. This was in 825, the same year as the triumph at Ellendun, and it is significant that there is no account suggesting any anti-Wessex uprising in Kent in the immediate aftermath of this regime change. But it was effectively the end of an independent kingdom of Kent, as Henry of Huntingdon acknowledged: 'The royal race of the kings of Kent then failed, and their right to the kingdom passed into other hands.'[21] Another piece in the puzzle of England had been slotted into place.

Significant though they were, these West Saxon successes were just the precursor for an even greater clash. The history of Anglo-Saxon England so far was a story of the waxing and waning of powers, of jostling for position, probing for weaknesses and seizing moments of opportunity. Kent, Northumbria, Wessex, Mercia and even Sussex had seen moments of triumph, the reaching of summits, but these had been fleeting, perhaps two or three generations of kings at most, before they were pushed off the peak and down into the dark, shadowy valleys below. Those periods of dominance had usually ended on the battlefield, and so it was to be now.

The *ASC* like to announce the arrival of momentous events with cosmic signs and symbols, comets being a particular favourite. At 2 a.m. on 25 December 828 there was a lunar eclipse. It was appropriate that, on that holiest of days, the moon should be hidden and then reappear, as if dying and then being reborn. It was an astronomical metaphor for the demise of one shining light in the firmament of England and the birth of another.[22] The chroniclers, as was their wont, were laconic. We are merely told that Ecgberht conquered Mercia and thus ruled all England south of the Humber. This is accompanied by the important detail that Ecgberht now became the eighth *Bretwalda*. The conquest of Mercia was followed soon after by the submission at Dore, near Sheffield, of Northumbria. Dore was on the northern border of Mercia, and it was here that Eaned, the Northumbrian king, symbolically submitted, further cementing Ecgberht's position.

Whilst we have few details to go on it is not too difficult to paint a general picture of what was most likely happening at the time. Mercia had lost two kings in battle against the East Anglians in as many years. It had been ousted from power both there and in Kent and Essex. These were visible signs of decline, and Ecgberht sensed an opportunity. Mercia already had another king, Wiglaf (a man whose parents may have thought a great deal of the magnificent poem *Beowulf,* as this was the name of the eponymous hero's nephew and successor, though we cannot be sure it was written yet). He was soon overthrown by Ecgberht, and the lack of the mention of a fight suggests that it is possible that there was none and that the demoralised Mercian army merely dissolved rather than take on a greatly superior opponent.

However, it was a surprise when just a year later Wiglaf became king of Mercia once more. The lack of surviving information for this sudden about-face is infuriating. Henry of Huntingdon suggests that Wiglaf returned as a tributary of Ecgberht,[23] but modern historians are sceptical about this as the *ASC* – our prime and most contemporary source for the period – mention no such arrangement, which it very likely would have if it was in place as it would further prove the power of the king of Wessex. In this case, the silence of the chroniclers is deafening. Possibly there had been a Mercian revolt after Ecgberht had overreached himself, conquering too much too soon.

Some historians suggest that Ecgberht had been relying on support from Francia that was no longer forthcoming.[24] Certainly domestic affairs in the Carolingian Empire were complicated by 830. They had started to fracture after the death of Charlemagne as his squabbling sons sought to achieve superiority over each other and in 829-30 the infighting reached crisis levels.[25] The withdrawal or at least diminishment of Frankish support is therefore a distinct possibility. Ecgberht in the meantime had launched a campaign in Wales in 830, another sign of empire-building. It is possible that Wiglaf took advantage of this suddenly messy situation to re-establish himself – and he would remain ruler of Mercia for the next decade. There are only a few charters surviving from Wiglaf's second stint as king but none of them refer to Ecgberht as an overlord, so he seems to have been acting as an independent ruler, albeit in a Mercia which had lost lands in the east and south-east for good.

The fact that Wiglaf enjoyed a second reign suggests that Ecgberht's power was built on shallow foundations. If the Mercian king had managed to reinstate himself without Ecgberht's permission, then it is tangible evidence that the king of Wessex was *Bretwalda* in name only, at least as far as the northern half of England was concerned. Wiglaf even issued charters for Middlesex, suggesting that the area around London had moved back into the Mercian sphere of influence.[26] Further, to compound Ecgberht's difficulties, a new enemy was about to emerge – or rather, an old threat was about to reappear.

The Vikings have a deserved reputation for both their ferocity and their adventurism, attributes which are in reality two sides of the same coin. For two and a half centuries they were the scourge of much of western and northern Europe. However, they were a more complex phenomenon than might first appear. Many near-contemporary accounts talk of the raiders as 'Danes' but in all likelihood the majority of the first visitors to Britain and Ireland hailed from what we now call Norway. Not that Norway (or for that matter Denmark or Sweden) yet existed. Scandinavia was then a hotchpotch of smaller polities headed up by warlords; not altogether different from what England, Scotland, Wales and Ireland then were. As the ninth century progressed, Norway would take the first step towards becoming a nation state under one overall king and Denmark and finally Sweden would follow suit. But that was some way off.[27]

There is growing evidence that the Viking raids on the West, first recorded in the 790s, were in fact preceded by similar activities in the eastern Baltic up to half a century earlier. The discovery in 2008 of an amazing ship burial at Salme in Estonia that can be dated to around 750 has many of the hallmarks of a raid gone wrong or possibly a Scandinavian – in this case Swedish – trade or political delegation that for whatever reason did not work out as planned. The development of small towns such as Ribe and Hedeby in Denmark or Birka in Sweden during the eighth century also suggest Viking activity – much of which may have been peaceful trading rather than raiding, though perhaps not all of it – decades before the first raids on England are said to have happened. This pushes the start date of the Viking period back a good half-century before the traditional start date of 793.

The first groups of Vikings (most likely mainly from Norway though over time the raiders became increasingly eclectic) had in effect 'island-hopped' their way down through Shetland and Orkney, then on to the Hebrides and south down the Irish Sea to Ireland. They had set up bases on the periphery of Ireland. At one time, historians believed that this did not take place until later on in the ninth century but archaeological finds in recent times have pushed dates progressively backwards. Whether full-blown Viking settlements were present in Ireland before around 840 is not yet proved, but it is entirely conceivable that temporary camps were set up and used as hopping-off points for raids across to Wales and England before then. Much of the loot taken from Britain and Ireland from this period has been discovered in archaeological sites in Norway, suggesting that many of the earlier raiders originated from here.[28]

This was not the first nor the last time that Ireland would be heavily involved in raiding activities, whether as victim or aggressor. After all, Patrick – the man who did much to establish Christianity in Ireland – was captured and taken there after an Irish raid on Britain in the fifth century. At the other end of the timescale, raids would be launched on England from Ireland after the Norman Conquest in 1066. After the Lindisfarne raid, Viking attacks on England were few and far between, at least as far as the *ASC* are concerned, though there is other evidence that suggests that this does not give the full picture. Further raids in Northumbria are noted in 794 but then there is nothing until 835. In the latter year 'heathen men' – by which we should assume Vikings – raided Sheppey off the Kent coast. The reference in the *ASC* to this is again laconic but for the next attack in the following year slightly more detail is given.

The chroniclers tell us that in 836 'King Ecgberht fought against thirty-five ship-loads at Carhampton, and great slaughter was made there, and the Danish had possession of the place of slaughter'. Carhampton was a royal estate on the North Somerset coast on the Bristol Channel. Given this location, it seems likely that the 'Danish' raiders were of Norwegian origin and sailed over from Ireland. The *ASC* were written up retrospectively at the end of the ninth century, when many of the Vikings attacking England were indeed Danes, but this may not have been the case in the 830s. The chroniclers tend to use the term 'Danish' as shorthand for any Viking and should not always be taken literally. How many warriors make up 'thirty-five ship-loads' is hard to assess. Ships varied in size and longships from the early eleventh century were larger than those in the ninth. But a reasonable assessment would be that it represented between 1,200 and 1,500 men.[29] To give this perspective, the first recorded raid on Portland consisted of three ships. This force was more than ten times greater, illustrating how the scale of the Viking threat was starting to escalate.

Henry of Huntingdon gives more details and suggests a different place for the battle (unless of course there are two different battles involved). He places the fight at Charmouth, on the west coast of Dorset, and there is indeed a local tradition suggesting that a holy woman was killed during a raid in the area; she later became St Wite and is commemorated at the church that still stands at Whitchurch Canonicorum, where her shrine can be seen today. Henry also gives the names of some of the senior Anglo-Saxon figures who died in the fight. Among them were Herefrith, bishop of Winchester, and another bishop named Wigfrith. Two ealdormen, Dudda and Oslac, also fell.[30] These were heavy losses indeed.

Ecgberht's defeat in battle was no doubt a shock. Apart from what might have happened in terms of any revolt in Mercia – and we simply do not have enough evidence to go on – Ecgberht had enjoyed pretty much unbroken success in his recent military campaigns in England and Wales. And whilst the attack on Lindisfarne had been traumatic, it was a raid on an undefended monastery off the coast. After that, when the Vikings had returned to Northumbria in 794, they had come off second best. But now the ruling *Bretwalda* had been bested. It was an early indication that the kingdoms of England had a challenge on their hands.

Some caution needs to be exercised at the silence of the *ASC* concerning Viking raids on England in the decades following 793. Whilst they are an important source, there are others. Recent research into Kentish charters suggests that Viking attacks had in fact continued despite them not being mentioned in the *ASC*. A charter from Kent dated 811 mentions the destruction of Viking camps, suggesting that even at this early stage attacks had become quite organised and were more than just hit-and-run raids. Charters from 814 and 822 also mention defences against raiders, and for the latter year there is record of an attack on Milton, over 10 miles inland. This is a very different picture than that suggested by the *ASC*.[31]

Encouraged by their success at Carhampton in 836, a Viking force returned to England soon after. The next attack recorded in the *ASC* fell on the west in 838. This time the raiders had allies. The Cornish were disconcerted at the way that the West Saxons had been raiding their lands and threatening their status as an independent state. Adopting the time-honoured policy that 'my enemy's enemy is my friend' they decided to throw in their lot with the raiders. Given the location of this next attack, an Irish point of origin for the Vikings is again possible. The armies clashed at Hingston Down near Gunnislake in Cornwall, which in the Anglo-Saxon age had the evocative name of *Hengestdun* or 'Stallion's Hill'. This was not far away from the River Tamar, presumably the entry point for the 'ship-army' that had descended on the region. News of their arrival had reached Ecgberht, who assembled his army to meet them. Details of the actual fighting are scarce, but the end result in the words of the *ASC* was unequivocal: Ecgberht 'there put to flight both the Britons and the Danish'.

This effectively ended the fighting between the West Saxons and the Cornish. A Cornish king named Dungarth ruled until 875 but may possibly have done so as a client-king of the West Saxons. He is linked to a King Doniert who is commemorated on a damaged cross shaft near St Cleer on the edge of Bodmin Moor. Doniert is recorded as drowning in that year; this might have been an accident, but accounts in Ireland suggest that he may have been executed in this fashion for cooperating with Viking raiders who had attacked Exeter. This could be the result of ongoing resistance to West Saxon rule over Cornwall. Distant echoes of these times still resonate with some; when I recently visited the cross there was a posy of fresh flowers laid by its side as if some still remember the fight to preserve Cornish independence more than a thousand years on.

This victory was the last act of Ecgberht's long reign to be recorded in the *ASC*. The following year, 839, they noted that the king passed away after thirty-seven years and seven months on the throne. It had been a long and eventful rule, indeed remarkably long by the standards of the time, but events had likely begun to take their toll on the ageing king who was probably in his late sixties. His early days had been marked by exile, which must have been a stressful experience, and he had spent many years campaigning. But he was in reality, if not by chronology, the founder of a great dynasty. His remains ended up at Winchester, where they are held in a later chest along with those of many other near-contemporary royals; or at least we think they do, for in an act of Cromwellian vandalism in the seventeenth century the contents of the chests were thrown about, and no one can be sure whose bones lie where anymore.

Records of Ecgberht's reign are sparse and we must rely on occasional archaeological finds to supplement our meagre resources. Sometimes though a pot of gold is unearthed – in Ecgberht's case almost literally. In March 2020 a metal detectorist came across a gold coin in a field in West Dean, Wiltshire. It proved to be from the reign of Ecgberht. Weighing in at just under half a gram, it is an extremely rare find – so far only eight other gold coins have been found from the reigns of English monarchs between 630 and 1257. In an age where the silver penny was ubiquitous, these gold 'mancuses' were only struck on special occasions. This one may have been minted in either Southampton or Winchester and is made of high-quality gold. What special occasion it marked we do not know, but it is a tantalising reminder of a great and largely forgotten king who set his dynasty on the road to supremacy in England.[32]

Ecgberht's crown passed without recorded incident to Æthelwulf. Perhaps inspired by his own bitter experiences in early life, Ecgberht went out of his way to ensure that his eldest son succeeded him, including having the succession announced at a major gathering in Kingston a year before his death.[33] It has been speculated that Æthelwulf was consecrated as the next king here in a formal religious ceremony – though precisely what 'consecration' meant is vague. The oldest surviving coronation rite, the first English consecration *ordo* ('order of service'), may even date to this time.[34] It is clear that Ecgberht's decision to apprentice Æthelwulf as ruler of Kent had been successful, giving the younger man a grounding in kingship and allowing him to build relationships with the powerbrokers who would decide on the succession. Æthelwulf adopted a similar policy now, giving the crowns of Kent, Essex, Surrey and Sussex to his son Æthelstan.[35] However, the term 'crown' should not be read literally. There is no evidence of a formal coronation ceremony for Anglo-Saxon kings before the tenth ceremony and coin evidence has been interpreted as suggesting that ninth-century kings were more likely to wear a ceremonial helmet than a crown.[36] There certainly existed a ceremony of some sort for this purpose, as King Ceolwulf of Mercia noted in a charter that he had been consecrated by the archbishop of Canterbury in 822.

Æthelwulf's delegation of so much power to Æthelstan was a big step for somebody who was presumably still young though some accounts, including later versions of the *ASC*, state that Æthelstan was Æthelwulf's brother rather than his son. Æthelstan's reign is confirmed by a number of Æthelwulf's charters in the 840s that were also attested by Æthelstan as king. Not only did it make sense to give him these kingdoms as a way of building the succession (if indeed he was Æthelwulf's son) but it was also entirely rational to spread the load of defending this stretched empire; for, although Æthelwulf might not yet know it, the Viking threat was about to start ratcheting up.

There were indeed extraordinary warnings about the danger that lay ahead. A letter from Æthelwulf to the Carolingian court in 839 told of a 'certain pious priest' in England who had experienced a disturbing vision of what lay in store should the people of Western Europe not change their ways. The letter went on to claim that dire days were ahead if matters continued as they were:

> If Christian people don't quickly do penance for their various vices and crimes and don't observe the Lord's day in a stricter and worthier way, then a great and crushing disaster were swiftly come upon them: for three days and nights a very dense fog will spread over their land, and then all of a sudden pagan men will lay waste with fire and sword most of the people and land of the Christians along with all they possess.[37]

This heightened threat affected Kent as well as Wessex. Viking attacks on Kent were recorded in 835, 841, 851, 853, 855 and 865 (though Æthelstan would be dead by 852). In an act arguably as shocking as the attack on Lindisfarne, Canterbury was sacked in 851. It is quite likely that its cathedral church, a prime target for Viking attackers, was pillaged.[38] The intensity of the attacks was clearly increasing, as was the raiders' ambition. This flurry of activity possibly resulted from a further evolution in the Viking landscape as new bands of raiders from Denmark joined those who had previously made their presence felt and who had probably largely come from Norway. Over the next couple of decades, the Viking threat to England would reach alarming levels.

The Threat Grows

In 840, just a year after Æthelwulf became king, there was another large raid, this time on Southampton. Coastal ports were a prime target for such attacks. They were full of portable wealth, a source of plunder that drew Viking raiders like bees to a honeypot. It is no coincidence that so many Viking raids targeted sites on the coast for here the dragon ships could swoop unannounced, hit quick and hard and then escape again before local forces had a chance to respond. Developments in shipbuilding in the eighth century had given the raiders a major technological advantage. Their ships were sleek and swift, and their shallow draft meant that they could journey upriver. In the case of Southampton Water, the river acted as a highway taking the raiders right to the edge of the trading settlement, then known as Hamwic, where they could be beached next to the port on the banks of the River Itchen. This was a significant place. Archaeological investigation reveals that it was a busy trading hub, full of cattle and sheep for slaughter as well as smithies and other industrial workshops. It also suggests that 'Hamwic was the only place in Wessex which sustained any urban community of a type that would be recognised by modern standards', though Alfred's building programme at the end of the ninth century would change that.[39]

Despite their fearsome reputation, the Vikings were not unbeatable in battle. On this occasion the defenders were either waiting in ambush or gathered quickly enough to fight them off. Thirty-three Viking ships were involved in the attack but the defenders, led by Ealdorman Wulfheard, beat them back after great slaughter. How much damage was done to the port itself we do not know but extensive excavations on the site suggest that it was still a vibrant town in 870.[40] However, the port was shifted a few hundred metres to the west early in the tenth century, to higher ground on the Test, approximately on the site of the modern port. The action might even have been fought offshore: Æthelweard's later account states that the ealdorman 'fought against the enemy fleet off Southampton'.[41]

The successful defence of Hamwic that year was counterbalanced by the results of another raid on Portland, about 70 miles to the west. Then an island but today linked to the mainland by a causeway, Portland jutted out into the English Channel and, judging by the number of times it was attacked by raiders, was a particularly lucrative target. Once again, an Anglo-Saxon force was at hand to attempt a defence, led by ealdorman Æthelhelm and the Dorset militia (or *fyrd* as it was known). The fighting was hard but this time it was the Vikings who were triumphant. Amongst the dead was the ealdorman, a significant blow to the defence of the realm in these parts. Æthelweard again adds a sliver of detail, saying that not only did the ealdorman perish in the fight but so too did his companions.[42] The Anglo-Saxon warlord, whether king or ealdorman, was traditionally honour-bound to his retinue (or hearth-troop) as they were to him. The chronicler's words suggest that they played their part and fell in heroic fashion, dying in the attempt to protect their lord, in line with the best traditions of Germanic warriors in times past.

It was proving to be a dangerous time to be an ealdorman. Wulfheard, who beat off the Viking attack at Hamwic in 840, had died the same year though probably not from any injuries he received (Æthelweard suggests he died peacefully). Then Æthelhelm had died in the battle at Portland. The next ealdorman to perish in 841 was Hereberht of Kent, who fell in a fight on Romney Marsh along with many of his troops. These were serious reverses from several perspectives. The losses inevitably took a toll on morale and manpower, and the elimination of several ealdormen was no small matter either. A king, however powerful, could not rule without a powerful coterie of supporters round him. The ealdormen looked after his interests in the shires. In charters of the period, they were referred to in Latin as *dux*, from which the modern 'duke' derives. Below them were the thegns, the Latin word for which was *minister*. The ealdormen gathered the local fighting men, the *fyrd*, and led them into battle. Ealdormen were often battle-gnarled veterans, and it would take years for replacements to grow into the role.

These attacks presaged an upswing in Viking raids, which are now reported in several successive years in the *ASC*, often with more than one per year. In 841 East Anglia and Lindsey were attacked as well as Kent; in the following year both Rochester and London were raided and suffered serious losses. Quentovic too was attacked. This was a major emporium on the Frankish coast, just across the Channel from England. It was assaulted several times by the Vikings over several years, causing its terminal decline. Given the reasonably close proximity of these locations, it is possible that the same group of Viking raiders was responsible for all of the attacks. Equally, though, there may have been a number of different groups involved; and certainly in the next few years there is conclusive evidence that more than one Viking force was on the move in western Europe simultaneously.

These were not yet massed, coordinated attacks. Viking forces from different kingdoms would coalesce, often for one-off raids. They were in some ways mercenaries, chasing short-term gains in wealth, slaves and probably in some cases glory. Whilst there might be one overall leader in control for the duration of a specific mission, accompanied by his men, many others would gather around him whose loyalty would be short-term, if even that. There is evidence from runestones in Scandinavia, carvings on rocks which sometimes serve as obituaries for the departed, that tell of men who served on at least three different missions with different leaders.

With the exception of the attack on Lindsey, these raids on England had a south-eastern focus. However, the one which was recorded in 843 was back in the west of England at the familiar location of Carhampton (though again Henry of Huntingdon places it at Charmouth). Indeed, it bears eerie echoes of the defeat suffered by Ecgberht in 836. Once more there were thirty-five ships involved. And, just as Ecgberht had been present and suffered defeat seven years before, now Æthelwulf was to suffer the same bitter taste. For reasons that are not hard to discern, the *ASC* gloss over the defeat but it must have been serious because news of it was recorded in Francia. The *Annals of St Bertin* record that 'the Northmen launched a major attack on the island of Britain, in that part which is largely inhabited by Anglo-Saxons. After a battle lasting three days, the Northmen emerged the winners: plundering, looting, slaughtering everywhere, they wielded power over the land at will.'[43]

There was another recorded raid in the west in 848 and the few details that have survived nevertheless serve to provide some interesting information. A battle took place at the mouth of the Parrett, where the river flows into the Bristol Channel on Bridgewater Bay. Although various drainage schemes over the centuries have transformed it, the river was once a watery artery into the heart of Somerset. It pushed towards the centre of the shire at Langport, a name which might mean 'long port' in Old English (though it might also mean 'long market'), and strategically close to the royal centre at Somerton.[44] Not far away was a small, nondescript hill rising almost apologetically above the waters of the Somerset Levels. This unknown and somewhat bleak spot, called Athelney, would assume a massive place in English history.

As the Parrett gave ingress to the shire it is unsurprising that Somerset was the site of frequent raids over the years. The Vikings in their shallow-draft ships, the water stallions that allowed them to push deep into the interior, were able to take full advantage. But on this occasion things did not go to plan for them. They were met by the *fyrds* of two counties, Somerset and Dorset, so clearly there had been a chance for the defenders to organise themselves. They were led by two ealdormen, Eanwulf of Somerset and Osric of Dorset, along with someone else who might seem an unlikely figure in this context: Eahlstan, bishop of Sherborne. Eahlstan was a vastly experienced man who had journeyed to Kent with Æthelwulf in 825 when the latter became king there. He was presumably a close confidante of the king, though a few years later he would show a very different side to himself as we shall see. For now he was involved in the hard-fought battle at the mouth of the Parrett, which saw the West Saxons unleash a 'great slaughter' on the enemy (though this little phrase is used almost formulaically by the chroniclers and appears repetitively in the *ASC*).[45]

Over the next few years there were a series of further attacks ranging over a fairly wide area. In 850, Ealdorman Ceorl of Devonshire defeated an army at 'Wicga's Stronghold', the precise location of which is uncertain though it has been tentatively speculated that it might be Wigborough in the south of Somerset.[46] Again, this was a West Saxon triumph with the obligatory 'great slaughter' being unleashed. This was followed in 851 by what sounds like the biggest attack yet. It was said that the raiding army came in 'three and a half hundred ships'. This veritable armada moved into the mouth of the Thames, attacking both London and Canterbury, which the *ASC* say were 'stormed'. London was perched on the frontiers of Mercia and Wessex and was therefore something of an Achilles' heel for the Anglo-Saxons.

There was a response, but it seems to have been disorganised. A Mercian army led by King Beorhtwulf came out to meet the Viking host but was soon put to flight. Beorhtwulf had become king in 840 and his reign seems to have been relatively stable despite the growing Viking threat, but there are no major military enterprises recorded for his reign and he proved to be second best in the face of the Viking onslaught. Given this heavy defeat, it presumably came as a relief to the Mercians when the raiders, rather than head further into their kingdom, instead pushed south into Surrey. This brought them into Æthelwulf's sphere of influence, and at Aclea – 'The Field of Oaks' – about 6 miles north of Horsham he and his son Æthelbald met the invasion head on. The *ASC* gloated of what happened next: the West Saxon army 'there made the greatest slaughter of a heathen raiding-army that we have ever heard tell of up to this present day, and there took the victory'.

Though we are indebted to the *ASC* for giving us information which would otherwise be lost to us, they have their limitations. They are often short on detail and frequently leave the reader wanting more after giving just a tantalising glimpse of some of the great events they cover. Thankfully, supplementary sources exist which can sometimes provide a little extra colour. Simeon of Durham compiled a *History of the Kings of England* in the early twelfth century and is slightly more expansive in his account of Aclea:

Ethelwlf [*sic*], the warlike king of the Saxons, together with his son Ethelbald, also assembled a numerous army in the place called Aclea (Oakley), that is, the Plain of the Oak. And when the flower of the English nation appeared, resplendent in clashing armour, there ensued a long battle between the English and the Danes; the former fighting bravely, when they saw their king conduct himself so fiercely in war; and in this they proved superior to their enemies in the contest. And when they had manfully contended for a very long time, and the fight was courageously and stoutly maintained on both sides, the greatest part of the pagan multitude was entirely overthrown and routed, so that never, in any one country in any one day, either before or since, had so many met their death. On that very day the Christians gloriously obtained the victory and remained masters of the field of slaughter; rendering thanks to God in hymns and confessions.[47]

Henry of Huntingdon exulted in the losses suffered by the raiders, describing it as one of the greatest battles in English history: 'The warriors fell on both sides like corn in harvest, and the bodies and limbs of the slain were swept along by rivers of blood.' He went on to say that 'God vouchsafed the victory to the faithful and caused the heathen to suffer a disgraceful defeat'.[48] Although they give little insight into the tactics, all the chroniclers agree that this was a significant triumph for Æthelwulf.

There was also a battle between the men of Kent and the Vikings around this time, though the exact chronology is unclear; two different versions of the *ASC*, the Winchester and Peterborough accounts, disagree on the precise order. Both versions state that the outcome was a triumph for the army of Kent led by King Æthelstan and Ealdorman Ealhhere and that the fight which took place at Sandwich saw nine Viking ships captured and the rest driven away. But the Peterborough version adds the intriguing detail that Æthelstan and Ealhhere fought the battle in ships. In other words, this was a sea battle, and the Vikings were defeated in what was supposed to be their natural environment.

The glow of victory would not have stopped the Anglo-Saxons from acknowledging the implications of this assault. Not only was the size of this attack of great concern, but this year saw the first instance of a Viking army overwintering at Thanet. Situated on the north-eastern tip of Kent, it was an ideal place for a Viking fleet to moor up for the duration of the campaign. Its strategic attraction to the raiders was further enhanced by the fact that it was actually an island, separated from the mainland by a channel known as the Wantsum, which acted as a cut-through from the English Channel to the Thames Estuary (though it silted up in the late Middle Ages).

Thanet seems to have provided many of the ingredients of a 'classic' Viking defensive position. Raiding parties liked to set up camp by the water's edge either on the ocean or on a river. They would ensure that at least one side of the camp was protected by water whilst on the remaining landward sections of the defences they would erect palisades, ending up with what was known as a D-shaped camp. Whether or not this was the case at Thanet we do not know, although many examples of such camps have been found dotted around Britain and Ireland. In any case, we can be confident that the experienced raiders would take full advantage of the landscape to assume a strong defensive position. And the waterside location would also enable them to keep their ships close at hand and make a quick getaway if necessary.

It seems that the site used by the Vikings in 850–51 was so suitable for their purposes that they used it again in 853. The Anglo-Saxons knew they could not leave the camp alone; if they did, the Vikings would simply use it as a base to launch offensive operations further afield. Moreover, their mere presence was a calculated insult to Æthelwulf and Æthelstan. Looking weak could be damaging, sometimes fatal, to the survival prospects of an Anglo-Saxon ruler. A counterattack on the Viking position was always likely, and soon it came. The attacking army was led by two ealdormen, Ealhhere of Kent and Huda of Surrey. According to the *ASC* it was another a hard-fought contest. The account is ambiguous, recording that the Anglo-Saxons 'at first took the victory', which implies that this might not have been the case by the end of the battle. It also records that many men on both sides were killed or drowned, suggesting a primeval battle of visceral intensity with no quarter given.[49] Simeon of Durham adds the further detail that both ealdormen were killed in the fighting.[50]

The situation was now serious enough that the two great Anglo-Saxon powers, Mercia and Wessex, decided to put aside their rivalry and cooperate. Mercia had a new king, Burgred, who had taken power in 852 after a vicious bout of dynastic infighting in the kingdom. Though he did not know it at the time, he would be the last independent ruler of Mercia. A great and glorious history was drawing to a close. However, that was not yet clear when the alliance between the two kingdoms was sealed by the marriage between Burgred and Æthelwulf's daughter Æthelswith at Chippenham, close to the borders of the two kingdoms. Æthelswith would live until 888 and appeared regularly as a charter witness during her time in Mercia. When she died, she would formally be recorded as 'queen'. This contrasted with the situation in Wessex, where royal wives generally were given a lower status.[51]

The armies of Mercia and Wessex now joined forces and moved together on a common enemy – not the Vikings but the Welsh. Wales was subject to attack from several different directions at this time. The *Brut y Tywysogion* records that in 850 'Meurug was killed by the Saxons', though this could have been in the course of a Welsh raid on Mercian territory rather than the other way round. That same year 'Cyngen was strangled by the pagans'. There was a Welsh king of Powys, Cyngen ap Cadell, though it was probably not him who was the unfortunate victim as he is reported as going to Rome on pilgrimage in 855 and dying there. Then, in 853 'Mona' (Anglesey) was attacked by the 'black pagans'. This is a particularly interesting if brief reference. Anglesey was renowned for the fecundity of its soil but from a Viking perspective was also perfectly placed for raids. It was a short hop over from Ireland, where Vikings had established coastal bases and where Dublin was starting to develop. Anglesey would become a prime target for the Vikings on many occasions. Even post-Conquest in 1098 Magnus Barelegs of Norway fought alongside the men from Gwynedd against a Norman army here. In that instance the Norse–Welsh alliance came out on top, killing the prominent baron Hugh of Montgomery in the process.

The mention of the 'black pagans' is informative. In 851, the fledgling Viking settlements in Ireland came under huge pressure, not so much from the Irish but due to fighting amongst themselves. Two competing groups emerged, set apart as fair or white and dark or black. Quite what divided these two different groups is a matter of great debate, but some have suggested the 'black pagans' were led by a man paradoxically called Óláfr the White.[52] Having fought with fellow Scandinavians in Ireland for power, Óláfr had then moved on to Anglesey.

This was the background to the joint Mercian–West Saxon attack on Wales. Together, say the *ASC*, they were triumphant and made the Welsh subject to the English; though it was a triumph that would prove only temporary. In fact, when the Welsh king Rhodri died in 877 he ruled a kingdom that stretched from Anglesey in the north to Gower in the south, the largest territory a Welsh king had ruled for some time and one that earned him the title Mawr – 'the Great'.[53] In any event, before long the Anglo-Saxon kingdoms would have something much greater to concern them. In 855, the Vikings were back. This time they were overwintering in Sheppey.

Like Thanet, Sheppey was on the northern coast of Kent though some miles west of it. The position of the 'isle of sheep' had great strategic value, situated not far from the mouth of the Thames in the estuary. From its shores, Viking raiders would be able to push far upriver, unleashing death and destruction in their wake. This emulated tactics they had employed in Francia, where they often seized river islands to act as jumping-off points for raids and strong defensive positions given their naval superiority.[54] It was an extremely dangerous situation for Wessex, or so it seemed. Despite this, at a moment of supreme peril, King Æthelwulf was about to disappear.

A Trip to Rome and a Kingdom Lost

Emulating his father, Æthelwulf took steps to secure the line of succession. He left instructions in his will that, on his death, Wessex should go to one of his sons, Æthelbald, and Kent along with Essex, Surrey and Sussex to another, Æthelberht. The welcome coincidence that the latter had the same name as a former king of Kent, and one who had been a *Bretwalda* at that, would surely help to make him acceptable to the people there. However, thanks to a trip to Rome, things would not turn out as neatly as planned.

Æthelwulf was a religious man but he also saw political advantage in supporting the papacy, although it was not yet the powerful institution that it later became. When Pope Leo III consecrated Charlemagne as Emperor on Christmas Day 800 he was doing so for his own protection. Just the year before he had barely escaped with his life when he was attacked in the streets of Rome and an attempt was made to cut out his tongue and gouge out his eyes. Although he escaped with his life, he was unconscious by the time he was rescued. Popes needed powerful protectors, and in return their sanction would give secular rulers greatly enhanced prestige and authority, forming a mutually advantageous arrangement.

Æthelwulf fathered a number of children. There was a big age gap between his eldest and the two youngest brothers, Æthelred and Alfred. Possibly these last two were born to his wife Osburh (Osburga), daughter of Oslac, butler to the king (and an important man through his connections to the traditional ruling house of the Isle of Wight), and the older ones may have been born to an earlier consort. Oslac held an important post, symbolic as much as practical, which provided personal access to the king. Æthelwulf and Osburh's youngest son, Alfred, was sent to Rome on a visit in 853. He was only about four at the time and was therefore unaware of the subtle arts of politics. However, the unfamiliar sights, sounds and smells of the city could make a huge impact on an impressionable child. Whilst Rome's heyday was long in the past, there were still glorious buildings to admire, notably churches like Old St Peter's, Santa Maria Maggiore and St John Lateran. There were also reminders of Rome's old imperial splendour in the shape of the shattered stumps of the Forum and the nearby Colosseum. It must have been an incredible experience for a young prince from Wessex.

For these years, we have a new source to consider. Asser, later bishop of Sherborne, was originally a Welsh monk from St David's. In around 893, he wrote a biography of Alfred the Great. This was the first full-blown biography of an English 'royal' and was stylistically based on the work written on the life of Charlemagne by Einhard about half a century earlier. It played a part in developing what was effectively a 'cult' around Alfred, who in Asser's eyes was a king without equal. Asser doesn't hesitate to build him up, and the visit to Rome is one of the first examples of this. He says that the Pope (Leo IV) 'anointed the child Alfred as king'.[55] It is not just Asser that says this either: the *ASC* does as well. However, it is very unlikely to have been true. Whilst the Pope's anointing of a ruler was certainly not unprecedented – after all, he had done the same with Charlemagne – why should he pick out a young child for such treatment? Alfred had older brothers, much more obvious choices to succeed Æthelwulf when he died. This feels like Asser suggesting divine sanction for Alfred's reign nearly forty years after the visit to Rome. To him, this was a replay of the young Christ visiting the temple in Jerusalem and being recognised as the Messiah by the holy men there. It is a claim that should be treated with great scepticism.

Alfred went accompanied by a large entourage of both 'nobles and commoners',[56] but not his father. Æthelwulf would make his own journey to Rome in 855. By then the king was a man in his fifties, which was close to old age at that time. Pope Leo died in the year of his visit and the papal throne was taken by Benedict III. Æthelwulf was at a point in his life where spiritual concerns and thoughts of his own mortality were starting to dominate his thinking. This can be read into another event in 855 when the king handed over a tenth of his land to the Church 'to the praise of God and his own eternal salvation'.[57] It was as if a ruler who was nearing the end of his time was hoping to purchase a ticket into Heaven by offering an extravagant tithe as a gift.

Anglo-Saxon kings of the past had sometimes gone to Rome to live out their last years humbly, offering repentance for sins committed in their lives. They hoped to avoid the wrath of God by spending their dotage in this holy city, which was draped in Christian iconography and blessed by the memory of saints like Peter and Paul who had both been sacrificed for their faith there. However, it seems as if Æthelwulf had no intention of going to Rome to die. He went to Rome in 'great state'. Asser says that Alfred accompanied him, visiting the city for a second time, although other sources are silent on the matter and it is unlikely a young child made such an epic journey twice in less than three years.[58] Æthelwulf stayed for a whole year, so perhaps there was a penitential aspect to his visit. However, that did not rule out political motivations. Throughout the medieval period, powerful secular authorities sought to reach an accommodation with the Church. There were mutual advantages to be gained, as Æthelwulf appreciated. During his reign, he ordered that an annual gift of 300 mancuses should be sent to Rome: 100 for St Peter, 100 for St Paul and 100 for the Pope.[59]

Important though this royal visit was, there was one even more potentially crucial alliance that Æthelwulf forged on the journey. Since the death of Charlemagne in 814, the Carolingian Empire had been creaking at the seams. Not only had Viking attacks increased in intensity, this extended territory which stretched from Hungary to Spain and from northern Germany down to Italy had proved too difficult for one man to rule. The work of the Vikings was often made easier by internal divisions within the states they raided and Francia was no exception. Charlemagne had been succeeded by Louis the Pious who sought to divide his empire between three of his sons, Lothair, Pepin and Louis. By the 830s his best-laid plans were starting to fail, made worse when he had another son, Charles, from a second marriage and tried to find space for him in the succession.

Bitter division followed, though it seemed to have been brought under control by the time of Louis's death in 840. However, his passing brought renewed infighting. In 843, Charles – known for unclear reasons as the Bald – became ruler of Western Francia, a territory roughly equivalent to modern France. The division of the empire and the accompanying internal conflict played into the hands of Viking raiders, who would grow increasingly ambitious in Francia just as they would in England. The Franks and the Anglo-Saxon kingdoms in England had a common enemy, then, and an alliance between the two would serve both their interests.

So it was arranged that Æthelwulf, now a widower, would marry Charles's daughter Judith, known to history as Judith of Flanders. This was quite a coup as Carolingian rulers did not generally like marrying their children to foreign potentates.[60] There was an enormous age difference between the two as well. Although exact years of birth are not known for either, the king of Wessex was probably well into his fifties whilst his wife was approximately thirteen. This was clearly not a love match – not that many noble marriages were at the time. The marriage may well have been arranged on Æthelwulf's journey out to Rome. The *Annals of St Bertin* record that the two kings had met at that time and Charles had treated Æthelwulf with great honour, escorting him to the borders of his kingdom. By the time that Æthelwulf had returned from Rome, Orléans had been sacked and the Vikings had overwintered on the Seine. There was a striking symmetry between what was happening in England and what was happening in Francia, which acted as a catalyst for closer links between rulers from the two regions.[61]

Judith made an almost unique impression on West Saxon royal history in the ninth century, when nearly all other royal wives are virtually invisible. Alfred's wife Ælswith is not even named in Asser's biography of that later king. Judith was consecrated before leaving Francia, which we should probably interpret as a determined effort by Charles the Bald to strengthen her (and vicariously his) status once she was overseas. Asser records that the wives of West Saxon kings were not even called queens but instead were referred to as 'king's wives'. The alleged evil behaviour of Eadburh at the start of the century when she was accused of killing King Beorhtric was blamed for this ongoing prejudice. In the light of these attitudes, it was a wise precaution to consecrate Judith as queen whilst the opportunity was there. Asser also makes the point that it was decided that Judith, uniquely, 'should sit beside him [Æthelwulf] on the royal throne to the end of his life', which perhaps we should take literally as well as symbolically. Certainly, Wessex was unusual amongst the Anglo-Saxon kingdoms in downgrading the status of king's wives in the way that it did.

In the event, the king would not be around for much longer, but his final years were possibly the most dramatic in an already eventful life. Instead of returning to Wessex in triumph, he came back under a cloud. He was about to find himself mixed up in a decidedly odd succession dispute. In this case, debate was raging over who was to succeed him whilst he was still alive. Æthelwulf had several older sons who had already played a role in his government. Æthelstan had of course been king of Kent but he is believed to have died around 852 judging by the lack of references to him in any of the sources after this date (although as previously mentioned he might have been Æthelwulf's brother rather than his son). Two others, Æthelbald and Æthelberht, were looking after Wessex and Kent respectively whilst Æthelwulf was in Rome. Æthelberht was the junior partner of the two, having not been recorded as a witness to any charters before 854 whilst Æthelbald had accompanied his father into battle before that date.

An Anglo-Saxon king did not have absolute power and had to rule with the aid of his councillors, both religious and secular in the shape of the bishops and ealdormen. The bishops were in a potentially complex position, having to serve two masters simultaneously. As religious figures they were answerable to the archbishop of Canterbury (or in the north to the archbishop of York) and ultimately through him to the Pope in Rome. But their role was also a political one. The Church obtained both power and wealth through the patronage of kings, and bishops at an individual level were beneficiaries of this. In return they not only gave him moral support but also practical advice when needed. Their role could be decisive in terms of reaching a decision and bringing waverers to the king's side. On the other hand, the withdrawal of support at a crucial time could have potentially disastrous results.

The ealdormen were the king's deputies, his local enforcers. In an age of fragmented communications and expanding kingdoms the demands on rulers were growing. They needed powerful supporters to be their local eyes and ears. In Wessex there were about a dozen ealdormen at any one time with each shire having one (though possibly Kent had two). There are currently sixty-six men known to have served as ealdormen of Wessex across the ninth century (though there were almost certainly more whose names have been lost). It is likely that other Anglo-Saxon kingdoms had similar structures to Wessex – certainly we know that Mercia did. Ealdormen played an important role in peacetime. They administered justice on the king's behalf and also had a fiscal and economic function, collecting taxes and dues and regulating trade. They were vital in war, when they would organise and lead the shire *fyrd* into battle.[62] They were essential allies of the king. But as Æthelwulf was about to find out, their local power made them dangerous.

What happened after Æthelwulf's return is not referred to at all in the *ASC*, perhaps out of embarrassment and a sense that some things are best left unsaid. Asser on the other hand is far from silent on what happened next. This is a good moment to say something about Asser's biography, which has caused a fair bit of controversy over the years (and it is important to note that the work, as far as it has survived after the disastrous loss of the only known original in 1731, appears to be an incomplete draft). Alfred P. Smyth was a much-respected historian of the period whose monumental work, *King Alfred the Great*, was published in 1995. This large volume has several chapters on what Smyth calls 'a thousand-year-old forgery'. Smyth contends that the work attributed to Asser was in fact a later forgery penned in the eleventh century. Smyth was not the first to assert this. A 1964 work, *An Introduction to the Study of History* by Professor V. H. Galbraith, suggested that Asser's work was the creation of Leofric, bishop of Devon and Cornwall, in 1046; and even before this, others were casting aspersions on the biography's authenticity.

Other specialists on the period have argued vigorously that the work attributed to Asser is authentic. Dorothy Whitelock, another prominent historian from the second half of the twentieth century, was a strong advocate of this argument. Whilst accepting that Asser may sometimes have exaggerated certain things, as she rightly pointed out our own age is not immune from such tendencies either. And the fact that Asser has some information included in his writings which is not mentioned elsewhere is hardly surprising given the limited number of alternative sources available. Indeed, a strong counterargument would be that Asser, whose existence no one seriously doubts, was personally very close to Alfred and would have access to detailed information that few other people would.[63]

These caveats are important because what happened next is described by Asser but not by the *ASC*. In Asser's account, when Æthelwulf returned to England with his new bride he received a frosty reception from Æthelbald, who had been ruling in Wessex in his absence. In fact, Asser told of 'a disgraceful episode' which took place 'to the west of Selwood', a forest in Wiltshire that broadly marked the division between the western and eastern parts of Wessex. This may well be significant because the episcopal power of Winchester in the east was rising at the time, sponsored by Æthelwulf, and the position of Sherborne in the west was diminishing accordingly. A very unholy rivalry was developing. The 'disgraceful episode' was nothing less than a plot to replace Æthelwulf as king of Wessex with Æthelbald on a more permanent basis. Implicated were Eanwulf, ealdorman of Somerset, and Eahlstan, bishop of Sherborne. It has been speculated that Æthelbald was unhappy at his father's marriage to Judith and the threat it posed to his own long-term prospects. But this seems unlikely. The bride was barely of childbearing age and the groom was old; even if the marriage produced a child, let alone a boy, it would be many years before he would be regarded as a suitable king.

More likely, Æthelbald had enjoyed the trappings of power in his supposedly temporary position and did not want to hand back the reins. Æthelwulf's long absence gave him the chance to build up relationships with men such as Eanwulf and Eahlstan who stood to gain a great deal if their man stayed on as king of Wessex with all the opportunities for patronage that went with it. Asser suggests that in the interests of the kingdom Æthelwulf backed down and accepted a division of the kingdom, keeping Kent but relinquishing Wessex to Æthelbald. But such generosity seems unlikely in a man who had been the leader of the pack for so long. Perhaps his grip on power had gone; maybe age was taking its toll. Retirement might have been tempting, for these were deeply unsettling times: on 28 December 857 Viking raiders descended on Paris and burned it, with Tours and Poitiers sacked in the same year. Even God was angry: a lightning strike on the church of St Peter in Cologne caused great damage and a priest and a deacon were killed; at Trier another church was struck by lightning and a mysterious dog appeared, ran round the altar and then disappeared in the bowels of the earth.[64]

These were ominous signs, suggesting that the world was on the verge of a huge upheaval. Æthelwulf however would not be around to see this, for in 858 the vastly experienced ruler breathed his last. A religious man, he had perhaps by now started to look forward to the blessings of Heaven after the trials and tribulations he had suffered on Earth. Æthelbald could now enjoy the trappings of power without threat from his father, though little good would it do him.

3

The Sons of Æthelwulf

Then was a splintering of shields, the sea-wolves coming on
in war-whetted anger.
'The Battle of Maldon', Anglo-Saxon poem

The Great Heathen Army Arrives

Æthelwulf was buried at Steyning in Sussex, where a Saxon grave slab possibly belonging to him can still be seen in the church. His body was later transferred to Winchester when his youngest son, Alfred, established a royal mausoleum there. Æthelbald not only assumed power – which he had of course already effectively seized before his father's death – but also sought something else of Æthelwulf's legacy in the shape of the late king's widow. Even in the twenty-first century, marrying a stepmother is potentially a complex legal issue. In Æthelbald's case it certainly raised Asser's hackles, though again the *ASC* are silent on the matter. While Asser was scandalised, perhaps he was not totally surprised at such actions from a man he described as 'grasping'. He wrote that 'Æthelbald ... against God's prohibition and Christian dignity, and also contrary to the actions of all pagans, took over his father's marriage-bed and married Judith ... incurring great disgrace from all who heard of it.'[1]

Æthelbald would only reign until 860. A couple of isolated charters are all that we possess to attest his reign, and the *ASC* say next to nothing about it. His seizure of Wessex from his father and his marriage to his stepmother are the only real imprints he made on history. On his death, he was buried in Sherborne, which seems quite appropriate given the part that the bishop of that place had played in his rise to power.

With Æthelbald's death, Judith was a widow for the second time despite probably not yet turning sixteen. She now returned to Francia after selling off her possessions in England. She had little reason to feel any real affection for the country, after all. Her father, Charles the Bald, was still dealing with his Viking problem. In 858 he had been forced to hand over 686 lbs of gold and 3,250 lbs of silver to get back Louis, Abbot of St Denis, who had been captured by raiders.

On Judith's return, Charles placed her at Senlis under the care of a guardian. She was after all a valuable asset in the marriage stakes, although her unfortunate track record might have put off some suitors. She soon showed herself to have a mind of her own. Without her father's permission she married Baldwin of Flanders, a man associated with dissentient elements within Charles's own family who had rebelled against his rule. Charles was understandably incensed. He summoned his bishops to pronounce their judgement against the marriage. It was said that it was as if Judith had 'run away with a thief', for in the legal constructs of the time the king should have had the final say on Judith's next husband.[2]

The remarkable story of Judith and her West Saxon connection was not quite over. Despite her father's anger, which resulted in Baldwin and Judith going into exile, the family dispute was patched up and they returned. An 'official' marriage ceremony was conducted which Charles pointedly avoided. Despite this frosty start, Baldwin later proved himself to be a staunch and reliable ally to Charles. The date of Judith's death is not known but is believed not to predate 870. She had a son from her marriage to Baldwin who became Baldwin II, one of possibly five children to result from the match. Sometime in the last decade of the ninth century he was married to Ælfthryth, daughter of Alfred the Great. Frankish–West Saxon marital relations had come full circle.

Æthelbald was replaced by his brother Æthelberht. Again, the chroniclers do not have much to say about his reign. However, in the *ASC* there is one brief but highly significant entry for the year 860 which says that he 'succeeded to the entire kingdom'. In other words, the experiment of having two kings, one for Wessex and another for Kent and the other kingdoms, was over. From now on, Wessex would be ruled by one overall king – an important but often overlooked development. Whilst the main sources have little to say on Æthelberht's reign, there is a charter (S327 in the numbering scheme developed for such documents) which although incorrectly dated appears to relate to the first year of his reign, 860. It is witnessed by leading men from across the extended kingdom, including the archbishop of Canterbury and bishops from Kent and Wessex, a clear sign that the king's council was composed of men from all over the land.[3]

Whilst details are sparse for this reign, the one main event that is recorded for it must nevertheless have come as a shock. Winchester was not yet the powerhouse it would become in Alfred's reign and after, but it was still a very important place and the home of the bishop for the east of Wessex. During Æthelberht's reign (860–865), a great Viking 'ship-army' descended on the city. The raid is corroborated in the *Annals of St Bertin*. Charles the Bald had promised these raiders tribute but it was not forthcoming, and they therefore made the short crossing over the Channel from their base on the Somme and fell on Wessex. However, as they returned to their fleet from an attack on Winchester, burdened with booty, they were assaulted by an army under the ealdormen Osric of Hampshire and Æthelwulf of Berkshire. The men of Wessex delivered fierce retribution on the raiders who fled in their ships.[4] Asser adds that 'the Vikings were cut down everywhere and, when they could resist no longer, they took to flight like women'. As far as surviving records are concerned, this battle was the only highlight of Æthelberht's reign. He died in 865 and was buried next to his brother in Sherborne. Asser pays tribute to the late king, saying that 'after governing in peace, love and honour for five years, Æthelberht went the way of all flesh, to the great sorrow of the people'.[5] It sounds like a genuinely warm epitaph, perhaps the result of Asser's relationship with Æthelberht's young brother Alfred.

Late in Æthelberht's reign (or possibly shortly after it) there was a serious development when a large Viking army set up camp in Thanet again. Those ruling Kent made peace with them, but it came at a cost. This deal, however, once struck was not honoured. When the raiders thought it over, they decided the payment they received was insufficient to dissuade them from raiding. Under cover of darkness, they stole out of their camp in Thanet and launched raids across eastern Kent. This was the first appearance of what was later known as the *Danegeld*, and the inherent flaws of paying protection money were already apparent. If a raider sensed weakness, they were unlikely to honour any commitments they had made. Like a predator stalking prey, they would sniff out fear and become ever bolder in their efforts. Asser even described the Vikings as 'crafty foxes'. The raiders saw a rich kingdom and a lack of vigour and resolve to defend it. This tempted them to seek for more, and so they did. The people of east Kent suffered for it.[6]

In 865, Æthelred I succeeded Æthelberht as king of Wessex. The sons of Æthelwulf were dropping by the wayside. Two older brothers had reigned before Æthelred and now just he and Alfred were left of

Æthelwulf's brood. Judged by the mores of his time, Æthelwulf had done his job by producing several sons but it was no longer clear that this was enough. Whilst Ecgberht and Æthelwulf had lived relatively long lives, an unfortunate and contrary pattern had started to emerge in their successors.

Specific details of Æthelred's reign are again in short supply as far as his own personal style of kingship is concerned. Not so for what was happening elsewhere in England, however, for in 865 there occurred an event that was, in retrospect, one of the most significant in Anglo-Saxon history. This was the arrival in East Anglia of what became known as the Great Heathen Army, or *se mycel hæpen here*. The arrival of this force changed the rules of engagement in England entirely. This horde was not here to raid and then leave again. Instead, it was intent on staying. It would move across the English kingdoms, knocking them over like dominoes. This was not about pillaging; it was about domination.

Whilst details at first sight appear typically sparse, by looking at various sources we can add some flesh to the bones as far as this Great Heathen Army is concerned. Æthelweard tells us that the Viking 'fleets' involved were led by the 'tyrant Inwær'. This equates to the name Ivarr, and it may be that here we have one of the famous Vikings of all, the infamous Ivarr the Boneless ('Beinlausi'), the quasi-legendary son of the even more legendary Ragnar Lodbrok (by tradition the son-in-the law of the renowned Sigurd 'the dragon slayer'). Ivarr the Boneless has become a notorious icon of the Viking Age. His very name is cloaked in sinister mystery. Was he 'boneless' because he had a physical disability? Did the sobriquet refer to some form of impotence? Was he so ruthless that he lacked basic humanity and therefore appeared to be inhuman? Was he snakelike in his character (the serpent had magical connections with his father Ragnar)? All of these have been suggested as explanations for his name. Yet it is an anachronism. It was first used centuries later when a twelfth-century source was one of the first to suggest that 'he was said to lack bones'.[7]

A prominent Viking called Ivarr had been active in Ireland for over a decade along with his ally Amlaib (or Óláfr). Based at Dublin, the two men, in alliance with minor Irish kings, had caused havoc in parts of that island between 851 and 864. This Ivarr may well be the same man, although Æthelweard tells us that his Inwær arrived from the north – and an entry into England from Scottish territory, some of which had long been under Viking control, is by no means unlikely.[8]

The Great Heathen Army made its way to East Anglia where it overwintered. Given its location, East Anglia was somewhat exposed to raiders from the east. One source, the *Historia de Sancto Cuthberto*, suggests that many of the raiders were *scaldingi*, a name that derives from the Latin *scaldis*, referring to the River Scheldt which flows through what is now the north of France and the west of Belgium and the Netherlands.[9] This would imply a short channel-hop across to East Anglia, a route of approach that makes perfect sense. England was increasingly surrounded by Viking bases in Ireland, the Low Countries, the islands off the north of Scotland and of course Scandinavia itself, rendering it ever more vulnerable to a large-scale attack. But this latest attack was to be very different. This time, the army wanted to stay.

The timing of the arrival of the Great Heathen Army in England may well not be coincidental. After decades of internal strife, Francia had unified somewhat. Innovative defensive systems had been constructed such as fortified bridges on the Seine upriver from Paris. These appear to have made things much more difficult for the Viking raiders. As a result, it is very possible that they looked around for easier targets. English defences were much less developed than those of Francia and this seems to have caused the Viking groups that had previously been engaged on the continent to change their focus. The Viking groups that were prominent during the period – for there were many of them, some on the Loire and others on the Seine or Somme – were very flexible; after all, this is precisely the advantage that their ships bestowed.

Ragnar Lodbrok does not appear in contemporary English histories at all; even Ivarr appears only briefly. It is also worth pointing out that Ivarr is a common Viking name and the contemporary chroniclers such as Æthelweard do not refer to 'their' Ivarr as being 'Boneless'. For the involvement of these two men in English affairs we are forced to rely on controversial sources in the form of later sagas. Many (though not all) were written centuries later in Iceland, which had been Christianised by then. The sagas reflect the requirements of their audience in thirteenth-century Iceland rather than aiming to provide a historically accurate account of what happened back in the ninth century. They are, after all, stories (evident in their frequent references to supernatural events). That said, the paucity of historical evidence for the period means we should be cautious before altogether rejecting the usefulness of sagas as sources. Neither did the mythologising of Ragnar end with the saga writers; some nineteenth-century historians even suggested that Queen Victoria was descended from him.[10]

One of these sagas is called *The Tale of Ragnar's Sons*. It is a very short work with uncertain provenance, but it is significant because of the link it makes between Ivarr the Boneless (and for that matter Ragnar Lodbrok) and England. It tells of Ivarr and his brothers raiding in the Baltic, apparently inspired by their father's awesome reputation and a jealous desperation to outdo him. So great were the tensions between father and sons that they came to blows. The story is repeated in more detail in *The Saga of Ragnar Lodbrok and His Sons*. However, the action as far as England is concerned relates to Northumbria in these two sources. In the event, if the 'Inwær' that Æthelweard refers to is indeed the same man as Ivarr the Boneless then his activities in East Anglia are omitted from both saga accounts.[11]

Two of the most difficult questions to answer about the era of Viking 'expansionism' concern what lay behind it and why it happened when it did. It is a hot topic of conversation amongst historians. In fact, contemporary historians do not like to talk about expansionism, preferring to talk of a Viking diaspora. In the past it was believed that land hunger, a desire for *lebensraum* so to speak, was the major motivation. Although Scandinavia has some fertile areas it also has others which are far less productive. On the coast of Norway many pockets of productive land were hemmed in by mountains, and much of Denmark's land was difficult to work. This paucity of good agricultural land, exacerbated by a possible rise in population, is said to have forced Vikings to look elsewhere.[12]

However, this attractively simple explanation now fails to satisfy a number of commentators. Factors such as political developments in Scandinavia itself seem to have been a driver. In the ninth century there was an increasing trend in Norway (and later in Denmark) for powerful individuals to develop the concept of kingship not just over small regions but increasingly over nascent nation-states too. In Norway, an increasingly powerful group of warlords emerged with the collective name *sekonungr* – 'sea kings'. These were powerful men with bases ashore but who spent much of their time adding to their stores of portable wealth by raiding. Perhaps the closest analogy would be to powerful pirates in the seventeenth and eighteenth centuries who grew so strong that they lived outside the law and set up bases in the Caribbean which became like small kingdoms; in this case, however, instead of names like 'Blackbeard' we get Scandinavian equivalents from the Anglo-Saxon period such as Jalkr 'the Screamer', Maevill 'the Seagull' or Mysingr 'the Mouse'.[13] Such men could get rich quick by falling on unsuspecting towns and religious establishments and making off with a large haul of booty.

Eventually some sea kings would expand their powerbase at the expense of others, and we end up with true kings like Harald Finehair in Norway. Such developments motivated sea-king types, dismayed at the prospect of being dominated by another individual, to leave Norway and push far out into the Atlantic. These men would establish a fledgling state (without an overall king at this stage) in Iceland and much later would eventually reach the fringes of North America. Viking adventurers would also go east, with the Rus' coming from Sweden and the fringes of the Baltic and pushing deep into the hinterland of Russia, taking advantage of mighty riverine systems like those of the Dnieper and the Volga that gouged out watery highways through the difficult terrain. That said, some of them may not have been running from anything; mere profit could be lure enough.

Material gain is a motivation that can easily be understood even today; there are many people in our world who are driven to strive for self-enrichment, albeit mostly through different methods to those employed by the Vikings. But there are other factors that are potentially more obscure to modern readers. Some have suggested there was a lack of marriageable women to go around. Viking society practiced polygyny, whereby men could have more than one wife or partner (there is strong evidence that not all 'wives' had equal standing and that, for want of a better word, some were effectively concubines rather than full-status wives). This could have led to an imbalance between male and female partners, driving raiders abroad in search of female partners whom they often obtained through enslavement. In this respect it is interesting to note that modern science suggests that the main genetic influence on the male side of the Icelandic population is Scandinavian, whilst on the female side it is more British and Irish.

Not only foreign wives were on the minds of Viking raiders though. Domestic (Scandinavian) brides of status demanded a bride-price. A man therefore needed wealth to fund his marriages, and raiding was one way to obtain it. Land was an important form of non-portable wealth, so much so that according to Snorri Sturluson, the doyen of saga-writers, Harald Finehair, the first king of Norway, set out on a campaign of conquest because the woman he wanted as his partner, Gyda, refused to accept him because he had insufficient land. Whilst sometimes the details of Snorri's stories might be taken with a pinch of salt, there is no reason to doubt the general suggestion that land was an important factor in attracting a partner.[14]

There is another factor that perhaps might seem remote from a modern perspective. The Vikings were a warrior culture, and as in many such cultures of the time status was found through glory. The warrior hall of Valhalla was no myth to a Viking warrior, who believed he would be picked up from the battlefield by Valkyries if he died heroically in battle. Such warriors wanted status and remembrance, living on after their deaths, as evidenced by runestones scattered around Scandinavia commemorating brave deeds. If a man were lucky (or, more crucially, rich and powerful) his deeds would be praised in the mead hall by a *skald* or poet. If he reached the ultimate level of fame, he might live on across the centuries in the sagas like Ragnar Lodbrok, Ivarr the Boneless or Egil Skallagrimsson.

Above all, one word best sums up the Viking attempts to settle: opportunity. The development of maritime technology in Scandinavia gave the people there a competitive advantage. Places like Francia and England were wealthy and fragmented, a dangerous combination which appealed to those who wished to settle as well as raid. These migrations, for such they were, certainly held risks for the Viking armies involved, which had suffered military reverses as well as triumphs in the past. But the leaders were playing for high stakes and could attract enough supporters to their side to launch a viable bid for land in a number of areas. The challenge varied greatly: in Iceland the *landnám* ('land-taking') took place on an island that was either completely uninhabited or at most was home to a few Irish monks in search of solitude. Parts of Scotland were already inhabited but were nevertheless overpowered. In Ireland, sea power enabled the Vikings to establish coastal bases though the hinterland proved stubbornly resistant to conquest. In England, as in Francia, the situation presented a much tougher challenge, but this was not sufficient to put off the Great Heathen Army.

East Anglia was protected on one side by the sea, though with Viking fleets in the vicinity that was a very dubious form of protection. This had long been the case. Not for nothing were a number of forts of the 'Saxon Shore' built in East Anglia when the Romans ruled Britannia. Now the descendants of those raiding 'Saxons' from half a millennium before were on the back foot. The size of the Viking force arrayed against the East Anglians was clearly too large to resist and the king of East Anglia, Edmund, was in no position to rebuff Viking demands. Judging by what happened next, the Vikings were allowed to stay where they were. As for their demands, East Anglia was renowned for its horse stock and horses were invaluable to the Vikings, who were good horsemen as well as good seafarers. East Anglia was not yet the Vikings' immediate priority, but East Anglian horses would prove useful against unsuspecting targets further afield.

Edmund was about a decade into his reign as king, having come to the throne of East Anglia in the mid-850s. By tradition he was crowned on Christmas Day 855. His story was written up over a century later by a French monk, Abbo of Fleury, who was visiting England and heard it from St Dunstan, an iconic figure of the period. Abbo gives us details which are not included in some other sources and tells his readers that the 'Danes' were led by Ivar [*sic*] and Ubba; other accounts in different contexts tell us that these two were brothers, both being sons of Ragnar Lodbrok. If Abbo's details are correct, the two generals decided that they should now head north, bypassing Mercia and falling on Northumbria. The Viking onslaught was well and truly underway.

Northumbria and Mercia under Attack

The Vikings now moved north. Their 'army' was in fact a cosmopolitan force made up of many different components, with individuals coming and going frequently. But in essence this force would be in England for the next decade, and some of its members would lay down roots in the country and (perhaps unwittingly at the beginning) help to shape it. Æthelweard implies that they used their ships to cross the Humber, the traditional boundary between the Mercian territory of Southumbria and Northumbria.[15] Most likely it was a two-pronged move with land forces using the horses that they had obtained in East Anglia whilst their ships moved up the coast. There were other occasions when Viking armies used this approach such as in later raids on Wessex, benefiting from an assault on two fronts. Viking naval superiority would also allow them to ferry land forces across the troublesome Humber Estuary unopposed.

Events in Northumbria played into the hands of the Vikings, who had sharply attuned political antennae. They often launched their attacks when their opponents were disunited, and this was no exception. Northumbria was in turmoil. Two competing kings were slugging it out for the right to rule in York (then called Eoforwic). One of them was Osberht, whose name suggests a connection to the legitimate ruling line in Northumbria (with former monarchs such as Oswald and Oswiu). The other was Ælle, whom the *ASC* call an 'unnatural king'.[16] This presumably means that he was not of the ruling bloodline. As noted previously, it was not necessarily the late king's son who inherited on his death, but any new king was expected to be part of the last ruler's family, an *ætheling*, which approximately means 'throne worthy' and more generally refers to a prince of the royal blood. Despite this, Ælle seems to have obtained the throne: the *ASC* tell us that the people of Northumbria had 'thrown down their king Osberht and accepted Ælle'. Æthelweard, in a similar vein, wrote that they 'all unanimously elected an ignoble king'.[17] In the context of the time, such comments suggest that what happened next was seen as divine chastisement for disturbing the natural order.

York appears to have been unprepared for the Viking attack when it came. It was a place with probably around 2,000 inhabitants, the largest settlement in England north of London.[18] However it's normal population would be swollen as this was All Saint's Day, 1 November 866, an occasion for celebration. The city, caught by surprise, was taken. According to Simeon of Durham, the Great Heathen Army destroyed churches and monasteries and left York a blazing wreck. Shocked, the Northumbrians afterwards put aside their differences and counterattacked, hoping to drive the raiders from their city. Asser suggests that York was not properly defended with strong walls and that some of the Northumbrians succeeded in breaking through. Several accounts state that the Vikings for a time were on the back foot and some of them even started to flee.[19] However, this promising start was misleading. Once inside, the Northumbrians were cornered by stronger Viking forces and many of them were slaughtered. The two warring kings had seen that the Viking threat was so serious that they should bury their differences and combine their armies, and both were killed in the attack on the city. The Vikings had had five months to erect their own defences and later actions at Reading and Repton suggest that they were capable of constructing these rapidly. It is very likely that they had built fortifications within York which proved too strong for the Northumbrians to breach. As far as York was concerned the Vikings were here to stay, although not until the tenth century would it become a true Viking powerhouse.

The Vikings undoubtedly left terror in their wake. In recent times it has become fashionable in some quarters to argue that their attachment to violence has been overplayed. It is certainly true that their reputation in this respect has on occasion overshadowed their qualities as traders, artisans and adventurers. But this was at heart a warrior culture. In the words of one of the foremost contemporary Viking historians, their militaristic ethos 'combined a violent aesthetic with sworn loyalty and a dazzling material culture of killing'.[20] This sums up rather well the core elements of a Viking army on the march. It was a formidable combination. These were warriors brought up in a strong military tradition. They were intensely loyal to their warlord (as long as he remained successful) and by sharing in the profits of raids they had a shared interest in succeeding. The Vikings also enjoyed a military advantage in that they were relatively manoeuvrable due to their skills on horseback and at sea.

In contrast, the Anglo-Saxons were always trying to guess at the Vikings' next move; or, in the case of the surprise attack on York, not trying to guess at all. Whilst the *fyrd* system meant that a local militia was available to the ealdormen of the shires, it would take time to assemble them to face any threat and by then it would often prove too late. Defences would develop further in later years, and early warning systems would be put in place to improve the situation including a series of beacons and improved *herepaths* – literally 'army paths' or military roads – that would enable a quicker response to major attacks. England was not yet on a war footing, and this deficiency would bring the Anglo-Saxon kingdoms to the brink of extinction.

The gravity of the Viking presence was now apparent, though it is unclear if it had yet been recognised as an attempt at all-out conquest. The fact that Northumbria was unprepared for an attack despite widespread awareness of a large army in East Anglia suggests that the true scale of the threat was not yet appreciated. For the Vikings' part, there was probably no coherent plan to conquer all the Anglo-Saxon kingdoms at the outset. Rather the attacks would be opportunistic, with attempts made to take land wherever and whenever an opportunity presented itself. East Anglia was the first port of call, though it had not yet been overrun. Northumbria was first to see a serious attempt at conquest, with Mercia effectively bypassed on the journey there. If the Mercians thought they had escaped the worst of it, though, they were much mistaken.

There is one story connected to the Viking campaign in Northumbria that probably owes more to the saga writers than to historical reality. It concerns Ragnar Lodbrok and his sons. Ragnar Lodbrok ('Hairy Breeches') is a figure so shrouded in mist that he is in a historical sense practically invisible. There was a Viking leader called Ragnar recorded at the siege of Paris in 845,[21] but there is little else on which to base any historical assessment. Still, several sagas have plenty to say. *The Saga of Ragnar Lodbrok and His Sons* for example tells us that Ragnar was jealous of the success of his sons and resolved to set off for England with just two ships. Both were wrecked in a storm, though the men carried on them reached England safely. It is also worth noting that Irish and later English sources also have tales of Ragnar which either add detail or provide information contradictory to the Scandinavian sagas, so there is circumstantial evidence that someone of this name did exist and made a big impression in several different regions, each of them perhaps visited by him during his remarkable life.[22]

According to the sagas, the English, in the form of Ælle, were ready for Ragnar when he arrived. Vastly outnumbered by Ælle's army, Ragnar's men were all struck down but he himself proved to be invincible, helped by a magical shirt that had been given to him by his wife Aslaug (this detail appears in another source, *The Saga of Ragnar's Sons*). In the end he was the last man standing from the Viking army and he was subdued by weight of numbers. He was taken before Ælle who demanded to know his name. Infuriated by his stubborn silence, Ælle ordered that Ragnar should be thrown into a snake pit to make him talk. At first the snakes would not touch him, but once his magical shirt had been removed they bit him vigorously. Feeling the life ebbing out of him, Ragnar presciently warned of his sons' vengeance: 'The piglets would grunt now if they knew what the old pig suffers.'[23]

It is unlikely that this tale is true. For one thing, there are no highly venomous snakes resident in England. The story also bears a close resemblance to that of Gunnarr Gjúkason, a legendary tale concerning the hero Sigurd who kills the dragon Fáfnir and falls in love with Brynhildr, the famous Valkyrie. Gunnarr and his brother Högni kill Sigurd and claim the dragon's treasure. However, when they in turn are captured and pressured to reveal where the treasure is, they refuse. Högni's heart is cut out and Gunnarr is thrown into a snake pit. For a time he enchants the snakes with a harp which his wife, Gudrun, has helpfully given him but this only works for so long before a particularly vicious serpent bites him in the heart and he finally dies.

The snake pit motif therefore is not unique to the tale of Ragnar Lodbrok. But in this story, fearful of the repercussions of what he had done, Ælle sent messengers to Denmark to placate Ragnar's sons. They were predictably enraged when they got the news. One of them, Bjorn Ironside, shook his spear so vigorously that the shaft shattered. Another, Sigurd Snake-in-the Eye, was busy paring his fingernails with a knife and he was so shocked that he cut through to the bone without noticing anything. His brother Hvitserk was holding a gaming piece – probably part of a set from the famous Viking strategy game *hnefatafl* – and he gripped it so hard that the blood poured out of his fingers. Only Ivarr remained calm in response to the terrible news.

The brothers made their way to England. After various machinations and twists in the plotline there was a final climactic battle, at the end of which Ælle was defeated and captured. His fate was terrible. In Ivarr's words, 'my advice now is that we remember the sort of death that he ordered for our father. Now the man who is the most skilled woodcarver shall carve an eagle on his back as carefully as is possible, and that eagle shall turn red with blood'. This is a reference to that horrific form of execution known as the 'blood eagle'. Historical references to such a violent method of killing are in short supply though there are other literary allusions to its use such as in the *Orkneyinga Saga* when Halfdan Háleg ('long legs') suffers such a fate. Significantly, Halfdan was no common man but the son of Harald Finehair, king of Norway, placing him in a long history of royal sacrifices in pagan Scandinavian society. It has also been pointed out that there are several accounts of Irish kings being killed in ritual fashion whilst Ivarr was on the island; he may be a common denominator in the king-slaying that took place during these years in England and Ireland (though he was not responsible for the execution of Halfdan Háleg).[24] If the story has a germ of truth in it, Ælle suffered a particularly brutal and painful end. Their vengeance achieved, all the brothers returned home – with the exception of Ivarr, who became, in the words of the saga, the ruler of England.[25]

A similar story is told in the *Tale of Ragnar's Sons*. This shorter work is where we get the story of the magical shirt. Further gruesome details are given about the blood eagle, of how the unfortunate Ælle had all his ribs smashed away from his backbone with a sword. The saga also refers to a famous poem, *Praise-Poem for King Knut*, which makes mention of how 'Ivar [*sic*] who resided at York ordered Ælle's back carved by an eagle'. There is another source of information that makes an intriguing suggestion about the end of Ælle, specifically that he was betrayed by one of his household servants. The source, *Fragmentary Annals of Ireland* (also known as the *Three Fragments*), is sometimes regarded as controversial, but the suggestion it is not at all farfetched. After all, if the king was regarded as a usurper, then the possibility of an enemy within cannot be discounted.[26] Whatever the case, Ælle's brutal end may have served a purpose beyond just disposing of a troublesome king. Another account of a blood-eagling in the *Orkneyinga Saga* suggests that it was done as a sacrifice to Odin.[27]

The writer who composed *The Tale of Ragnar's Sons* is less dramatic in his claims than other sources, stating that Ivarr only ruled over a portion of England rather than inferring that he took all of it.[28] Probably inspired by these sagas, the later Danish historian Saxo Grammaticus repeats many of the details in the thirteenth century.[29] However, he makes Ragnar the king of Denmark in his account, something that some modern historians are very sceptical about as it contradicts the chronology given for other rulers of parts of the country during the period.[30] In fact, much of the fragmentary evidence that does exist, weak though it is, suggests that Ragnar had strong connections with Norway (specifically the Viken area, around modern Oslo) though that does not preclude a link with Denmark too, particularly Zealand. After all, the Baltic at its narrowest point is less than 2 miles wide and its northern shore in Sweden is not only close to Norway but is visible at the tip of Denmark on all but the foggiest of days.

Whilst the tale of Ragnar's death may not be true (a lesser-known source, the Danish *Annales Ryenses*, has him dying on campaign in Ireland in 854),[31] the success of the Viking raids in the north is unquestionable. The conquest of Northumbria was a major coup for the Vikings, and the capture of York a huge achievement. They now had control over a vital trading centre in the north of England, later giving the city the Viking name of Jorvik. It also had substantial political status and, with its bishopric, was the religious centre of the north. During the following decades the Viking hold on Jorvik would mostly remain strong. It would also form part of an extended Viking sphere of interest stretching not from north to south but from east to west, even extending across the watery frontier of the Irish Sea to Dublin; later, both cities would be controlled by the same ruling dynasty. They did install a client king in Northumbria, with the very Anglo-Saxon name Ecgberht, but before long the kingdom was effectively dismembered. Ecgberht was given the area beyond the Tyne – basically Bernicia – as his part of the realm but the remainder – Deira – they kept for themselves.

The fall of Northumbria might have seemed enough for the time being but instead its capture seems to have fed a lust for more amongst the conquerors. At the beginning of the ninth century Mercia was the most powerful kingdom in England. That position of prominence had slowly been eroded, with Wessex becoming more significant at its expense. Mercia's weakening had not gone unnoticed by the Viking armies. They had bullied East Anglia into tacit acceptance of their presence and now Northumbria was theirs. En route to the latter they would have passed through Mercian territory, and the lack of resistance would have registered with the Vikings. It evidenced a lack of fighting power and intent, and that was a very dangerous signal to send.

With ambitions fired up by success, in 868 the Great Heathen Army set its sights on Mercia. Nottingham was in a key position as far as the kingdom was concerned. Situated in the Trent Valley, it was an attractive target for river-borne Vikings who could supplement attacks from land-based armies moving in from the north. Up until the seventeenth century, Nottingham was the navigable head of the Trent. In the east it flowed out into the North Sea through the mighty Humber Estuary, as inviting to a Viking fleet as an open door to a burglar. The capture of Nottingham would dangerously expose the heart of Mercia, the remainder of which might then fall into Viking hands. The kingdom was not strong enough to face up to the threat on its own and in recent times had fostered closer ties with the emerging power of Wessex through marriage alliances. Now it was time to call in a favour.

Burgred, king of Mercia, sent for Æthelred I of Wessex, his brother-in-law, to come to his aid. Since his marriage to the daughter of Æthelwulf over a decade before, Burgred's reign appears to have been largely successful. Campaigning against the Welsh had continued and in 865 he had managed to push through the country as far as Anglesey. However, he suffered from the loss of Kent to Wessex. This had cost him wealth, prestige and also influence in the form of the archbishopric of Canterbury.[32]

Æthelred responded energetically to the request for help, marching north along with a large army gathered from across his kingdoms and his younger brother Alfred at his side. They made it to Nottingham, which Asser noted was called *Tig Guocobauc* in Welsh, an inclusion which reminds us of his origins and also suggests that his audience was at least partly Welsh. He also quotes Nottingham's Latin name, *Speluncarum Domus* or 'house of caves'. This was an allusion to the honeycomb of caves beneath the city.

When Æthelred's army arrived at Nottingham, it found that the Viking force had put up strong defences to keep them out. The Vikings may have adopted familiar tactics, setting up a D-shaped camp or something similar that took advantage of the river as part of a defensive perimeter. However 'immense' the West Saxon army was according to Asser, it was not sufficient to shift the Vikings. Asser noted that 'since the Christians were unable to breach the wall, peace was established between the Mercians and the Vikings'.

It was a fairly safe bet that this peace came at a cost. Details are lacking, but based on what we know of similar situations it is likely that substantial quantities of gold and silver were involved as well as food and other mundane provisions. The Vikings, bought off for the time being, moved back to Jorvik where they would spend the next year.[33] They had certainly not finished with Mercia, nor with the other English kingdoms. Æthelred and Alfred returned south with their army. The younger brother may well have noted the strength and success of the Viking defences, which had proved impervious to the attacks of the Anglo-Saxon army, tucking this knowledge away for future reference. Alfred also gained something else from Mercia, for in that same year he married Ælswith, daughter of Æthelred Mucel, an ealdorman of the Gaini, and his wife Eadburh who hailed from the Mercian royal family.[34] This was another important building-block in the dynastic progression of the West Saxon dynasty.

Edmund and East Anglia – Creating a Martyr

The next stopping point on the Vikings' violent progress around the Anglo-Saxon kingdoms moves us close to the realms of mythology. That does not mean the salient events were insignificant, for many stories in the development of a nation have at their core events that seem inherently unlikely: Robert the Bruce and the spider in the cave, Romulus and Remus being suckled by a she-wolf as infants before founding Rome, and William Tell shooting the arrow from off the top of his son's head to name but a few. Yet such quasi-mythological events can inspire others to extraordinary things. What actually happened becomes less important than what was believed to have happened. The effect is exaggerated when the societies within which these stories develop are not populated by sceptical rationalists as they are in many modern nation-states (though even today the ability of misplaced nationalism and associated myths to enflame passions should not be overlooked). In a young, newly Christianised Anglo-Saxon England, the miraculous seemed entirely believable. Enter Edmund, king of East Anglia and later saint of England.

Little is recorded of Edmund's reaction when the Vikings first arrived in his kingdom in 865, but he probably felt he had little option but to negotiate with them. There is no record of any battle at this stage. The *ASC* say only that 'they made peace with them' and provided the Vikings with horses. The Vikings had set up their winter camp in the kingdom, a move which one assumes came with a large element of threat. The East Angles had provided them with horses and let them be. It was presumably something of a relief with the Great Heathen Army made off to the north and left East Anglia alone for a while. However, this was a temporary reprieve. After the Great Heathen Army faced off against the combined forces of Wessex and Mercia at Nottingham, they had soon gone back to Northumbria, possibly deciding to focus on easier pickings. On reflection, despite what later hagiographers suggest concerning the martial qualities of Edmund, it seems a very plausible argument that the Vikings, remembering their previous success in East Anglia, felt that the kingdom would be easier to subdue than the combined might of Mercia and Wessex.

And so in 869, seemingly without warning, the Vikings of Jorvik stormed south – via Mercia and also, according to Abbo, from the sea – and fell on East Anglia.[35] Like one of Thor's mighty hammer-blows, they smashed all resistance in their path. The monastery at Medeshamstede – Peterborough – was an ancient and proud institution. Founded in the middle of the seventh century, it was a venerable place. Although it was in Mercia, it was close to the frontier with East Anglia. A raid on it, apparently led by Ubba, was devastating. The abbot and his monks were killed and the buildings there pillaged and burned. When the Vikings rode off, leaving death and a blazing funeral pyre in their wake, they had ensured that 'what was earlier very rich was as it were nothing'.[36] What may have made the attack even more grievous was that, according to the later Anglo-Norman chronicler Geoffrey Gaimar, there were levies from both Mercia and Northumbria included in the Viking host.[37]

After this opening salvo, they fell on East Anglia. It is possible that Ubba did not take part: Abbo says he had been left in charge at York and the main assault was led by Ivarr.[38] Possibly Ubba only pushed forward to Medeshamstede and no further. Henry of Huntingdon says that the Viking army marched from Mercia to East Anglia led by Ivarr (Hinguar as he calls him). However, one version of the *ASC* notes that the Danes were led on this campaign by Ivarr and Ubba, so the question of leadership is confused in our various sources.[39] The initial target of the assault was Thetford, next to a ford across the Little Ouse. Once more they set up a winter base in East Anglia, which made sense as the town was then closer to the waters of the Wash than it is in modern times. The Viking army could therefore be shipped in as well as crossing over land. Although details are sparse, this time Edmund does not appear to have been willing to let them stay. A battle followed; laconic as ever, the *ASC* merely note that 'the Danish took the victory, and killed the king, and conquered all that land'. Æthelweard gives largely similar details, adding the significant snippet that not only did Edmund die that year but so too did Ivarr.[40] It is striking that, if these details are accurate, the sons of Ragnar were directly responsible for the deaths of two English kings. No wonder that the name of Ivarr in particular resonates down the centuries.

So far this is a fairly straightforward story. The death of Edmund in these accounts is not discussed in great detail but the most obvious assumption to make is that he was killed in battle against the invaders. Asser follows largely the same line but gives slightly stronger suggestions about Edmund's end: 'In the same year, Edmund, king of the East Angles, fought fiercely against that army. But alas, he was killed there with a large number of his men, and the Vikings rejoiced triumphantly; the enemy were masters of the battlefield, and they subjected that entire province to their authority.'[41] This clearly suggests that the king died in battle.

This is not the end that we now associate with Edmund, whom we are led to believe was taken captive by Vikings, tied to a tree and shot to death with arrows. For that particular version of events we can thank Abbo of Fleury, who was in England between 985 and 987. Abbo came to England after he missed out on a prestigious appointment back in Francia; just because he was a holy man, it did not mean that he lacked ambition. Whilst he was in England he met St Dunstan, a great religious reformer of the time. Dunstan gave him an account of the end of King Edmund which he had himself been told by a very old man over half a century before whilst he was at the court of King Æthelstan. The old man had been Edmund's armour-bearer and had witnessed his end. In his account Edmund had virtually offered himself up as a sacrifice to Ivarr, disdaining to fight. He was put in chains – explicitly in imitation of Christ before Pilate in Abbo's account. He was beaten and then tied up and whipped, again emulating Christ. Finally, he was riddled with arrows, so that he was 'like a hedgehog or a thistle fretted with spines'. Abbo says he was executed in a way that emulated the great medieval icon St Sebastian, a late third-century martyr who was shot through with arrows during the reign of the pagan emperor Diocletian, though he did not die from these wounds. Instead, he was later clubbed to death.

Interestingly in Abbo's account the arrows did not kill Edmund either. Instead, whilst he was still alive, he was taken down from the tree and subjected to further brutality. 'His ribs [were] laid bare by numerous gashes, as if he had been to the torture of the rack, or had been torn by savage claws', bringing to mind the agonies of the blood-eagle. Finally, he was finished when his head was hacked off. Beating, whipping, being shot with arrows, blood-eagling, beheading – this was truly overkill. In Abbo's version, the martyr Edmund was subjected to a terrifying catalogue of violent actions before he died.[42]

This was not the end of Abbo's story though – far from it. Edmund's head was carried off in macabre triumph into a wood, Haglesdun. In the heart of that place it was thrown into a dense thicket of brambles so that it would be denied the dignity of a proper burial. Edmund's people were devastated and later formed a search party, intent on finding the gruesome relic. They duly organised themselves, but the thickness of the forest severely hampered them. Just as all seemed hopeless, they heard a cry from the midst of the trees: 'Here, here, here.' It was nothing less than the severed head calling out to them so that it could be found and reunited with its body. And that was not the end of the miracles. When they at last reached the source of the shouting, they found the head lying on the ground, protected from further damage by an attendant wolf. The kings of East Anglia were supposedly part of the bloodline of the Wuffing dynasty, whose name is remarkably similar to that of the Wulfings, a people who feature in the great Anglo-Saxon epic *Beowulf*. Here was an appropriate guardian spirit for the last king of the Wuffings.

The head was duly taken back for burial and reunited with the body. As the solemn procession made its way out of the forest with its precious relic, it was dutifully followed by the wolf, who only disappeared back into the trees once the sad cortege had reached its final destination. Edmund's remains were interred in a humble shrine, but they were later ceremonially transferred to a spot at what became known as Bury St Edmunds. This would prove a key destination for later pilgrims, who in turn provided a great source of wealth for the abbey that was built there.

As was often the case with medieval saints, the miracles did not stop with the death of the king. When his body was later disinterred it was found to be miraculously incorrupt, a sure sign of sanctity that was only found with the truly holy such as St Cuthbert. In fact the head and the body had apparently become reattached, with a thin red line round the neck the only indication they had ever been parted. This imagery replicates that found in other medieval saints' tales such as that of the Welsh St Winifred. She was also beheaded but her head was miraculously reattached to her body, leaving a permanent mark around her neck, though in her case she also came back to life A woman was appointed to tend to Edmund's body decades after his death, cutting his nails and hair – we even have her name, Oswen. Once a year she would dutifully perform this macabre ritual on the anniversary of the Last Supper (though the anniversary of Edmund's death was on 20 November). It was a way of reminding the people of the special nature of the corpse, which needed looking after as if its owner was still alive. Probably the Last Supper was adopted as the anniversary date for this ritual because it was on the eve of two enormous events in the life of Christ: His brutal execution and then His miraculous resurrection. Just as Edmund's death had emulated the first of these events, so surely would he enjoy the blessings of the second.[43]

Even in death the body had magical, dangerous powers and those who overlooked this fact put themselves in mortal jeopardy. One night, eight thieves broke into Edmund's mausoleum. However, in the middle of carrying out their work they found themselves paralysed. When dawn broke the next day, they were discovered in their frozen state. The bishop at the time, a man named Theodred, was so incensed at their sacrilegious temerity that he had them all hanged, though he later bitterly regretted this act as churchmen were not allowed to pass sentence of death.

Then there was the story of Leofstan, who was so obsessed with Edmund's sanctity that he demanded to see his body. Many advised him not to do so but he was insistent. Being a man of 'great position', he got his own way. But when the coffin was opened, he was immediately overtaken by madness. His father, Ælfgar, was so appalled at his actions that he threw him out of his home. Leofstan's life was effectively destroyed, and he lived out his days as a pauper, eventually dying consumed by worms.[44] Clearly one took liberties with the saint's body at one's peril.

These developments, which led to the dead king being seen as a martyr and a saint, belong in the tenth century. It is ironic though that the Vikings, by killing Edmund in whatever fashion, helped to create a national icon that would serve to assist in the forging of the concept of a country called England. Indeed, when the West Saxon kings drove forward their plans for an expanded kingdom, they were quick to appropriate the East Anglian saint for themselves. Neither was this a unique action on their part; they would also in their own way appropriate Cuthbert, who was originally a saint of the north. So Edmund's death was not the end of his story, merely a transition to a quite different direction in his tale. Of his life we know little, though this could be because East Anglian sources have not survived, and the West Saxon-focused *ASC* have little use for him at the time when the various strands were written. We know much more about his second 'existence' after his death. It is intriguing to note too that the Vikings in their own way were seduced by his legend even though they had played such a violent part in writing it.

After Edmund's death the Great Heathen Army took East Anglia for itself. Two kings followed, known only from the few coins that have survived from their reign: Oswald and Æthelred. Either these men were Vikings who took Anglo-Saxon names to make themselves more acceptable to their subjects (there were others who did this, though from later times when the context was different) or they were puppet kings installed by the Vikings. However, the Christian cross that had previously marked East Anglian coinage remained. Incredibly, just two decades after Edmund's death the Viking-held kingdom he had once ruled was issuing coins which read *Sancte Eadmund Rex* – 'Saint Edmund the King'. It was a remarkable change in fortune for a man who had been killed by the Vikings and was now seen as a saint by the inheritors of those killers. But there was a great deal of water to flow under the bridge before that point was reached, and before then it would sometimes seem as if no Anglo-Saxon kingdom would survive the chaos unleashed by the Vikings.

There is one other aspect of this story which is now little remembered. According to William of Malmesbury, Edmund had a brother, Edwold (Ædwold). In several accounts Edmund is either implicitly or explicitly a virgin, which was another key requirement for many a Christian saint of the time. If Edmund was indeed childless, then Edwold would have had a very strong claim to replace him. However, he was in no position to profit from this claim. In any event, according to William, Edwold was so distraught that 'he was tired, so men said, of the delights of the world, in which misfortune had overtaken both him and his brother'. The chronicler suggests that these dramatic events turned Edwold's mind towards God and he lived out his life in a tiny hermit's cell in a remote corner of Dorset. When he died, he was buried at Cerne, where, in the tenth century, an abbey was built and did well out of pilgrim traffic visiting his tomb.[45]

St Edwold is now little more than a footnote in history, and it is fitting that the church dedicated to him at Stockwood, a few miles from Cerne, is the smallest in Dorset and one of the smallest in England. Nestled in a bucolic setting, it remains a fine and fitting place to stop and muse a while about the long-lost world of Anglo-Saxon Wessex. It is in its own way an East Anglian prince's corner of a foreign field. I first visited it one

Easter Sunday in the midst of a pandemic, when a world I thought to be secure and immutable was suddenly under unprecedented threat. It felt an appropriate time to be in such a sanctuary of peace and tranquillity. For a few brief moments, the so-called Dark Ages did not seem to be so very far away.

Wessex under Threat

By 870 the position of the English kingdoms was increasingly precarious. East Anglia and part of Northumbria had gone, and Mercia was under threat. Even Wessex was not safe. But respite came that year as Ivarr moved north, firstly reuniting with Ubba and then heading across Hadrian's Wall. Roger of Wendover, who wrote in the thirteenth century, described how the nuns of Coldingham, a convent in the Scottish borders, cut off their noses and upper lips to make them unattractive to the Viking raiders. If Roger is to be believed, they succeeded in a way: the convent was destroyed and everyone in it killed.[46]

Ivarr took part in a four-month siege of the great rock at Dumbarton, the main base of the Britons of Strathclyde, along with his old ally Óláfr from whom he had been parted for some time. The defenders' fate was sealed by a shortage of water and food. This was a very long siege for the period and suggests powerful motives for the Vikings to prosecute it with such vigour. When the fortress finally fell, Óláfr and Ivarr returned to Ireland. They had been away for a few years and in that time Viking fortunes on the island had deteriorated. The two Viking leaders did not travel alone. They were accompanied by 200 ships, packed to the gunwales with English, British (from Strathclyde) and Pictish slaves. This is a very large number of ships, and if accurate it is stark testimony to the awfulness of the situation for those unfortunates caught up in the Viking onslaught. It is not out of kilter with other near-contemporary incidents. In 882 the famous Viking warlord Hæsten required a similar number of ships to take his captives back to Scandinavia from Francia.[47]

The racial origin of these slaves is suggestive. Scotland at the time was divided into two main power blocs, the Scots in the south-west and the Picts elsewhere. The Vikings added a third powerful ingredient to this cocktail. There is evidence that the Scots were in alliance with the Vikings, an arrangement that would continue on and off for decades thereafter, and it is telling that no Scots are mentioned as being amongst the slaves shipped back to Ireland. From here, the slaves could be 'processed' either for use in Ireland or for onward sale to overseas markets from the growing trading hub of Dublin. This is an important reminder of the dark side to Viking life. Other raids such as one in Armagh a few years earlier had also resulted in the capture of hundreds of slaves. Men like Óláfr and Ivarr became powerful and rich on the back of this harrowing trade.

Ivarr probably never returned to England despite some recent suggestions to the contrary, and his presence presaged a terrible time for the Irish. Over the next century there are frequent references in Irish annals to Viking raids on the hinterland, with hundreds taken captive. Sometimes, the more important hostages would be ransomed for large amounts; if more wealth could be gained through this means rather than enslavement, then the Vikings were quite happy to take advantage of the opportunity.

Even with Ivarr gone, the army left behind in East Anglia was far from finished. Only one kingdom had escaped the recent attacks of the Viking armies thus far: Wessex. The Great Heathen Army duly fell on Reading, at the confluence of the Kennet and the Thames, over the Christmas season of 870/71. This was a royal *vill*, the centre of an estate with responsibilities including the collection and storing of taxes. Reading was perfectly sited for a Viking attack. Their ships, their 'sea stallions', could gallop without interference upstream from the Thames Estuary, a short hop round the coast from East Anglia. At the same time their land forces, now enjoying unfettered access to the equine reserves of that subdued kingdom, could converge on it from the landward side.

Refreshed with the bountiful provisions that they had captured, the Viking army then reinforced the fortifications which seem to have previously been totally inadequate to resist them. The position again was perfect for them, allowing for the construction of their favoured D-shaped camp. Archaeological research has suggested that a water-filled trench known as the Plummery Ditch linked the Kennet and the Thames, and this would make this a formidable position from which to resist an Anglo-Saxon counterattack. If so, the enclosed area could shelter about 1,000 Vikings.[48]

That counterattack was not long in coming. News travelled quickly down to the heart of Wessex, where King Æthelred hastily assembled an army to fight back. Even before the relief army arrived, the Anglo-Saxons scored a success outside Reading at Englefield. A Viking raiding party, pushing out from Reading, was met by Æthelwulf, ealdorman of Berkshire, a man of some reputation who had already bested the Vikings when they were driven back from Winchester in 860. The Vikings, led by two jarls and consisting of a good body of men, were badly mauled. According to the *ASC*, Æthelwulf stood firm and 'although his band was small, their reserves of courage were mighty'. The Viking jarl Sidroc

(Sigurd) was amongst those whose corpse lay on the battlefield at the end of the fight.

This news would undoubtedly have raised the spirits of Æthelred and his army when they arrived outside Reading. He had already seen the Vikings up close several years back at Nottingham. Now, as then, his younger brother rode at his side. By this time, Alfred was around twenty-three years old, and even though Æthelred had two young sons Alfred was at this moment the most obvious heir should anything happen to his elder brother. They rode through the frosty January air, musing on the tactics and range of possible outcomes of the forthcoming fight. The elder brother, though his personality made next to no impression on the chroniclers of the day, may well have felt the weight of responsibility heavily. He was probably also well aware of the brutal fate that had awaited other conquered Anglo-Saxon kings at the hands of the Viking host. Alfred, whom Asser suggests was a serious young man, may have retreated into his thoughts, hoping that he would be able to act manfully in the looming battle. He was at the start of a year that would change his life and write him and his dynasty into English history.

4

On the Edge of a Precipice

Then out of the night came the shadow-stalker, stealthy and swift; the
hall-guards were slack, asleep at their posts...

Beowulf

The Rise of a King

Early in January 871, the two brothers arrived with the army of Wessex
and prepared to assault Reading. The success of ealdorman Æthelwulf
at Englefield had raised their spirits, and filled them with confidence for
the fight ahead. Perhaps too much so, for the Vikings had regrouped
and considerably strengthened their position. At the outset the Anglo-
Saxon army appeared to be doing well, with many Vikings hacked
down. It appeared as if a great triumph was about to be won, until the
Vikings inside the fortress came charging out 'like wolves', slashing at
their opponents. The fight was keenly fought but inch by inch the Anglo-
Saxons began to edge back until the Vikings drove them from the field.
Amongst the dead was Æthelwulf, the victor of Englefield and Winchester.
This was a loss that could be ill afforded. His remains were taken to
Northworthy (Derby) for burial, for he was a Mercian. Berkshire was
on the frontier of Wessex and Mercia and had changed hands several
times over the years. It was in some ways part of both kingdoms, which
is worth recalling when we consider that Alfred was according to some
sources born in Wantage which was in the shire.[1]

It was now the Vikings' turn to feel exultant. The might of Wessex
had been driven off and the Anglo-Saxons were in retreat. Now the
Vikings would go on the attack. The army of Wessex drew back 'in grief

and shame' according to Asser. The Vikings gave chase, but the West Saxons escaped by fording a river. The later writer Geoffrey Gaimar said that this was at Whistley and that the ford was across the River Loddon. The Vikings, without local knowledge, could not find the ford and abandoned their pursuit. However, a few days later they began to move out from Reading in force and came up against the West Saxons at a place called Ashdown. It is not clear exactly where this was, but it is often associated with either Kingstanding Hill, about 25 miles west of Reading, astride the old Icknield Way, or Aldworth in Berkshire, which was slightly closer to the Viking base. The battlefield was marked by a 'small and solitary thorn tree', hence its name. According to Asser (who claims he saw the tree still standing when he visited the battlefield roughly two decades later), when the Vikings launched their attack King Æthelred was at prayer. He refused to budge until the solemn ceremony was finished and it was therefore left to Alfred to take the brunt of the Viking assault.

The Vikings had the advantage of attacking downhill and they smashed into the Saxon shield wall with fearsome effect. They had divided their force in two, one half led by two kings and the other by several jarls. Alfred fought back 'like a boar' according to Asser. The fight grew hot and fierce around the ash tree, but the Anglo-Saxon force stood firm. When Æthelred at last joined the fray, the Vikings were slowly but surely forced back. They at last broke and fled. They left behind them a dead king, Bagsecg, and five dead jarls: Sidroc the Old, Sidroc the Young, Osbern, Fræna and Harald. They did not pause until they had returned safely to Reading, with the Saxon army hot on their heels. It was, said Æthelweard, a great triumph: 'Neither before nor after has such a slaughter been heard of since the race of the Saxons won Britain in war.'[2]

It is worth bearing in mind that Æthelweard was a direct lineal descendant of Æthelred and was talking about an event that played a glorious part in his family's history. With that said, what happened next does not really fit with the suggestion of a massive Viking defeat. Just two weeks later, they were involved in battle again, this time further west at Basing. Despite their headlong retreat, the Viking army was now pushing deeper into the heart of Wessex. It may well be the case that the losses sustained by the West Saxons at Reading, Englefield and Ashdown were mounting and proving as crippling in their own way as those suffered by the Vikings. In addition, the Viking force was made up of men who had in some cases been fighting for years and whose skills and battle-hardness were well honed by now. The fight at Basing ended in a Viking victory, exposing the heartlands of Wessex to further depredations.

Matters were gradually worsening for the West Saxons, and they were about to deteriorate still further. There was a break of two months whilst both sides licked their wounds, but at the end of this period a rejuvenated Viking army went on the attack again. The scene was set for a titanic clash, and it would take place at Meretun. It has never been proved where this was, but a strong candidate is Martin near the borders of Hampshire, Wiltshire and Dorset. There are several reasons for this assumption. Martin is close to an old Roman road, the Ackling Dyke, which may have remained in use long into the Anglo-Saxon period (much of it can still be walked as a well-marked footpath today). Nearby is the Bokerley Dyke, regarded by archaeologists as most likely being a fortification contemporary with the period. The hilltop position of Martin Down bears the hallmarks of a classic site for battles of the era. It is also deeper into Wessex than Basing, the site of the last Viking victory, and as such a logical next step for their advance.[3]

The battle at Meretun was a hard-fought confrontation. The *ASC* suggest that the West Saxons had the best of it for much of the day but in the end the Vikings held the field. Æthelweard tells us that 'a multitude were killed on either side'. From Asser all we have is a spectacular silence; the end result presumably did not fit with the required outcome for his hero, Alfred. Amongst the Saxon dead was Heahmund, the bishop of Sherborne. He had not long been consecrated, becoming bishop in 867 or 868. He was later venerated as a saint in both the Catholic and the Eastern Orthodox traditions. His saint's day is 22 March. As such a day is usually assigned to the anniversary of a saint's death, it is possible that this was also the date of the battle at Meretun. The battle at Ashdown is usually dated to around 8 January that year, and given the information we have on other battles in the campaign that means that the Viking assault started towards the end of December 870. The campaign had therefore been going on for eleven or twelve weeks, and a heavy toll was being exacted from both sides.

The bishop of Sherborne was perhaps not the most notable casualty of the battle. In typical laconic style the *ASC* briefly note that 'afterwards, after Easter, King Æthelred died'. He had only been king for five years or so and was by no means old, probably around thirty-four years of age. There are no details about what caused his death, but coming so soon after the battle of Meretun it is tempting to speculate that he was badly wounded in fighting there and lingered for a few weeks before he finally breathed his last. His body was brought back to the minster at Wimborne where he was buried. A fifteenth-century brass by the high altar in the church still commemorates the fact that he was buried there. There is a tradition that the dying king was taken through Witchampton, a few miles to the north of Wimborne, where the parish church is dedicated to St Cuthburga, the same saint who is commemorated at Wimborne Minster. Cuthburga was a member of the West Saxon royal dynasty, the sister of King Ine, and in around 705 she became the first abbess of the convent at Wimborne which later became a double monastery with monks as well as nuns. The pedigree of the church and its founder made Wimborne the ideal location to commemorate a Saxon king with all due honour and dignity.

Although Asser insists that Æthelred designated Alfred his heir before his death at a meeting held at the sadly unknown site of Swineborg, there was no guarantee that he would ultimately succeed to the throne. In fact, Asser goes too far in insisting that Alfred's virtues were so great that 'he could easily have taken the throne while his brother ... was still alive, had he considered himself worthy to do so, for he surpassed all his brothers both in wisdom and good habits; and in particular because he was a great warrior and victorious in virtually all battles'. This is a nonsensical comment on several accounts. For one thing Alfred had tasted defeat as well as victory in battle and indeed only one victory, Ashdown, had so far been recorded that could be at all attributed to him. For another, the enthronement of a king was a highly charged religious act, sanctioned by God. It could not easily be put aside. This reads like a propagandist overstating his hero's qualities to the nth degree.

But in many ways Alfred was now the only viable candidate. It was of course not necessary that the king's heir be his eldest son, but it was expected that he was an *ætheling*. The king took his throne after election by the witan, the ruling council of the kingdom. There would be a great deal of horse-trading going on behind the scenes before the election process was held, when the various candidates made their bid for votes, offering patronage in return for support. If Æthelred had been some time in dying, Alfred would have had time to build support within the witan for his claim, if we do not take Asser literally and he had not already been designated the late king's heir. This was no time for a child to be taking over with a Viking army on the doorstep, so Æthelred's infant sons were never major contenders. Alfred assumed the throne.

It was not long before the new king was on the defensive again. This time we can identify the site of the battle with much more confidence: Wilton in Wiltshire, a place which was significantly a royal estate and therefore an attractive target both for the wealth that was likely to be found there and possibly also for the potential to undermine royal prestige, which could have a very damaging effect on the status of the new ruler. This was about one month after Alfred had become king, and according to the *ASC* he led a small army out to meet the threat. All the surviving Anglo-Saxon accounts say that, heavily outnumbered, they fought gallantly; Asser even says that at one point the Viking forces fled, though when they saw the small pursuing force they turned about and overwhelmed them. It is possible of course that the Vikings were feigning retreat to break up the West Saxon formation – an echo of events at Hastings two centuries later. If so, the tactic was very successful. The Vikings again emerged the victors.

These basic details are recorded in both the *ASC* and Asser, but Æthelweard adds further intriguing details. He suggests that Alfred was almost caught off guard as he was busy attending to the obsequies for his late brother. He also mentions the arrival of a Great Summer Army (*sumorlida* in Old English). Assisted by the men who were already there, it was this new force that launched a vigorous attack on the West Saxons and won the day. Wessex was on its knees.

But there was no final push by the Vikings. Why they did not press the advantage must remain a matter of speculation. The various accounts that survive suggest that both sides had suffered heavy losses during this year of nine battles – though intriguingly none of them name all nine. It is also striking that only two of the battles were West Saxon victories, and only one of those (Ashdown) involved an army partly led by the new king. Not all the battles are named, and Asser ignores Meretun altogether. Of those battles for which no details are given, we should assume that these were West Saxon defeats too; otherwise they would surely have been mentioned for propaganda purposes.[4] Perhaps the new arrivals were more interested in plunder than conquest, and the very heart of Wessex, which we can assume was around Wimborne at the time, might still have been a tough nut to crack. The most likely reason that the campaign petered out was that Alfred opted to buy off the Vikings. In their victories and close defeats his army had done enough to dampen Viking confidence; Asser suggests that thousands of lives had been lost amongst the raiders and, whilst he may be prone to exaggeration, all the indications are that the campaign had been long and bloody. In any event, the Vikings withdrew and set up a camp near London.

The year 871 had been hugely important for Wessex (and ultimately for England too) as it felt the sharp edge of the Viking assaults for the first time. Viking attacks on Northumbria, East Anglia and Mercia had elicited only a passing interest by the West Saxon chroniclers. That had now changed for good, and a significant change in emphasis becomes evident. Soon after, the *ASC* give more details concerning the leaders of the Viking onslaught. As far as the *ASC* is concerned, earlier names that are famous today such as Ragnar Lodbrok and Ivarr the Boneless are invisible. There is a very good reason for this: such men did not attack Wessex, and the *ASC* were a creation of that kingdom about two decades after these events. But in the next few years we are given the names of men like Guthrum, Oscetel, Anund and Halfdan, and whilst we cannot be sure they were all there in 871 it is a strong possibility that at least some of them were.

The End of the Great Heathen Army

With the campaign in Wessex over – for now at least – the Great Heathen Army began to discuss its next move. However, there are indications that it had already started to fragment. Ivarr had, according to Irish sources, already returned to Ireland following his highly successful attack with Óláfr on the Strathclyde-British citadel at Dumbarton Rock. The arrival of the Great Summer Army in 871 signified a new influx of Vikings intent on achieving success in England, but there might not have been a consensus on what success meant. Some may have been motivated by those traditional rewards of glory and plunder but for others settlement may have been as attractive a prize, if not more so. There is a clue in Æthelweard that the latest arrivals were no insignificant party of reinforcements: he describes it as 'an innumerable summer army'.[5]

With the campaign against Wessex suspended, what this new influx was to do was a moot point. Ivarr's brother Halfdan was still on the scene, as was a new Viking leader by the name of Guthrum. There was of course East Anglia, which had been subjugated, and further north there was Jorvik and surrounding Northumbria. But between them lay another kingdom which may have looked ripe for the picking: Mercia. Not only was there attractive, fertile land and riches available there, but the kingdom had also been an ally of Wessex in recent years and neutralizing the former would indirectly affect the latter. Since the stalemate at Nottingham a few years before, Burgred had remained king. According to the later chronicler Roger of Wendover, the Mercian king had bought them off. Several coin hoards uncovered in the London region at Barking, Croydon and Westminster Bridge may well date to this time. They could either represent an individual Viking's share in the collective loot or an Anglo-Saxon's attempt to squirrel away some of their wealth.[6] A lease from Bishop Wærferth of Worcester to a Mercian thegn named Eanwulf, dated 872, states unequivocally that the bishop was entering into the arrangement because he was struggling to raise the funds for his contribution to the large tribute owed to the Vikings.[7]

Even paying tribute was insufficient to guarantee security from Viking attacks, though. Charles the Bald had found this out in Francia a decade or so previously and famously Æthelred II, 'the Unready', would learn this painful lesson far into the future in the early years of the eleventh century. Rudyard Kipling may not be to everybody's taste but there was a germ of exaggerated truth in his poem 'that if once you have paid him the Dane-geld you never get rid of the Dane'.[8] Burgred was to find out for himself how true this sentiment was. But before he did so the Vikings in the south had to deal with a rebellion in Jorvik. After taking the city in 867 they had installed a puppet king, Ecgberht, as ruler there but in 872 he was driven out in a rebellion led by a Northumbrian nobleman named Ricsige. The puppet king escaped to Mercia along with the current archbishop of York, Wulfhere. The archbishop seems to have had a wonderfully elastic conscience in quickly coming to terms with the demands of *de facto* pagan Viking rulers. It is not exactly clear how or if the rebellion was put down, but Ricsige stayed as ruler in Jorvik until 876, after which the Vikings moved in and took over again. For the moment, though, the rebellion was a stroke of luck for Alfred and Wessex as it diverted Viking attention from the battered kingdom.

Part of the Viking force overwintered further south on the borders of Mercia. During the winter of 872/3 they stayed at Torksey in Lindsey, where recent archaeological excavations have yielded some fascinating results. It was a temporary camp composed of tents, large enough to accommodate several thousand people comfortably, meaning contemporary accounts of at least one hundred ships are quite believable. There appear to have been no fortifications, but none were needed. The site is on a small but prominent bluff in what is quite a flat landscape. On one side ran the Trent (the course of which has changed since) and on the others the camp was surrounded by marshland, likely impenetrable except for a few paths.

Large coin finds from Torksey include over 200 Northumbrian *stycas* (small coins) which are not found in such numbers anywhere else outside Northumbria. These may well have belonged to individuals who campaigned there a few years before. Perhaps most intriguingly, over 100 *dirhams* have been found, the largest concentration yet discovered in England. These were Central Asian coins and may have originally come from major trading centres like Baghdad, though they probably did not arrive directly but through important Scandinavian settlements such as Birka in Sweden. There were many weights found, as would be used in trading, and many lead gaming pieces which are a distinctive feature associated with Viking camps of the time, being cheap, roughly made and expendable. It is not difficult to let the imagination run wild and picture groups of Vikings hunkering down by a fire, retelling today's events or discussing tomorrow's plans, drinking mead and arguing over the best tactics to use in a game of *hnefatafl*. Only a few fragmentary human remains have been found but included amongst them is a skull which is marked by at least two blows from a heavy implement. Clearly, this individual met a violent end.[9]

Comparatively little is known of Lindsey in Anglo-Saxon times although its boundaries at least are clear enough, with the mighty Humber Estuary on the north, the North Sea to the east and the Fens on the south. The Trent and the Ouse ran into the Humber, providing Viking ships with easy access to the heart of Mercia and leaving Lindsey highly vulnerable. The Mercians seemed powerless to resist. The *ASC* note that 'the Mercians made peace with the raiding party' but we can be confident that it was not as part of some amicable agreement and that a sizeable payment in some form or another was required.[10] Just a few years later the Vikings would occupy Lindsey in force and Lincoln would become one of their main settlements.[11]

The following year, the Viking army overwintered in what became their most famous camp in England at Repton, Derbyshire. There is a reference in the *ASC* to this event in 873. Fairly recent archaeological discoveries, which are even now in the process of being interpreted, have added greatly to our understanding of this site. They were made by a team led by husband and wife Martin Biddle and Birthe Kjolbye-Biddle in the 1970s and 1980s, though intriguing evidence was first uncovered here centuries earlier. In 1726 Dr Simon Degge recorded in his journal that he had visited Repton and was told a story by a labourer, Thomas Walker, then eighty-eight years of age. Walker related that about four decades earlier he had been digging in the area when he came across an old stone wall framing a square enclosure. In this he found a coffin and saw a skeleton which he claimed was 9 feet tall, surrounded by the remains of about 100 other individuals. Perhaps unsurprisingly, the 9-foot skeleton has since disappeared but plenty of other remains were found in the more recent dig.

These twentieth-century investigations focused on a mound that was approximately 13 by 11 metres in diameter. Beneath this was a two-roomed stone structure, possibly originally the mausoleum of the Mercian royal family: its east–west alignment certainly suggests Christian overtones. This would make sense, as Repton was a place of both strategic and symbolic significance. Its strategic importance lay in its position on the Trent, an important route into Mercia. But it was perhaps equally important as the last resting place of some of the former royalty of Mercia. Most notably, here lay the body of St Wystan (also known as Wigstan), who according to legend could have been king but instead chose the life of a holy man. He was later martyred in an internecine Mercian dispute and his body was carried in great ceremony to Repton where he was interred in the tomb of his grandfather, King Wiglaf (though it was later moved to Evesham).

Wystan's tomb had become a place of pilgrimage and that must have made the Vikings' actions after occupying Repton all the more distressing to the Mercians. The church was close to the Trent, the river forming one natural side of the defensive perimeter that was now constructed. They built a D-shaped ditch enclosing their camp on the other three sides and at the heart of it was the church, now forming part of a fortress rather than a holy place. It was a remarkable transformation. However, the camp footprint at Repton seems tiny compared to that at Torksey and recent excavations suggest that it in fact extended well beyond the constrained area that the Biddles' results (as yet not fully published) suggested.[12]

One of the rooms excavated at Repton contained the remains of 249 disarticulated individuals, hinting that this was a charnel house where bones were interred after corpses had decayed elsewhere. The other room was empty of human remains, but material items found there included gold and silver and coins dating from a short period between 872 and 874. Of the skeletal remains found, 80 per cent appeared to be males between fifteen and forty-five. None of these seemed to have died of war wounds, though there was evidence of injuries that had subsequently healed. Other finds are also revealing, including a shield boss of a style similar to examples found in the Isle of Man, Cumbria and Dublin. This is suggestive of links with the Irish Sea region, which in turn confirms the peripatetic nature of Viking warriors operating over a wide geographical area.

These were all interesting finds but they were overshadowed in the public eye by the remains discovered in a double grave. The grave had two males interred in it, labelled G295 and G511 – mundane titles masking incredible stories. The older man, G511, was buried with the tell-tale evidence of a Thor's Hammer and a sword of Viking provenance. DNA interpretation suggests that the two men were related in the first degree on the paternal side. Osteological evidence suggests that the older man was between thirty-five and forty-five and the younger between seventeen and twenty years old, so they could possibly have been father and son. Isotope analysis shows that they came from Scandinavia, probably from Denmark. These two men had both suffered violent deaths, G511 especially so. A deep wound to his left femur provides evidence of a cut that may well have removed his left testicle and penis. There were also two spear wounds above his eye. This man had been buried with a boar's tusk which may have been a symbolic replacement for the severed penis. It is perhaps significant that evidence of particularly pronounced boars' tusks has been found at a ritual site at Frösö in the north of Sweden, where indications of human and animal sacrifice have been discovered. The pig was linked to Freyr, a Viking deity associated with fertility.[13] Using a tusk as a surrogate for a dismembered penis therefore seems entirely appropriate.

We have no firm evidence of who these men were, and various theories have been proposed as to their identity. Biddle and Kjolbye-Biddle suggested that one of them might be no less a person than the legendary Ivarr the Boneless, though the admittedly limited historical evidence we have suggests that he died in Ireland. An alternative and more recent suggestion is that one of the two men might be Óláfr, Ivarr's long-term associate in Ireland and more recently in Scotland. These are fascinating theories but unfortunately there is a lack of solid evidence to prove them. The consensus is that the men buried in this double grave were important, but it is pushing a point to link them to specific individuals. Nevertheless, the slight possibility that these might be particularly prominent Vikings cannot be ruled out.

Another intriguing find near Repton is a classic Viking cemetery at Heath Wood just a few miles off. This contrasts with the finds in Repton itself as the burial mounds cover cremations rather than inhumations (some appear to be cremations done *in situ* and others were from ceremonies performed elsewhere with some of the ashes then being reinterred). There are about sixty such mounds and the site is unique in England so far. Very close by at Foremark – a Norse name – was another camp. Here were found lead gaming pieces, Islamic coins and Scandinavian- and Saxon-style brooches. It is assumed that the Foremark camp was erected at the same time as the one at Repton; it has not yet been confirmed, but the finds there are of a similar date. The Foremark camp is larger than that at Repton, so it may have been the main Viking base in the area. It is intriguing, if they are contemporary, that the cemeteries at Heath Wood and Repton use different burial practices; perhaps at this time there was no one orthodox approach to such matters.[14] Some have suggested that the difference in interment styles might even symbolically mark the point where the Great Heathen Army splintered.[15] It is often the small details that fascinate: the warrior buried with an earring or the skeletal remains of a horse that came from Scandinavia rather than England are just two of many such examples.

The archaeological finds at Repton and Heath Wood/Foremark add colour to the somewhat monochrome picture presented by the *ASC*. Nevertheless, another brief comment in the *Chronicle* speaks volumes. It tells how the Viking army decided to move against their next prey: the remainders of Mercia. Burgred was driven off and ended up, according to William of Malmesbury, at Pavia in Italy, where he died (though Asser states that he died and was buried in Rome in the Church of St Mary in the Saxon Quarter). Despite their previous support for the regime in Mercia, the men of Wessex on this occasion made no attempt to intervene. Burgred's wife, Æthelswith – Alfred's sister – went with him, dying in Pavia in 888.

Burgred's place was taken by Ceolwulf, one of his advisers, who does not come across well in contemporary records. In the memorable words of the *ASC* he was no more than a 'foolish king's thegn', whilst William of Malmesbury, presumably inspired by this source, calls him a 'driveller'. But some historians feel that he has been harshly treated and point out that during his reign he acted in many ways as expected of an independent contemporary king.[16] One of Ceolwulf's coin issues is very similar to that issued by Alfred and may have well been minted by a Wessex artisan. It has been suggested that the king of Wessex was unlikely to have been working closely with Ceolwulf if he was so inept. Ultimately, these harsh judgements may have been made with the benefit of hindsight and Ceolwulf may have been marked down as he was ultimately seen as a collaborator with an occupying Viking army.[17] Perhaps at the time he felt that he had little choice; it is easy to be wise after the event. The accusations made against him might be no more than propagandist efforts to inflate the virtues of the chroniclers' hero, Alfred, by comparison. Indeed, finds of so-called 'Two Emperor' pennies with images of Ceolwulf and Alfred alongside each other on them suggest that the two men were rather close allies, calling into doubt the *ASC*'s picture of the maligned king.[18]

The time spent at Repton was seminal to the future of the Great Heathen Army. They had been on campaign for nearly a decade now and, whilst there would have been much attrition, with some of the original members moving on to other things or dying off and their place being taken by fresh blood, it was understandable if some of those who remained were tired and wanted to settle down. A decision that the army should divide appears to have now been made. With typical brevity, the *ASC* note that in 875 some of the army made its way north to Tyneside.

This splinter was led by Halfdan, who had been at Repton and was supposedly another son of Ragnar Lodbrok and brother to Ivarr the Boneless. Halfdan's move led to what was for the Anglo-Saxons a hugely symbolic event in the shape of the final abandonment of Lindisfarne. The church there had struggled on despite its portentous sacking in 793. Now Bishop Eardulf decided that the holy relics of St Cuthbert and the head of St Oswald (as well as some bones of St Aidan, the first bishop of Lindisfarne) could not be left to the invaders, ordering that they should be removed to a safer place. The trouble was that it was not at all clear where was safe. Indeed, this was the start of a seemingly endless peregrination for the sacred remains.

Halfdan launched an orgy of destruction, with monasteries and churches firmly in the firing line: 'Fire and sword were carried from the eastern sea to the western.'[19] There is evidence of a sizeable camp (albeit smaller than Torksey) at Aldwark, north-west of York, the identity of which was until recently obscured under the nondescript acronym ARSNY – A Riverine Site North of York. This camp probably played a key role in the Viking conquest of the region. From Northumbria they then raided north into what is now Scotland but was then the separate kingdoms of the Picts and the Strathclyde Britons. Halfdan was next recorded dividing up Northumbria before his people settled it. This process can perhaps be viewed as the true birth of the Viking kingdom in Northumbria centred on Jorvik. In any case, Halfdan himself was not cut out for domestic life. He was apparently a failure as a peacetime ruler, and one senses that he missed the warrior's way. According to Irish accounts he took himself off to Dublin and died in a failed attempt to take the city for himself. It seems a fitting end to a restless and relentless adventurer, a true heir of Ragnar and companion-in-arms for the legendary Ivarr.

This was the end of Halfdan, but the Viking threat was alive and well. Having had a little time to take a breath, Wessex was soon to be in the raiders' sights once more.

Renewed Threats to Wessex

When Halfdan moved north, he effectively brought an end to the Great Heathen Army in its original form. The part of the army that did not go with him stationed itself at Cambridge, illustrating that East Anglia and its surrounding area was now firmly in the Viking sphere in England. From here the raiders could move west into Mercia or south into Wessex. The force was led by three men, Oscetel, Anund and Guthrum, the last of whom was poised to play a particularly significant role in the story of Alfred and his dynasty in Wessex. Æthelweard suggests that the division of the force was part of an agreement to share England between the men led by Halfdan on the one hand and Oscetel, Anund and Guthrum on the other. However, if the latter wished to stake a claim to the riches of Wessex, they would have to work hard for the privilege.

Alfred had now been king for four years. After the trauma of 871, when Wessex had been under serious attack, the absence of any firm evidence to the contrary leads us to conclude that the Vikings had largely left his kingdom alone, although it is certainly not inconceivable that the occasional raid might have taken place. The king was still a young man, and his experience was as yet shallow. As the youngest of four brothers, he had not been groomed for kingship unless we accept Asser's improbable suggestion that Æthelred I had nominated him as his heir. All this might explain why the Vikings' next move appears to have caught Alfred on the hop. Without warning, the force in Cambridge decamped and marched into the heart of Wessex. They managed to reach Wareham in Dorset, deep inside the kingdom and only 10 miles or so from the important West Saxon settlement at Wimborne, which had important connections to the royal dynasty of Wessex. Wareham itself also had royal connections, being the last resting place of King Beorhtric. Whilst Viking finds in this area are rare, a cosmopolitan cluster including weights from Mercia, a Frankish sword-belt mount, Irish metalwork and a gold ingot suggests the Vikings raided and traded over a wide area.[20]

It was alarming that the Viking force had managed to make its way this deep into Wessex seemingly without even an attempt at interception. Indeed, this highlighted an Achilles' heel in the defences of all Anglo-Saxon kingdoms: the lack of fortifications. It had been an issue in Francia too, but Charles the Bald had started to address it in recent years. In contrast, the Anglo-Saxon kingdoms had been slow to recognise the threat and little had been done about it. Alfred was certainly culpable here. Wessex had come close to being overwhelmed in 871 and yet the problem of weak defences remained as acute as ever. This situation was both politically embarrassing and, worse, potentially fatal to the future of the kingdom which was now effectively the last independent Anglo-Saxon state in England. Alfred had not learned his lessons well, or perhaps the task was just too big for him so early in his career. It is important to avoid being governed by hindsight when we assess Alfred's achievements. Because we know of his eventual greatness, we might easily be misled as to his blind spots. He was not a ready-made great king as Asser would have us believe. Perhaps his greatest achievement was to recognise his own weaknesses for what they were and find a way of dealing with them. Bitter experience would be a harsh teacher for Alfred, but he was a hugely conscientious student.

Æthelweard suggests that the incursion into Wareham was part of a wider and devastating raid: 'The greater part of that province [possibly Dorset, maybe Wessex as a whole] was ravaged by them.' In his version of events, the army took up camp 'near the town called Wareham' though the *ASC* state that the Vikings went 'into Wareham', which is a slightly different thing.[21] Certainly, it was an attractive target with its rich nunnery on the dual banks of the Frome and the Piddle, and its position as a port for the royal town of Dorchester upriver.[22] It may not have been as rich a prize as Hamwic (Southampton) some 30 miles east along the coast, but it would still tempt a Viking raider.[23] There is also a possibility that the town's defences were not as effective or complete as they should have been. Although Wareham certainly had some strong defences later on in Alfred's reign on its northern, eastern and western sides, no such traces have been found on the southern side which rests on the bank of the Frome. Further, the later tenth-century document known as the *Burghal Hidage*, which gives approximate dimensions for the area covered by the defences of various Wessex *burhs* (fortified towns), suggests that those around Wareham were equal to the length of the walls on the northern, eastern and western sides only. This may suggest that the riverside fortifications were insubstantial.

The raid was part of a two-pronged attack, with part of the assault probably coming overland. Now that they were in full possession of East Anglia, the Vikings in Cambridge had complete and potentially unfettered access to the prized equine stock of the region. Given their skill as horsemen this would have been very welcome. Many boasted fighting skills honed by years of regular campaigning in England, and they were able to move swiftly across country on horseback, outmanoeuvring any defensive force despatched to stop them. But the Vikings' traditional talent as seafarers also played a part in this major raid. In the same year, the *ASC* record a confrontation between some of Alfred's ships and a Viking force. The latter was not very large, with only seven ships mentioned, one of which was lost with the remainder fleeing; but it may have been just part of a bigger fleet. Certainly, there is strong evidence that soon after a force with well over 100 ships was in the area. Such 'joint operations' as we would now call them, where land and sea forces worked in strategic conjunction, seem to be a fairly regular feature of Viking strategy at the time. The Viking move on Northumbria a few years before appears to be one such example and another would be witnessed in 878 in Wessex.

Alfred belatedly managed to coordinate an effective response to the raid at Wareham, and the Vikings ultimately agreed a truce. They gave hostages for their good behaviour, with several accounts suggesting they included the more distinguished men amongst them, though the West Saxons also had to hand over men themselves. The existence of this truce suggests that the raid had not been as successful as the Vikings had hoped. But there was one element in the deal which, whilst not mentioned in all sources, Æthelweard is very clear about: Alfred paid off the Vikings.[24] Essentially, he did what the later king Æthelred II ('the Unready') would be castigated for and paid them what would later be called Danegeld. No opprobrium would attach to Alfred for doing this – it would not fit with the caricature of the flawless king which writers such as Asser wanted to develop. Such matters were best glossed over.

In return, the Vikings took an oath on a 'sacred ring' that they would leave without further trouble. The nature of this 'sacred ring' is slightly unclear. Asser's version of events suggests that the ring was sacred to Alfred whilst historians have noted that there is evidence from works such as the *Eyrbyggja Saga* which show that the Vikings also had rings that were of symbolic significance to them which were used for the purposes of oath-taking.[25] Suffice to say, whomever the ring was sacred to it did not have the desired effect as far as the West Saxons were concerned. Rather than return to East Anglia as desired, instead the Vikings stole out under cover of darkness and moved rapidly west to Exeter, further into Wessex. They killed their hostages before doing so (presumably the West Saxons did the same with theirs). Alfred was again caught off guard, and his situation looked certain to get worse before a stroke of luck (or, as Alfred would have it, an act of God) intervened.

There was by now a large Viking fleet in the area. It was moored up in Poole Harbour, referred to at the time as 'the mouth of the Frome', a magnificent anchorage sheltered from wind and waves by one of the largest natural harbours in the world. The fleet soon headed off to follow the land army down to Devon, presenting a major threat to Alfred's army. Just a few miles out of the harbour, the Viking ships made their way past Old Harry Rocks and on to Peveril Point. They then planned to sail west along the Dorset coast, arriving soon after at the mouth of the Exe just downriver from Exeter. But somewhere in Swanage Bay, disaster struck.

The precise nature of this disaster is somewhat unclear. Some versions of the *ASC* say it was a storm, others a mist which could indeed have been disastrous given the treacherous rocks scattered around the area.

Whatever the case, 120 Viking ships were lost. Such a large number suggests a storm rather than mist; if the latter had been the problem, the bulk of the force would have been sufficiently warned by the misfortune of the first ships to come to grief. The loss of so many ships was a major blow to the Viking raid, but the fact that it still went ahead perhaps gives a clue to the scale of the Viking fleet, implying as it does that there were more ships available. A Victorian-era monument erected by a local magnate, John Mowlem, proudly records Alfred's great victory over the Vikings at Swanage. It is in every way an anachronism. Cannonballs from the Crimean War adorn it and there is no evidence whatsoever that this disaster was a victory for anything other than the elements, welcome though it surely was to Alfred.

Exeter was a place with a long military history and in Roman times had been a legionary base known as Isca Dumnoniorum. The *ASC* hint that it was already fortified though the Roman walls might not have been maintained as well as desired; certainly, that would be the assumption based on what had occurred a few years before at York, which was also built on a Roman site. Whatever defences existed were insufficient to keep out the Viking force and they duly took possession. Alfred came chasing after them but was not able to eject them. He knew, after the experience he and his elder brother Æthelred had suffered at Nottingham and Reading during the past few years, that the Vikings were skilled in erecting or improving fortifications and would be hard to budge.

Just as Alfred could not batter his way in, nor could the Vikings fight their way out. The loss of 120 ships at Swanage must have made serious inroads into their available manpower. In addition, this was no longer the entire Great Heathen Army, part of which had moved north with Halfdan. It is not even certain that the men of this remainder were prepared to fight; after years in the field some may well have been ready to settle down, and the lands of East Anglia would be an attractive proposition for them. Faced with another stalemate, the two sides agreed another truce. Hostages were again exchanged, though after what had happened at Wareham this move must have been treated with some scepticism on the part of the West Saxons. But this time the arrangement was honoured. During the harvest period of 877 the Vikings took themselves off to Mercia, which they proceeded to divide between themselves and the supposed puppet king Ceolwulf. But Mercia and Wessex were close neighbours, and the Vikings were still in a good position to launch surprise attacks on Alfred's fragile kingdom. It would be foolish to assume that they had left Wessex alone for good.

Alfred on the Brink

We cannot be sure how harsh or inclement the winter weather was in 877/78, but we can be confident that the West Saxons did not expect to be going to war anytime soon. This was no time for fighting; that must wait until the late spring. Many of the fighting men were back in their homes, making the most of the festive season with their families. The harvest was in, the winter cull had taken place and the meat had been salted and stashed away. Christmas would be the last time to eat, drink and be merry for a while before the long, cold days of Lent. There would be no need to worry about fighting for months. But apparently no one had explained this to Guthrum.

Christmas would be a particularly enticing time for a Viking raider to attack a royal settlement. It would be crammed full of supplies, especially if a king and his court were in attendance. The laws of Ine may come from the beginning of the previous century but they were probably still a good reflection of the situation, particularly in the details they provide of the food and drink that was needed for just one night when the king was in residence: ten jars of honey, three hundred loaves, twelve casks of ale and thirty of clear ale, two old oxen, ten geese, twenty hens, ten cheeses, a cask of butter, five salmon, one hundred eels and twenty pounds of fodder. All this was part of the food rent, the *fearm*, a form of tax in kind which such estates were required to stump up.[26]

Many Viking attacks were on royal centres, *vills*. Dotted around the countryside, these are the places where food rents due from the local population would be collected. Kings and their entourages would travel around, staying here and there until supplies ran low. Given the nature of the *vills* they were attractive locations, as much for large Viking warbands with mouths to feed as for kings. Indeed, royal sites like Reading and Carhampton had been attacked in recent years. This meant that such places should be closely watched, especially at times of the year like Christmas when stocks would be particularly high. Unfortunately, over the Christmas period of 877/78 such caution was not observed at Chippenham.

Without warning, a Viking raiding party led by Guthrum fell on Chippenham sometime after Twelfth Night, 6 January 878, though it cannot have been much later as we are told it was midwinter. When the attack came, it seems to have taken everybody unawares. Some have even suggested that treason was at play and the Vikings were let in, though the evidence to back up such a claim is flimsy.[27] The Vikings, according to Æthelweard, were now based at Gloucester, around 50 miles to the north. There are no suggestions that there was a long fight, and the Vikings were soon in total control of Chippenham. It is possible that Alfred was not even there at the time. If he was, he would have been of great value to the raiders as a prime bargaining chip or perhaps a quisling king. A worse fate than this might have been in store, though, more along the lines of that faced by Ælle of Northumbria or Edmund of East Anglia: brutal, bestial, bloody. Alfred in any event escaped, if indeed he had been at Chippenham in the first place. He made his way to a watery, wasteland sanctuary, to his appointment with destiny in the Somerset Levels at Athelney, travelling 'with a small troop ... with difficulty through woods and into swamp-fastnesses'.[28] It was not much of a place, prominent only because its low bump rose above the even flatter wetlands round about. This was as far from the grandeur of a royal palace as it was possible to get. Presumably Alfred's family were with him, his wife Ælswith, his daughter Æthelflæd and his young son Edward. It was not much of a life for them either.

Alfred's future was now very uncertain. There are no records of any major battle between 871 and 878: the Viking raids in recent times had certainly been worrying but they had not led to any full-scale confrontations as far as we know. Yet there is an inexorable feeling that the raiders had slowly but surely been gaining the upper hand. There is also indirect evidence that Alfred was being compelled to pay what was in effect protection money. A letter from Pope John VIII to Archbishop Æthelred of Canterbury written in late 877 or early 878 recognises the problems that the archbishop is having because of the financial exactions being placed on the Church by the king. There is reference in that letter to a missive that the Pope had sent directly to Alfred reminding him of his responsibilities to protect the Church. Unfortunately, the original letter from the Pope to the king does not survive and is not mentioned in the *ASC*. This latter situation is hardly surprising: it does not fit comfortably with the image of a Christian paragon that the chronicler wishes to project for Alfred.

There is other evidence which suggests that Alfred was not quite the stalwart defender of the Church that his apologists would like him to be. Later chroniclers of Abingdon Abbey were positively scathing about the king. One even likened him to Judas Iscariot, the disciple who betrayed Christ. The abbey had been totally ransacked during the war of 871 and in its dereliction passed into the hands of the crown. Once he had it, Alfred proved very reluctant to hand it back. He was not unique in this though. Such measures had been initiated in the reign of Ecgberht and picked up by his successor Æthelwulf. Alfred's son and successor Edward would do the same. With many monastic establishments put out of commission by Viking raiders, there were plenty of abandoned properties to go around.

In a supreme irony, the depredations of the Vikings had directly benefited the income streams of the nascent Anglo-Saxon monarchy.[29]

Yet there was an element of inevitability about all this. The financial demands made by the Vikings were substantial and it would be impossible to meet them from the king's revenues. As a very rich player in the country, the Church would inevitably be tapped for substantial contributions towards the payments necessary to placate the Vikings. This was also the case across the Channel in Francia. That said, Guthrum's attack on Chippenham may have been a last throw of the dice. There was perhaps a sense that the Great Heathen Army was rapidly becoming a thing of the past. Certainly its numbers must have been well down on their peak by now as the force had been divided into different fragments several years previously. Perhaps Guthrum reasoned there was one last fight in them – but also that it was now or never if he was going to take Wessex for himself.

The *ASC* suggest that the raiders now swept all before them in Wessex. Droves of West Saxons either gave up the fight or fled the kingdom. We have no real evidence for Guthrum's military strategy at this point but perhaps some speculation can be allowed. Our task is made a little easier because we do have some snippets of information on which to build. In that same winter, a brother of Ivarr the Boneless and Halfdan was also in Wessex. Geoffrey Gaimar, a twelfth-century Anglo-Norman chronicler, identifies him as Ubba. Asser, without naming Ubba, gives other details about this Viking warlord. He tells his readers that he sailed from Dyfed, a kingdom in south-west Wales, with twenty-three ships (Æthelweard suggests thirty). Asser would be well placed to know this as he came to Wessex from St David's in Dyfed not long after the events he describes. He noted that the unnamed leader had slaughtered many of the Christians in Wales before sailing to Devon.

When he landed, Ubba was faced by a force providing a defensive screen for the western approaches to Wessex. It was led by Odda, the ealdorman of Devon. This force was protected after a fashion in a hilltop fortress at Cynuit. This could have been the Iron Age hill fort known as Wind Hill, close to Lynmouth. At some 260 metres (about 850 feet) above sea level it was in a powerful position, but no 'modern' defences had been built by the defending force and they seem to have relied on earthen ramparts which may have been little different than they had been a thousand years before. This location does not have an undisputed claim to be Cynuit though; an alternative suggestion is Cannington in Somerset, site of another Iron Age hill fort. It was also close to the coast and at the mouth of the Parrett, which flows down into the Levels close to Athelney. The latter suggestion has some attractive features to it.

It would be an ideal spot to launch one half of a pincer movement against Alfred if carried out in conjunction with a land force led by Guthrum coming from the east. But contemporary accounts, including the *ASC* and Æthelweard, clearly state that the action took place in Devon and the latter also tells us that the defensive force was led by the ealdorman of that shire.

There are also several other possible sites that might have been Cynuit. One near Bideford in Devon is evocatively called Bloody Corner. Indeed, there is a monument nearby which states unambiguously that near the spot lies buried 'Hubba [Ubba] the Dane who was slayed by Alfred the Great in a bloody retreat'. Unfortunately, this claim is of recent vintage with little by way of evidence to support it. Indeed, ascribing the victory to Alfred rather than Odda, as more contemporary sources do, is part of that hero-worshipping tendency which often took hold of antiquarians in certain periods of history. Such commentators can conceive of no one except the target of their adulation being capable of such triumphs. Neither was Ubba killed in a bloody retreat – he was overwhelmed in a surprise attack. To add further gloss to this arresting fable, local legend suggests that there was a large stone on the local shoreline beneath which Ubba was buried, though it has long since disappeared if indeed it was ever there in the first place.[30]

However antique the defences of Cynuit might have been, they were sufficiently formidable to deter the Vikings from attacking. Instead, they decided to starve out the garrison. They were in a good position to do so, especially as the fortress had no direct access to water. However, the defenders were in no mood to go down without a fight. Inspired by God (according to Asser), or perhaps fuelled by desperation given their lack of supplies, the garrison launched a sudden attack down the hill, seeking either 'death or victory'. Their momentum proved unstoppable, especially as their charge came at dawn whilst the Vikings might well have still been sleeping. The hapless besiegers were totally unprepared and were soon overwhelmed. Only a few Vikings managed to get to their ships and escape. Ubba was not one of them. He fell in the slaughter along with at least 800 others. This was a huge toll if correct given that Ubba's fleet was only between twenty-three and thirty ships strong. Odda had won a stunning victory which no doubt seemed miraculous to the West Saxon army. It was also a massive fillip to the morale of a beleaguered king and his people.[31]

The psychological boost was further strengthened by a prize taken in the battle in the form of Ubba's raven banner. The *Annals of St Neots* says that it was woven by three daughters of Ragnar Lodbrok and had magical properties. If the raven image on it fluttered, then victory for the bearer was certain; if it drooped, defeat must follow. The raven was Odin's bird. Two of them, Huginn and Muninn ('thought' and 'memory') flew around the world, gaining information on what was happening and reporting back to the deity. They were also associated with the carnage of battle, where they fed on carrion amidst the devastation left after combat. Viking sagas tell of other raven banners. The *Orkneyinga Saga* records that one was carried by Sigurd, earl of Orkney, at the epic battle of Clontarf near Dublin in April 1014. No one else would carry it into battle so the earl did so himself. Little good did it do him; his men were defeated and he was killed. Cnut is reported to have had a raven banner with him in his crushing victory at Ashingdon in 1016. Clearly the raven banner did not guarantee success, but its loss was nevertheless a heavy blow to the Vikings. To them, the banner was a sacred object, as significant as a holy relic would be to a devout Christian.[32] And indeed it lived on long into the future: when William of Normandy rode into battle at Hastings, according to the evidence of the Bayeux Tapestry, two banners fluttered in the breeze before his army: one with a Christian cross and the other with the age-old totem of Odin's sacred bird.

The Turning of the Tide

Sometime after Easter (23 March in 878), Alfred ordered defences to be constructed at Athelney. We can infer from Viking successes in recent years at places such as Reading, Exeter and Chippenham (and before that at York) that Anglo-Saxon defences were not in a good state of repair. It is unlikely that the defences at Athelney amounted to very much: whilst we can perhaps read too much into individual words or phrases in the various surviving chronicles, Æthelweard's description of 'something of a fort' built there has a slightly dismissive ring about it. However, the location had some strong natural advantages. Marooned in the middle of a vast marsh, half land, half water, it was very difficult to approach by either. There was only one land connection of note from Athelney, a causeway to East Lyng a mile or so away on higher ground. That made Athelney reasonably easy to protect, which was just as well. There were also nearby hills such as the atmospheric Burrow Mump, providing excellent lookout posts to ensure any approaching Viking force was detected early.

Even now, long after the wetland surrounding Athelney has been drained (though that does not stop it flooding from time to time), this is an evocative and mysterious landscape, apt for a place so closely associated with decisive events in England's history. It is a phantasmagorical place, haunted by spirits of events and people far in the past but still somehow hugely relevant to the ongoing story of the country. Sometimes when visiting a location with historical connections in modern times, it is hard to sense the spirit of the place, especially when all that one sees is a series of bumps and depressions in the ground. Not so with Athelney.

Alfred's small force was joined by men led by Æthelnoth, the ealdorman of Somerset, and it is easy to imagine the two plus the king's inner circle talking long into the night in this forlorn and remote place, plotting a counterattack. For a time, Alfred resorted to raiding, launching guerrilla attacks and generally reminding the Viking forces in the area that he was still around. He knew that a king could not stay hidden from his people for long before becoming irrelevant and losing power, but to fight back in a more meaningful way he needed an army and that was not easy to come by. In theory, the king had access to the *fyrd*, a militia which provided men to assist him when required. Each shire was responsible for its own *fyrd*, to be led by its ealdorman. In times of war, they would be ordered to assemble at a designated meeting point and then march off on campaign. To be more effective, such *fyrds* would sometimes combine forces, merging those from several shires, and there are a number of examples where two or more went into battle against a Viking enemy.

The *fyrd* of Devonshire had already proved its worth against Ubba, and it was still needed to guard Alfred's western flank against further attack from a Viking ship army. Alfred now sent out instructions to the *fyrds* of Somerset (some of whom were already at his side and participating in his guerrilla raids), Wiltshire and Hampshire to assemble at a place called Ecgberht's Stone, ready for battle. The absence of the *fyrd* of Dorset, which given the geography of the region would have been logically expected, asks some nagging – but currently unresolvable – questions about the loyalty of that part of Wessex to Alfred's cause. The precise location of Ecgberht's Stone is unclear, though a popular candidate is the spot marked by Alfred's Tower on the border between Wiltshire, Dorset and Somerset; indeed, there is a corner of this triangular structure in each shire. Other possible sites include the Upper Deverills, a group of villages to the south of Warminster. Asser gives us some clue in saying that Ecgberht's Stone was in the eastern part of Selwood. Selwood Forest was a traditional boundary dividing the eastern and western parts of Wessex: west of Selwood was the bishopric of Sherborne whilst to the east was the bishopric of Winchester. But this is not much help in narrowing things down.[33]

The eastern side of Selwood is about 30 miles to the east of Athelney. When the men of the three shires arrived there, we are told that they were overjoyed to see their king, some having expected to never see him again. Alfred would also have his own personal hearth-guard with him. This combined force camped at Ecgberht's Stone overnight before moving to Iglea or Aecglea, widely regarded as a reference to Iley Oak near Warminster. This was a well-known meeting spot where the local courts of Warminster and Heytesbury used to convene. It was probably hoped that more men would join to supplement those who had already assembled with the army at Ecgberht's Stone. This was sometime in the seventh week after Easter, which places these events between 4 and 10 May in 878, fitting well with the conventional start of the campaigning season.

One needs to resort to imagination to recreate images of the last night in the camp at Aecglea. Yet it is likely that they were much the same as many other armies over the centuries. Some men no doubt were boisterous, excited at the thought of an imminent fight. Others would have been quiet, contemplative, wanting to be alone with their thoughts and, in that religious age, their God. The task before them was formidable, their enemy strong and determined. Yet perhaps they were also beatable. The slaying of Ubba was a great victory which gave them hope. And their king was with them again, as if back from the dead. Perhaps God really was with him and with them.

It was time for the decisive battle. This might have been Alfred's last chance. Enough men had stayed loyal for him to raise an army, but if they lost their next fight they would either be dead or deprived of hope to such a degree that, as far as the king was concerned, they might as well be. If Guthrum and his men were to prevail, it might open the floodgates to other Vikings who would carve up Wessex between them as they had already done in Northumbria, Mercia and East Anglia. Guthrum had led his men out of Chippenham, determined to stop Alfred's resurrection dead in its tracks, and the two forces were destined to meet at Ethandun, which most historians believe was at Edington in Wiltshire. There are other claimants to be the site of this decisive battle, including another Edington in Somerset, but the Wiltshire location makes sense given Alfred's recent movements. Furthermore, an important priory was later set up in the Wiltshire Edington and Alfred left the estate there to his wife Ælswith in his will. Clearly this was a place that was significant to him.

This part of Wiltshire is the very quintessence of England in May, a land of gently rolling hills festooned with glorious late spring flowers, their yellow, scarlet, white and purple heads kneeling in obeisance before the warm and gently blowing breeze. It is difficult to imagine now that this beautiful spot was where the future of a country would be decided. It is possible that Guthrum's men had used the nearby Bratton Camp as a temporary fortress: in fact, given the defences that were already there, it would be surprising if they did not take advantage of it. The Iron Age fortress was in a strong natural position and its man-made earthen banks made it still more formidable. Even if the defences had gone to rack and ruin since its heyday many centuries before, it remained a very useful position for the Vikings as they prepared for battle.

The two armies moved into sight of one another in the rolling hills. The ridge that snakes from east to west above the villages of Edington and Bratton is, given its perspective, a dominating humpback. At its feet, the flat plain stretches for miles to the far horizon, closed off to the distant north by another impressive ridgeline. The sun rose in the sky, bringing a balmy warmth to the day, but the men did not notice it. Their eyes were fixed on their opponents. The pinpricks of sweat that increasingly glossed their brows were the result of nervous anticipation as much as the sun's rays. Both armies were arrayed behind compact shield walls, presenting a solid line to the opponent. It would come down to pushing and shoving, of axes crashing into flesh and bone, of swords and spears thrusting, of arrows arcing in deadly flight. Above all it would come down to which side held their formation and their faith in victory.

It was probably the West Saxon army that moved first. Given Guthrum's likely position up on Bratton Camp, this would not have been easy. The Vikings were already masters of much of Wessex and there was therefore no necessity for them to take the initiative, though they would of course welcome a final victory over their stubborn foe. If Alfred were to perish – on the field of battle or beneath the scarlet wings of the blood eagle, it mattered little – then surely the war would be over. However, they waged war for land and riches. The West Saxons were fighting to ensure their very survival and the future of their families. Their spirits ignited by such considerations, they fought the fight of the desperate.

The conflict raged for a long time. Both armies stood firm. The war shouts of the warriors, the shrieks of the injured and the diminuendo groans of the dying mingled, a haunting battle symphony on an epic scale. Men hacked and slashed at each other, gore carpeting the ground, but there was no quarter from either army for some time. And suddenly it came. It was just a small gap at first – and then another and then one more. As long as the shield wall – the *skaldborg* as the Vikings knew it – held, neither side could win; but when it was breached it would be as if an ocean had broken through the dykes. The flood would be unstoppable, deluging all in its path. As the tsunami gained in force, the panicked Vikings ran for their lives. Some of them made it to safety of a sort in a fortress, though whether this was close by at Bratton or in their main base at Chippenham is not clear (given its proximity the former seems more likely). For any Viking overtaken in retreat, only Valhalla beckoned.

Alfred's men on the other hand were exultant, their spirits raised to impossible heights by the heady cocktail of victory against the odds. For those Vikings who survived behind their fortifications a demoralising two weeks lay ahead. They were without adequate provisions and, more than that, without hope. Finally, they sued for peace. There was no obvious need for Alfred to be magnanimous, but he was. The Vikings would be allowed to leave but there would be a price – nothing less than their faith. Guthrum and thirty of his chief men were to be baptised as Christians. The ceremony of baptism would take place at Aller, near Athelney, on the very edge of the wetland which had protected the king at his moment of greatest danger. Guthrum surrendered the protection of his gods, abandoning Odin, Thor and Freyja for Christ. As he emerged from the waters he did so with a new name, Æthelstan, which he would use for the rest of his life. It was a name with real significance in the Wessex dynasty both before and after, which is indicative of Alfred's patronage. A church still stands near the spot, bearing a highly idealised stained-glass window of Alfred looking on. It is, inevitably perhaps, Victorian, that later era acquiring the king for itself and recreating him in a very romanticised form.

Baptism was something that would have seemed very alien to a Viking. Pagan Viking religion and Christianity could not be more different; there was not even such a thing as organised Viking religion. A man or woman could choose to follow whichever god or gods they wanted. There was no theocracy in the sense of a priesthood telling followers what they should and should not do. There was no text setting out a code to follow; there was not even a name for the Viking religion. People simply referred to it as *forn sidr*, 'the old ways'.[34] Conversely Christianity was highly regulated. The Church, still developing admittedly but increasingly assertive, was on its way to becoming a dominant, all-embracing bureaucracy which wielded great power. Vikings had been baptised before, particularly in Francia when they had been bested in battle or when seeking an alliance, but they had not always proved to be loyal adherents to the new faith. There is a revealing story from the reign of the Carolingian ruler Louis the Pious, earlier in the ninth century, in which a Viking about to be baptised complained about the quality of clothes that had been given to him for the occasion. He bluntly exclaimed, 'I have already gone through this washing business twenty times already, and I have been dressed in excellent clothes of perfect whiteness; but a sack like this is more fit for swineherds than for soldiers.'[35]

But Guthrum, or Æthelstan as he now became, seems to have retained his Christian identity for the rest of his life with his 'Christian name' invariably used on his later coinage as king of East Anglia. This flexibility of conscience contrasts surprisingly with the picture of convinced and confirmed pagans painted by various chroniclers of the time. The writers of English, Frankish and Irish records consistently emphasise the non-Christian beliefs of the Vikings, referring to them as pagans, gentiles or heathens. The *Annals of Ulster* refers to Irishmen who adopted a Viking way of life as either apostates or 'sons of death'. Yet in the late ninth and throughout the tenth centuries an increasing number of Scandinavians and Vikings would become adherents of the Christian flock, though in a good many cases they also retained various aspects of their old pagan customs. Indeed, just two years before at Ponthion in Francia, a group of Vikings had been baptised but, the chronicler sniffily noted, 'afterward, like typical Northmen, they lived according to the pagan custom just as before'.[36]

Baptism, however, was not just about religion. It gave the sponsor symbolic power over the man or woman being baptised. In effect, they became the godfather and the baptised became the godchild. By becoming Guthrum's sponsor, Alfred was asserting his symbolic superiority over him. We do not know why Alfred adopted this approach towards his captured enemy rather than some of the more violent alternatives. Perhaps he saw something in Guthrum which gave him hope that he could work with him in the future. In any case, a treaty was agreed at Wedmore in Somerset. It was very much a carrot-and-stick approach, for the thirty-man Viking delegation was showered with gifts. However, this was not just a nice gesture. The giving of gifts was a way of establishing overlordship, an action that the Viking warriors understood only too well; their own culture involved, for instance, giving objects such as arm-rings as a way of establishing superiority over others. Guthrum's army would be required to retreat to Mercia, stopping at Cirencester before finally ending up in East Anglia, a truly conquered land. Here many of them set down roots and sought out a different life for themselves. It is a strange thought, and few would have foreseen it, but these individuals would play a crucial and positive part in the formation of England.

The fightback was complete. As we shall see, Alfred would face further challenges from the Vikings in the years ahead, but never again would he be so close to the edge of the precipice as he had been in the fragile sanctuary of Athelney. A nagging thought remains, though: if the king had truly been so near to oblivion as Asser suggests, how could he have survived? If his people were so devastated in the aftermath of the debacle at Chippenham, how had the fallen king managed to raise more troops? Perhaps Asser overemphasises the powerlessness of his hero's position at the time in the interests of building up his achievements yet further. After all, Alfred was still able to summon the *fyrds* of Wiltshire, Somerset and Hampshire; and there is no suggestion that his lands to the east – Sussex, Kent and Berkshire, for example – had been lost to him.

It is also suspicious that, despite allegedly having won a crushing victory at Edington, Alfred was so generous in victory. It is very possible that a good part of the Viking army remained intact after the battle and that the 'gifts' Alfred gave them were nothing more than a generous helping of Danegeld. But this is nit-picking. In the final analysis, it would be wrong to underestimate the enormity of Alfred's achievements. It was not yet the beginning of the end as far as the Viking threat was concerned, but it could certainly be argued that it was the end of the beginning.

5

Alfred the Great

They said that of all the kings upon the earth he was the man most
gracious and fair-minded, kindest to his people and keen to win fame.

Beowulf

Rebuilding Wessex

Guthrum took his men back over the border to Cirencester, still ominously
close to the borders of Wessex. He stayed here for a year before moving to
East Anglia where he settled down to the challenges of kingship, dividing
the land between his men. Further ominous news arrived with the landing
of another Viking force at Fulham on the Thames, but the threat came to
nothing; perhaps the treaty with Guthrum was already doing its job and
the tamed king wanted to reap the benefits of peace. The force at Fulham
stayed for a year and then, like the peripatetic animal that it was, made
its way over to Ghent, then in Francia, where it stayed for a further year.
Surprisingly, for the next few years the producers of the *ASC* focus their
accounts on events on the continent rather than England. An exception
is found in the year 881 when we are told of a triumph in a battle at sea
between Alfred and Vikings, but as only four Viking ships were involved
this was a very minor encounter indeed. Two ships were destroyed with
their men whilst the crews of the other two surrendered.

The reason for this concentration on Frankish rather than Anglo-
Saxon affairs in the *ASC* during this decade has never been satisfactorily
explained. Various theories have been put forward, but none are
particularly convincing. It is also hard to believe that very few Viking
raids were taking place during this decade when we know that they were

a regular occurrence in Francia. This was a very extended coastline, with the south-east around Kent exposed to attack from the continent whilst the south-west was open to raids from Ireland and south Wales, both regions with a significant Viking presence at this time. It is hard to believe that the Viking threat to England had simply melted away.

There is, however, a glimmer of light which does give some insight into what was happening in England during this decade. There was a large raid in the south-east in 884. A sizeable force – which the chronicler implies was one of those that had been causing trouble in Francia – fell on Rochester. Asser relates that the Viking force in Francia had captured many horses and brought some of these over to England. This raiding force established itself in a fortress they constructed outside the city, emulating tactics used by Viking armies many times before. However, the defenders had clearly made good preparations as they held out until the arrival of a relieving force led by Alfred compelled the Vikings to abandon their fort. They rushed back to their ships and sailed off, leaving their horses behind them as well as many prisoners they had taken – a signal triumph for the king.

Alfred was not yet finished though. He sent his men on a raid into East Anglia in 885. This is an interesting development, as the kingdom was under the rule of Guthrum. Perhaps East Anglia had been offering sanctuary to the force that had raided Rochester; maybe some of the raiders remained there even now. This is one case where Æthelweard gives more detail than the *ASC*. He tells us that the large force that had been raiding Francia had split into two, one part attacking Rochester whilst the other remained on the continent and moved on Louvain. Agreeing with other accounts, he says the invading force was driven off when Alfred arrived and 'the foul plague was overcome'. But not all returned across the water. Some stayed behind, and hostages were exchanged as a surety for their good behaviour.

But the raiders did not stick to the terms of the deal. Several more raids followed. The 'foul people who then held East Anglia gave support and suddenly made an expedition outside their own boundaries to Benfleet [Essex]'. It was, according to Æthelweard, in retaliation for this that Alfred sent his men into East Anglia where they attacked sixteen ships at the mouth of the Stour. Guthrum was perhaps not quite the paragon of a Christian king that Alfred hoped he would become after his baptism. Initially the West Saxon force was successful: the Viking ships were cleared and the leaders on board were killed. But as the West Saxons made off, burdened with the spoils of victory, a 'great raiding ship-army of Vikings' fell on them. Ultimately, the *ASC* note that 'the Danes had the victory'. It was a salutary reminder to Alfred. The Vikings remained a potent threat, and his army which had seemingly won a great victory remained vulnerable, lured into complacency by the narcotic effect of hubris.[1]

London was a key point in all this, having been occupied by the Vikings in the aftermath of the campaign in Wessex back in 871. It was, as it still is, in a prime position for trade and a linchpin of communications. Archaeological finds reveal long-distance trading for objects such as lava querns and glass vessels along with pottery from the Rhineland, northern France and Flanders. Bede had called London 'the mart of many nations coming to it by land and sea'.[2] It was then in Mercia though the Thames, on which it stood, formed a vital riverine artery into Wessex too. Alfred felt that it was high time to acquire London. It had declined since its Roman heyday and was based now at Lundenwic, to the west of the Roman city walls, but it remained an important place in its own right. Alfred moved on it and took it in 886. He then handed control of the city to his Mercian son-in-law, Æthelred, who married Alfred's first-born, Æthelflæd, in the same year. He also decided to rebuild London on the ruins of the old Roman city, setting up what was in effect a *burh*, a fortified settlement which served a dual purpose as a trading centre. It was at this time that the *ASC*, closely echoed by Asser, recorded that Alfred was recognised as king by all Anglo-Saxons except for those living under the Vikings in territory that they had taken. This may even have involved a formal oath-taking by all Anglo-Saxons in those regions, including those outside of Wessex – a major development in the making of England.

Now Alfred sought to put Guthrum back in his place through other means. Another treaty was agreed between the two. It defined the boundaries of land to be held by Alfred and by the East Anglian Vikings. Rivers and roads marked the dividing line: the Thames, the Lea and from there in a straight line to Bedford. Then the border followed the Ouse up to Watling Street. The eastern side of the country was split in two by a diagonal line. It was also agreed that the value of a Dane and an Englishman killed would be the same – this was a reference to the Anglo-Saxon concept of *wergild*, which put a value on human life so that capital punishment for offences like murder could be avoided if blood-money were paid instead. It was also affirmed that no slaves or freemen (who owed tribute on their land) could desert one side and join the army of the other. It was an interesting agreement, made as if between equals. Clearly Alfred was a long way from governing the whole of England. At this point in time, the Danes simply had to be tolerated. The treaty was clearly for the long-term too, as it noted that it was for 'both the living and the unborn'.

At some point in the mid-880s – the exact year is not clear – the archbishop of Rheims in Francia wrote to Alfred, using a new regnal title: *Regi Anglorum*. The recognition of Alfred as king of the Anglo-Saxons, and perhaps his own pretension in giving himself such a title, marks an important step in his own ambitions and also a widening of his powerbase. It should not be overplayed – there were many Anglo-Saxons further north living under Viking rule – but it was important in suggesting how the dynasty of Wessex now saw itself.

In the introduction to Pope Gregory's *Pastoral Care*, which he commissioned to be translated, Alfred wrote in sad reflection some words which spoke eloquently of the effect that Viking attacks had wrought on his kingdom: 'In the past men from abroad came to this land in search of wisdom and teaching, and ... now we must get them abroad [again].' He also mourned the fact that 'before it had all been ravaged and burned, the churches throughout all England stood filled with treasures and books'.[3] The attacks on the Church had decimated English learning, though some felt that it was already in decline even before the Vikings had launched their ferocious assault. Fulco, archbishop of Rheims, noted in a letter to Alfred probably written in 886 that the ecclesiastical order had 'in many respects, as you say ... fallen into ruin, whether by the frequent invasion and onslaught of Vikings, or through decrepitude or through the carelessness of its bishops or the ignorance of those subject to them'. Perhaps the raiders from the north were not solely responsible for the decline, then.[4]

Even if this is true, they certainly had not improved the situation. There is a good deal of tangible evidence of the destruction unleashed by the Vikings. By the 870s, Leicester and Lindsey in Mercia were without bishops, as were Elmham and Dunwich in East Anglia. In Northumbria, Hexham was no longer viable, and the monks of Lindisfarne were forced to evacuate their sacred isle, fleeing to the mainland taking the mortal remains of the venerable Cuthbert with them. Important churches such as Dover and Minster in Kent disappear from the records without trace. Many other churches were ransacked; and whilst some historians argue that the damage was far worse in some areas than others, not all of the impact was visible. When Vikings destroyed churches, they not only caused huge material loss but destroyed fountains of knowledge. In those days, most literate people were connected to the Church, and with the decline of the institution there was an immense societal fallout which Alfred was keen to address.[5]

Alfred devoted much of his spare time to studying the scriptures and divine contemplation. There was so much on his plate that it was all too easy to get distracted and not give sufficient time to God. His was a busy world, and his attitude to surviving it is summed up eloquently in the introduction he wrote to the work he commissioned on the *Dialogues* of Pope Gregory: 'There is the most urgent necessity to calm our minds amidst these earthly anxieties and direct them to divine and spiritual law.' In some ways this is as much a message to our own world as it was to his.[6] One cannot understand Alfred without understanding his spirituality. The Vikings were a warning from God that His people should reform themselves. They could not do so without reading His word, and due to the decline in standards of literacy this was not an option for many. The situation could not be tolerated.

For one thing, to govern a kingdom a ruler had to have a civil service with men who were not only loyal to his cause but also skilled in their job. So he set about reforming the country through education. In order to do so, he pulled in the best men he could find from all over England and beyond. One of those recruited was Wærferth, the bishop of Worcester in Mercia. He had been close to those ruling in the kingdom, particularly the former king, Ceolwulf II, and ealdorman Æthelred, Alfred's son-in-law. The bishop was very familiar with the Viking threat: this was the very same man who in 872 had pleaded poverty when having to sell off land because of the taxes levied to placate them. He was also a skilled translator and is regarded by many as the man who translated Pope Gregory's *Dialogues* into Anglo-Saxon for Alfred.[7] The work became very popular in the Middle Ages and focussed in particular on the life of St Benedict, one of the founding figures of medieval monasticism, which provided the subject for one of the four books that made up the work as a whole.

Another scholar recruited by Alfred was Plegmund, also a Mercian. Later tradition asserted that at some point he lived as a hermit, but he also earned a reputation for his learning. He was part of a team that worked on a translation of Gregory's *Pastoral Care*. He rose to great heights, becoming archbishop of Canterbury in 890, the ASC proclaiming that in that year 'Archbishop Plegmund was elected by God and all the people'. This was possibly after the post had been offered to Grimbald, a Flemish scholar who had also been invited to Alfred's court, arriving in 886. Grimbald was a monk from St Bertin's in Flanders who was under the patronage of Fulco, archbishop of Rheims, whose correspondence with Alfred has survived. The king had approached Fulco for help in rebuilding the state of learning in his kingdom, sending a delegation to him which bore gifts including five hunting dogs, an export for which England had long been famous. In Fulco's letter to Alfred, it comes across as if he is 'doing Alfred a great favour' by letting Grimbald leave.[8] Grimbald, who was multi-talented – he was described as an 'excellent chanter' – may have made a particularly significant contribution. Both the *ASC* and Asser show a decent knowledge of recent Frankish affairs, and this might well have come from him.

At around the same time, another man from overseas, John 'the Old Saxon', also joined this academic coterie. A man of 'acute intelligence', he would be appointed as the abbot of the religious foundation that Alfred established at his place of destiny, Athelney. This was a very cosmopolitan foundation as there were monks of various nationalities there, even including one who came from Viking stock. But contemporaries suggested that this was out of necessity. Partly due to Viking raids and partly because of monasticism's lack of appeal to the English people, it was difficult to attract new recruits from Anglo-Saxon England alone.[9] John had a colourful career subsequently. Attacked in the church at Athelney by some of his own monks in an assassination plot, he survived despite severe wounds. His would-be killers were captured having tried to hide in the marshes and died a gruesome death after 'various tortures'.[10] He would go on to witness a number of charters in the reign of the next king, Edward the Elder. The monastery itself, despite royal patronage, was never a total success. Perhaps it was too remote to become firmly established.

The best-remembered recruit to Alfred's court was probably Asser, the king's biographer. Some negotiations were required to tempt him away from his role as a monk (and quite possibly bishop) at St David's, that beautiful and lonely establishment in the far west of Wales perched on the edge of the Irish Sea. His first visit to Alfred at Dean in Sussex lasted just four days. He returned to his community at St David's, explaining to the king that he would have to talk to them before removing himself to Alfred's court on a longer-term basis as the king had requested. An illness that laid him up at Caerwent delayed him for a year, but then he returned and for a while split his time between Wessex and Wales. The beginning of his long-term relationship with Alfred in Wessex has been dated to around 887. After this time, he split his year between Wessex and St David's, eventually becoming bishop of Sherborne. Alfred gained a scholar and a bishop whilst Asser hoped to win the king's protection for his 'home' establishment in the west of Wales, which had suffered the unwelcome attentions of Hyfaidd, king of Dyfed, on several occasions.[11]

In Asser's slightly dubious account, the king himself soon developed a skill for translation which he supposedly put to good use in taking on such activities himself. Whilst Alfred copied many ideas from Francia, albeit adapting them to an English context, by using Anglo-Saxon as the language of state he was completely innovative in Northern Europe where other 'civilised nations' used Latin. Asser claims that the king learned to read and translate on the same day, giving Alfred an intellect that would seemingly rival that of Einstein. Alfred is regarded as being behind the translation of four major works: Pope Gregory's *Pastoral Care*, Boethius's *The Consolation of Philosophy*, Saint Augustine's *Soliloquies* and the first fifty psalms of the Psalter. The Psalter is particularly appropriate as many of the Psalms are literary lamentations written by the biblical King David in the face of the tribulations inflicted on him by his pagan Philistine enemies.[12] Other translations appeared as part of Alfred's programme (though he himself was not the translator) including Bede's *Ecclesiastical History* and Gregory's *Dialogues*, which considered the immortality of the soul, a subject that interested Alfred greatly. He was clearly an enthusiastic scholar, and he carried a small notebook, an *enchiridion*, around with him to scribble down words that interested him.

Pastoral Care appears to have held special importance for Alfred. It was the first work to be translated, and copies were circulated to all his bishops. It has been said that it is the equivalent of St Benedict's Rule for secular clergy. But its content possibly touched Alfred at a personal level. Its injunctions for men to stay steadfast in the face of earthly tribulations may have particularly appealed to the king in the light of all that he had experienced.

The Consolation of Philosophy by Boethius was also hugely influential across the medieval period and beyond. Boethius was an early sixth-century scholar in north Italy who was sentenced to death after being implicated in a plot against Theodoric, an Ostrogoth who in effect conquered Italy and would therefore be considered by many as an interloper just like the Vikings who had attempted to take over Wessex. Boethius wrote his work whilst awaiting his execution. It is in essence a dialogue between a doomed man and the personification of philosophy, and ends with him accepting his fate as a good Christian should. It is not difficult to see why this work appealed to Alfred given what he had been through. It is an interesting aside that in the sixteenth century Queen Elizabeth I of England was inspired to undertake her own translation of this work into the English of her age, which she allegedly accomplished in twenty-seven hours[13] – a reminder that almost supernatural qualities have been attributed to many rulers across the ages.

Alfred's translation of Boethius was a loose rather than a literal one. So too was the translation of Augustine's *Soliloquies*, which majored on the complex question of the immortality of the soul in a similar way to Gregory's *Dialogues*. Alfred was no pedant, and he was more interested in making these works accessible rather than philologically perfect.

His greatest insight as far as learning was concerned was perhaps to arrange for these works to be available in Anglo-Saxon rather than Latin. He felt that using the language of the everyday would make it easier for his people to learn. A school was set up to educate the children of Alfred's nobles as well as members of the royal family. He did not underestimate the value of Latin but felt that it should only be studied after the basics had been learned in Anglo-Saxon. Further, Latin should in the main only be taught to those who planned to enter holy orders.

One of the most intriguing authors to be translated as part of this programme was Orosius, an early fifth-century writer who composed a work known as the *Histories against the Pagans*. The title alone is suggestive of the work's appeal to Alfred. It is ironic that perhaps the most fascinating part of the translation is what is effectively a postscript which tells of a visit to Alfred's court by a man from the remote north, on the far fringes of Viking Scandinavia. This man, named Ohthere, was a sailor who had journeyed into the largely unknown lands on the edges of the White Sea. This apparently friendly visit is a reminder of some potential complexities around contemporary relationships. Not all Scandinavians were hostile Viking raiders.

Several other works were produced by this busy group. There was a *Martyrology*, a compilation of several hundred saints' lives. Perhaps most interesting of all from a cultural perspective was the *Leechbook* of Bald, a fascinating compendium of medical recipes in an age where treatment relied on basic herbology rather than complex pharmaceuticals. Whilst we might be dubious about the efficacy of some of these recipes, Alfred's sponsorship of the work at least suggests that he was interested in practical issues as well as complicated theology and philosophy. According to Asser, the king even designed a primitive kind of clock using candles.[14]

The translations that Alfred was directly or indirectly responsible for frequently discussed profound spiritual issues, which reflects a strong personal interest in such matters. He was remarkably well read and, given his piety, was probably familiar with the rule of St Benedict. If this was so, he may have also been familiar with Benedict's injunction that 'idleness is the enemy of the soul' and taken it to heart. Certainly, the actions he took to improve standards of literacy and his unstinting efforts to persuade or cajole others to advance their own education would suggest so. It seems significant that Gregory's *Pastoral Care* emphasises that those in positions of power should devote themselves to learning, something that Alfred instructed his ealdormen to do. 'Do as I do as well as I say' seems to have been his maxim for government, which one suspects may have become tiring to some of his advisors, especially the older ones amongst them.

The translations were made in the later years of his reign and provided a core part of his strategy for the education of the English, in its own way an element in helping to build a stronger kingdom and an important legacy for the king.

Alfred was also a lawmaker. His law code was put in place in the late 880s or early 890s and was essentially a combination of several elements. Unsurprisingly there was reference to God's law in the shape of the Ten Commandments. There were also elements of the laws of one of Alfred's predecessors as king of Wessex, Ine, as well as references to those of Offa and Æthelberht of Kent. Alfred included his own direct rulings too, among them a requirement that 'each man keep carefully his oath and his pledge' or face forty days' imprisonment. Plotting against the king's life would, unsurprisingly, result in the offender forfeiting his own. If a man drew his sword in the king's hall, then it was up to the ruler to decide whether he should live or die. There was mention of what was to be done about sexual offences, and what a man was allowed to do if he found another in bed with his wife. A popular element, one assumes, was the requirement that all free men should be allowed twelve days' holiday at Christmas, though this did not include slaves or unfree men – a poignant reminder that there were many such in those days and that slavery was not just a Viking phenomenon. A further fourteen days' holiday would be granted to free men at Easter along with odd holy days here and there throughout the year.[15]

This was another facet of kingship that was important. As well as being a warrior, a ruler of the period should also be a lawmaker. It was no coincidence that Alfred consciously sought to emulate other great Anglo-Saxon kings in his laws. It showed that he had significant pretensions to greatness – pretensions that he would ultimately prove were more than justified.

Fortifying Wessex

Alfred's translation of Boethius, which he says was 'sense for sense' rather than 'word for word', gives us a fascinating insight into the way that he, and no doubt most of his successors, thought concerning what was required to be a successful king of the period. He needed several fundamentals with which to support his people: land to live on, gifts, weapons, food, ale and clothing are specifically mentioned. A king had to provide both sustenance and patronage. The need for the former is obvious, while perhaps for the latter it is less so. But although divinely appointed by God, this on its own did not guarantee successful rule.

A king was supported by powerful counsellors which in England took the form of a *witan*. If he lost their support, then he might lose his kingdom. Indeed, this is one interpretation of the state of affairs in 878 when Wessex almost slipped from his grasp. So a king had to be generous; and Alfred won himself a reputation for his generosity. The author of the preface to a copy of Gregory's *Dialogues* – probably Bishop Wulfsige of Sherborne, Asser's predecessor – described him as 'the greatest treasure-giver of all the kings he has ever heard tell of'.[16]

Boethius also talks about a widely referenced medieval view of society, namely that it was composed of three classes of men: those who pray, those who fight and those who work.[17] Alfred would have seen the importance of all of them but also of the need for balance. Those who fight became more important in the latter part of Alfred's reign. Nicholas Brooks estimated that around 27,000 men could have been deployed as Wessex effectively went onto a war footing. This equates to a remarkable one in every five or six available men.[18] Theoretically this was one man to every three feet of wall that formed part of a *burh*. The underlying principle was that gaps between *burhs* should be no greater than 20 miles. They were supported by an early-warning system in the form of beacons – there is evidence of even ancient landmarks such as Silbury Hill near Avebury being brought into use. *Herepaths* – 'army paths' – were put in place which would allow West Saxon forces to travel quickly. Twenty-two out of thirty-three places named in the later document known as the *Burghal Hidage* were at river crossings, so bridges and fords would both have been important. Another five – Southampton, Christchurch (Twynham as it was then), Watchet, Hastings and Portchester – were in important coastal locations, some of which were at critical points giving access into major river systems. Exeter and Chichester were also very close to the coast. The proximity of the *burhs* to water is a powerful indicator of the importance of sea power as far as the Viking threat was concerned.

Anglo-Saxons were not unused to being taxed for the building and maintenance of bridges and fortifications as well as giving military service – the 'Common Burdens' as they were known. But this was something on an altogether different scale. It was certainly needed, but it was also unpopular. In a revealing passage, Asser tells us that Alfred had to instruct, cajole, urge, command and ultimately chastise some of his people who were, in his words, disobedient and sometimes stupid and stubborn. Those who continued to resist his commands were in the end punished by 'virtual extinction' at the hands of raiders. Then they repented their stubbornness; but, the writer wondered, 'what use is their accursed repentance ... having lost their fathers, spouses, children, servants, slaves, handmaidens, the fruits of their labours and all their possessions', and when they were reduced to tears?[19]

Of course, Alfred was not the first to build defensive fortifications in Wessex, but he introduced a structure of interconnected sites that took the defence of the kingdom to a whole new level. Inspired by major fortress-building schemes in Francia which had been deployed against the Vikings, Alfred threw himself into similar projects in Wessex. It is also very possible that he had been inspired by the Vikings' skills in defensive construction too, having learned of them the hard way at Nottingham and Reading. There were similarities in design between many of the fortresses as far as we can tell. They were typically surrounded by a deep ditch, the soil from which would be piled up to form a rampart that was topped with a timber palisade and towers. But there was in reality no such thing as a generic burh. They varied enormously in size from large *burhs* such as Winchester, with an estimated wall length of just over 3,000 metres, to very small sites such as Lyng, which measured a mere 171 metres.[20] Often sites with Roman walls were reused, such as at Exeter, Winchester, Bath, Portchester and Chichester. Inherently strong natural positions were fully utilised where available such as the hilltop locations of Shaftesbury and Malmesbury (Wiltshire) or the deep gorge at Lydford (Devon), which made the place virtually impregnable from several directions. Particularly fine examples of *burh* fortifications can still be seen at Lydford and Wareham, the latter significant enough to be strengthened and brought back into use as recently as the Second World War.

Whilst some such locations had a long history dating back to Roman times, in other cases Alfred built on sites which were either new or had a very modest heritage. An example was Shaftesbury, which had little provenance to speak of yet was chosen to host a *burh*. It fitted into the invisible gridline of places 20 miles apart and its defensive position was superb. It had an extensive outlook, especially to the south where it lowered menacingly over the flatlands of the Blackmore Vale. William of Malmesbury tells us that he had seen a carved stone which told how 'Alfred made this town in 880', a wonderful piece of evidence that very soon after the Viking attacks had been driven off, the king was hard at work on his fortification schemes. Bringing William's account to life, the very same stone was unearthed eight centuries later in 1904.

Alfred's building schemes also gave him the opportunity to make a political point, and this is rarely acknowledged. Shaftesbury again provides a good example. A new town, which Shaftesbury effectively was, needs institutions to support it. The king founded a nunnery there which would rise to be amongst the richest and most powerful in England. Its first abbess, Æthelgifu – 'a virgin consecrated to God'[21] – was Alfred's daughter, though she was not installed until some years later in 888. Royal patronage was key to such institutions thriving and it must have come as a blow to Wimborne, just 20 miles away, which already had a nunnery. It is an early sign that all might not have been well with Alfred and Wimborne.

The *burhs* had several significant purposes. They were places where those under attack could take shelter behind strong prepared positions which raiders would struggle to breach. But they were also places where Anglo-Saxon forces could assemble in safety before going on the offensive. Garrisons could be installed which could if needed go to the aid of friendly forces in the area that were under attack. It would be wrong, though, to see these places as mere military strongholds. They were in effect fledgling towns where trade and commerce could flourish in secure conditions. This had huge potential benefits for the king in particular. His agents could keep an eye on trade, monitor markets and regulate mints, the latter of which were particularly financially lucrative – every so often the coinage would be reissued, a process from which the king through various means would make a profit. Also, taxes could be collected with greatly reduced opportunities for evasion by taxpayers. This helped build the centralised power of the monarchy, a process that Alfred's son Edward and his daughter Æthelflæd would fully exploit after his demise, building burhs deeper into Mercia.

The garrisons therefore had an economic as well as a military impact. Significant numbers of men living together would inevitably have a knock-on effect on trade. Food and drink needed to be provided and goods had to be obtained, encouraging traders to come and sell their wares. Women would have also made an input, perhaps sometimes as wives and on other occasions as more informal companions. Such has always been the way with armies. If one were to travel back over half a millennium, a similar situation would have been witnessed around Roman legionary establishments. Evidence of the impact of Saxon development can still be seen if, for example, one walks around the streets of Winchester, where names such as Parchment Street, Silver Hill and Tanner Street hint at the existence of now long-gone occupations.

Yet for all the benefits of these fortifications, it should not be assumed that they were universally popular. Far from it in fact. Men would not take kindly to being conscripted to garrison them, and their construction contributed to a heavy tax burden. The cost of building the defences, not to mention the other expensive measures that Alfred had taken over the years such as the various payments of 'protection money' to persuade raiding armies to leave Wessex alone, had hit hard. There are several items of evidence from Alfred's reign which suggest that the Church was unhappy with what it was expected to contribute towards this national effort. The community at Abingdon, as already mentioned, was especially bitter in its criticism of the king.

The development of the *burh* system was a critical part of Alfred's strategy against the Vikings, and he remained committed to it throughout his later reign. Indeed, although the *ASC* are largely silent as to his activities in any respects in the last two years of his rule, we know from other sources that to the last such issues remained on his mind. A charter from either 898 or 899 granting land at the important site of Queenhithe on the Thames in London suggests that he was thinking about improving the fortifications of this crucial strategic site even then.[22] In fact, the system of fortifications that he created would be put to the test severely in the earlier part of the 890s. The course of events then would demonstrate very clearly just how successful his strategy was in keeping the Viking threat at bay. However, even by this later stage his plans had not yet all reached fruition. The words of Asser imply that in or around 893, when he wrote up his biography of the king, some fortifications had not yet been completed and in some cases construction had not even started.[23]

Alfred was also a skilled politician, and one of his areas of political focus was Wales. At the time, Wales was divided into several smaller kingdoms. It was a volatile region, the target of attacks from Mercia and Viking armies on an ongoing basis. The Welsh kings were also frequently at each other's throats. An alliance with the growing power of Wessex made sense to them as well as Alfred, leading to a pact between Wessex and the kings of Dyfed, Glywysing (in the south-east), Gwent and Brycheiniog (around Brecon). Gwent was particularly happy with the deal as the kingdom had been subject to frequent pressure from Ealdorman Æthelred of Mercia, which Alfred would be in a good position to stop. One king, Anarawd ap Rhodri of Gwynedd in the north of Wales, initially formed an alliance with the Vikings of Jorvik but found he gained little benefit from this and soon changed sides, later visiting Alfred's court. This is just one example of Alfred's approach to international relations. Surviving correspondence and comments made by various chroniclers suggest communication further afield with Ireland to the west and Francia to the east, not to mention frequent exchanges with the Pope in Rome and even with Elias, the patriarch of Jerusalem. Correspondence with the latter is especially interesting for it is not limited to matters spiritual, with Elias sending some suggested remedies to Alfred for complaints as varied as constipation, diarrhoea and 'internal tenderness', whatever that might be.[24]

Alfred's Last War

The relative lack of attacks on England in the 880s (at least as far as surviving records are concerned) may be because major Viking incursions in Francia were taking place, culminating in an epic siege of Paris in 885–86. But a disastrous defeat on the River Dyle in 891, followed the year after by a devastating famine in the region, led to a Viking army leaving Francia for Kent. The 250 ships which bore them across the Channel were followed by eighty from another force, suggesting that roughly 3,000 to 4,000 Viking raiders were on the attack, presenting a sizeable threat. Their arrival, ushering in a time of crisis worse than anything seen for more than a decade, may have prompted the compilation of the *ASC*. It was a powerful reminder that the Viking threat was far from over. This probably also coincided with the creation of Asser's biography of Alfred, which owed much to the *Chronicles* but was written with a different audience in mind. The *ASC* were probably primarily prepared for Alfred's court, whereas certain passages in Asser hint that he was writing for his own compatriots, the Welsh. As many of the sub-kings of Wales now acknowledged Alfred as their overlord, albeit whilst retaining significant autonomy, this made political sense.[25]

One of the main figures in the Viking attack on England was a remarkable character called Hæsten. If the legends and sagas are to be believed, he had been involved in a raid on Luna on the Italian coast as far back as the 850s. This was part of an incredible Viking probe into the Mediterranean, also involving another figure shrouded in legendary mist in the shape of Bjorn Ironside, son of Ragnar Lodbrok. Even in the great Viking epics, this adventure stood apart. True, it was a costly one and many ships did not return home; and it was embarrassing to realise that when attacking Luna, the raiders thought that they were besieging Rome. But the boldness of the mission was striking even by Viking standards. It was an epic adventure in the best Viking tradition.

Hæsten (if indeed it was him involved in this epic) later turned his attentions to Francia, where he played a prominent part in events over many years. He clearly survived the debacle on the Dyle and, realising that the pendulum had swung against the Vikings in Francia, sought for an alternative. The lure of England just across the narrow waters was too strong to resist. Much had changed there. Guthrum/Æthelstan of East Anglia had died in 890, an event that merited comment in the *ASC*.

The absence of adverse remarks in that august work, and the reminder to its readers that he was Alfred's godson, suggests that on the whole he had been a loyal ally, though the actions of some of his people may have been suspect at times. However, before long the emerging pattern of Viking settlers proving trustworthy allies (or at least neutral) would be placed in jeopardy.

For the campaign that followed, the *ASC* are positively verbose compared to their normal fare. The fleet of 250 Viking ships made their way over from Boulogne to the mouth of the Lympne, which is now called the Rother. The river flows through what is now East Sussex and Kent but in the Anglo-Saxon period its mouth was in a different place, entering the Channel near Dungeness. This was close to the great wood known as Andred at the time, better known today as the Weald. The chroniclers note that it was 120 miles long and 30 miles wide. The Viking fleet sailed 4 miles up from the river's mouth and reached the forest. On its edge they came across a half-finished fortification manned by 'a few peasant men',[26] which they quickly destroyed. Clearly Alfred's building programme was far from finished. The army then placed itself at Appledore, on the northern edge of Romney Marsh and at the time an important port on the Lympne/Rother.

It was only now that Hæsten himself arrived, moving with eighty ships to the mouth of the Thames on the northern side of Kent and basing himself at Milton. Kent was on the fringes of Alfred's kingdom. On the other side of the Thames was East Anglia and people who could turn out to be allies of the raiders. Alfred was concerned enough to obtain oaths from them and the Northumbrians. He also obtained six hostages from the East Anglians. There was a pregnant pause for a time, as if a storm was coming over the horizon and was about to break, and then the action began.

The campaign that followed was very different than those of 871 or 878. Back then it was as if there were two young prize-fighters going at each other hammer and tongs, hoping to land a knockout blow. This time it was a battle between two gnarled pros, sparring and jabbing, probing for an opening, looking for a weakness. Attacks came from all directions: Kent, East Anglia, even Northumbria. The raiding parties in Kent were first on the list. Alfred got his army together and moved towards them, his force apparently strong considering the raiding army opted not to emerge from behind its defences on more than two occasions.

Alfred was presumably delighted at his ability to keep the raiders under control when disturbing news reached him from the West: 140 ships had been gathered in Northumbria and East Anglia and had sailed right down to the far south-west of Alfred's kingdom. Forty ships had attacked a fortification on the coast of the Bristol Channel in Devon, and the rest had laid siege to Exeter. This was a serious threat and could not be ignored. No doubt with some reluctance, he began the long march down towards Exeter. It was left to his son, Edward, to take the lead against the raiders elsewhere. These marauders were ranging far afield, and Æthelweard notes that they caused major damage in Berkshire and Northamptonshire. When they moved deeper into Wessex, Edward took his forces out to meet them. The two armies collided at Farnham. Edward drove them back, wounding 'the barbarian king' (unnamed, though this may have been Hæsten) and forcing them north. A siege was laid on the marshy island of Thorney in the Thames close to Westminster. No longer an island, this hugely important spot is now home to one of England's foremost Christian sites in the shape of Westminster Abbey as well as its most significant secular location in the form of the Houses of Parliament. Significantly, there may have been a ford nearby which formed part of Watling Street, now the border between Anglo-Saxon and Viking-held territory. A charter of Offa about a century before had described it as 'a terrible place'. Æthelred, Alfred's son-in-law, came down from nearby London to support Edward. Hostages were exchanged and the Vikings agreed to leave.[27]

The Viking forces in Kent abandoned their camps at Milton and Appledore, opting to combine their strength at Benfleet in Essex on the northern side of the Thames Estuary, where Hæsten had earlier made a fort. Its position close to the water and the nearby Viking inhabitants of East Anglia made it a perfect place from which to launch raids further afield, and it was whilst Hæsten was away on one such raid that the Anglo-Saxons attacked Benfleet. They put the raiding army to flight and broke down the fort, seizing all that was inside, which included both material wealth and women and children. This booty was brought safely into London and all the Viking ships that were taken were either broken up or burned, save for a few that were taken back to London and Rochester.

Amongst those who were captured was Hæsten's wife and his two sons. One of these sons was Alfred's godson and the other was the godson of Æthelred of Mercia, the king's son-in-law. The fact that these boys had previously been sponsored at baptism by Alfred and Æthelred is significant. A deal had been struck between Alfred and Hæsten at the time that the baptisms took place. Hæsten had been given generous gifts (which again sounds like Danegeld) to leave the kingdom, but as soon as he reached Benfleet he reneged on the deal and recommenced his raids. The fact that Hæsten himself was not a godson is suggestive; perhaps he had already been baptised previously and could therefore not go through the ceremony again. This indicates one of those situations which have been mentioned before whereby a Viking would undergo baptism for the sake of convenience but might afterwards relapse and break the agreement with his sponsor. Hæsten certainly seems to have done so.

The presence of Hæsten's wife also indicates that there were women with the army. Whilst English accounts rarely mention the presence of women and children in the Viking incursions, contemporary accounts from Ireland and Francia do, so it is highly likely that some accompanied the armies that had been attacking the Anglo-Saxon kingdoms since 865. The peripatetic lifestyle of the Vikings was therefore shared by some of their families, though as settlement in England became established a degree of conventional domesticity would have followed.

Surprisingly, Alfred allowed Hæsten's wife and sons to return to him. If he hoped this seemingly altruistic gesture would buy off the troublesome Viking, he was sadly mistaken. The *ASC* suggest that he released the two sons because they were his and Aethelred's godsons. Possibly Alfred wanted to make a point that this was not how Christians behaved, but any such moral lesson was wasted on Hæsten. A real problem was now brewing. A Viking army had assembled at Shoebury, on the eastern tip of the Thames Estuary. It was composed of the two raiding-armies that had previously been in Kent and also men from East Anglia and Northumbria. To compound the problem, Alfred was far away, campaigning in the south-west. The Viking fleet sailed up the Thames and then up the Severn into Mercia.

This army posed a substantial threat, and Alfred's response reflected that. In an almost unprecedented move, he called up men on something resembling a national scale. Those from the West Country were ordered to assemble, from both east and west of Selwood, led by ealdormen Æthelnoth of Somerset and Æthelhelm of Wiltshire. Naturally given the location of the Viking attack, Æthelred of Mercia was there too. There were men from 'every stronghold east of the Parret', from north of the Thames and west of the Severn. There were even 'a certain part of the Welsh race' involved.

This large force marched north and chased after the Viking army. They caught it at Buttington, which was probably a hill fort near Shrewsbury. The Vikings were soon in trouble. Under siege and running short of supplies, they were so 'weighed down with lack of food' that they were forced to eat their horses. Desperate, they tried to break out. Fired on by their awful situation, they took a number of the Anglo-Saxons down with them including several king's thegns. The chronicler claims it as a Christian victory, but some of the Viking army managed to break free.

The Viking army returned east, licking its wounds but still capable of posing a threat. It camped at Benfleet, where clearly the destruction wrought by the Anglo-Saxons had not been total. The last battle proved only a temporary setback for the raiders, who teamed up with more men from East Anglia and Northumbria and struck north again. Leaving their women and their treasure in East Anglia, the Vikings made their way to the deserted city of Chester, once home to the Roman legions in its heyday as Legaceaster. They managed to get there safely but an Anglo-Saxon army was in close pursuit and laid siege to them. The cattle outside the walls were seized and the grain stocks destroyed by the Anglo-Saxons, and again the Vikings were soon starving.

But it was still not over. The siege was not tightly laid, or perhaps the period of service for Alfred's levies expired and they returned home. For soon after the Vikings at Chester broke out into Wales. They raided there and then made it back to Mersea, an island off the coast of Essex. They were forced to take a long and circuitous route to get there, journeying through Viking-held territory in Northumbria and East Anglia. From here they then sailed up the Thames and into the River Lea. In the meantime, the Viking force which had been besieging Exeter in the south-west also made its way back. Deciding that they weren't yet done, they attacked Chichester en route but were badly mauled and some hundreds of their number were killed and some of their ships captured.

A Viking camp was set up on the Lea about 20 miles from London which would place it in the region of Hertford. Again, the wording in the *ASC* suggest that using time-honoured tactics they built a fort there. Here, in the summer of 895, they were attacked by an Anglo-Saxon force. This time the Vikings successfully defended themselves in a bloody action in which four of Alfred's thegns were killed. Perhaps alarmed by this loss, the king arrived to lead a force against them in person. Arriving in harvest time, he paused to protect those reaping the crops whilst they worked. This gave him time to observe, and he noticed that the Lea could be blocked. Using tactics employed a few decades earlier by Charles the Bald in Francia, he built fortifications on either side of the river.

The Vikings now realised that their ships were trapped, or would be once the fortifications were finished. They broke out to the north-west, making their way to Bridgnorth on the Severn where they erected another fort. The Anglo-Saxons rode after them, for although they did not seem to use cavalry in battle they were good horsemen and comfortable in the chase on horseback. Although the Vikings escaped, their ships did not. The garrison from London came to capture them, burning those they could not drag off with them. The Vikings overwintered in Bridgnorth.

It was now three years since this major attack had been launched on Alfred's kingdom. His resources had been stretched to the limit. He had not managed to land a knockout blow, it is true, but neither had the raiders been able to overrun him. Despite this, his realm was not in a good state. There had been 'three years with pestilence among cattle and men' and some of the king's closest supporters had died. These included Swithwulf, bishop of Rochester; Ceolmund, ealdorman of Kent; Beorhtwulf, who held the same position in Essex; Ealhheard, bishop of Dorchester; Eadwulf, the king's thegn in Sussex; Beornwulf, the reeve in Winchester; and Ecgwulf, the king's 'horse-thegn', who presumably was responsible for some of Alfred's stables.

By now, the latest Viking threat was waning. Some of the raiders, disheartened by their lack of success, sailed back to Francia. But during 896 raids were still launched on Wessex from East Anglia and Northumbria. At around this time, Æthelweard notes two raids led by a Northumbrian 'pirate' called Sigeferth.[28] Interestingly, Northumbria was by now ruled by a Christian Viking, Guthfrid, who was buried in York Minster when he died a few years later. He had allegedly been singled out by no less a person than the long dead St Cuthbert to be ruler, a proposition that was made a reality by the intervention of an abbot called Eadred. Guthfrid had thereafter proved a generous benefactor of the Church, probably through gratitude as he had been a slave before his freedom was purchased so that he could become king.

The account of these events, found in Simeon's *History of the Church of Durham*, is highly suspect. Not only is it replete with miracles, one of which involved a Scottish army attacking Lindisfarne before being swallowed up by the earth, but it also uses one of them involving Guthfrid as the basis of a claim to sizeable amounts of land for the Church between the Wear and the Tyne. In other words, the writer is not an objective observer. He also mentions close cooperation between Alfred and Guthfrid and efforts to build closer relations between Wessex and Northumbria. Ealdorman Æthelnoth of Somerset is said to have visited Jorvik in 894, presumably to foster good relations. This may have been prompted by attacks from Northumbria on Alfred's kingdom.[29]

Guthfrid was succeeded by Siefred, and it is tempting to assume that this was the same man as 'Sigeferth the pirate'. Some of Yorkshire at least had now become thoroughly Viking. Archaeological evidence suggests widespread abandonment of Anglo-Saxon settlements in East Yorkshire and their replacement by Viking equivalents instead, though the latter may not have been permanent but temporary bases before longer-term roots were established.[30] Intriguingly, there is evidence from finds suggesting more than one visit from Vikings in the late ninth century. On the first occasion, places such as Cottam in Yorkshire were sacked, probably when Halfdan's army passed through in the 870s. But later a Viking settler would establish a farm there, though probably ejecting the Anglo-Saxon residents before doing so.[31]

Alfred had ordered ships to be built to fight back against seaborne raiders, large vessels with sixty oars or more. Their design was innovative; they were 'neither of Frisian design or of Danish' according to one chronicler. Viking raids were now on a smaller scale. One on the Isle of Wight was composed of just six ships, though these did much harm to coastal settlements as far off as Devon. Alfred's ships caught up with them at a battle by a river-mouth which may have been the Exe in Devon or Poole Harbour in Dorset. The Viking ships were stranded by the tide, three on either side of the mouth. Two of the three on one side were captured, and their crews put to the sword. A third escaped but with only five men left alive; they got off because Alfred's larger ships had also run aground when the tide went out and their larger size meant they were stuck for longer. The three Danish ships stranded on the other side of the river then attacked three of Alfred's beached ships. There was a large-scale fight in which sixty-two Saxons and their Frisian allies died, as did 120 Danes. Amongst the dead was Alfred's reeve, Lucumon, along with prominent Frisians named Wulfheard, Æbbe and Æthelhere.[32] The mention of Frisians is interesting. They were renowned for their shipbuilding skills, and some had possibly been helping Alfred to construct his fledgling navy. Certainly, the Frisians had also suffered grievously from Viking attacks over the years and were therefore natural allies of the Anglo-Saxons.

At some point in the melee, the three Viking ships were able to escape as their shallow-draught vessels were first to float free. But they were badly damaged and two of them were driven ashore in Sussex. The crews were captured, marched before Alfred in Winchester, and promptly hanged. The remaining ship made it back to East Anglia, though many of the men aboard were wounded. During that year another twenty ships perished off the coast. Although Alfred's navy struggled with the manoeuvrability of its vessels, it was still an encouraging performance.[33]

This was the last recorded attack suffered by Alfred's kingdom during his life. At the end of this campaign, perhaps Alfred pondered one of the biblical quotes he had translated, Psalm 9, verse 14: 'I will rejoice in Your protection, which You grant to me; and the enemy peoples persecuting me are trapped in the same difficulties which they had intended for me, and their feet are caught in the same snare which they had concealed and set for me.' The Viking raiders had been outmanoeuvred. Wessex had faced the nightmare scenario of multi-pronged attacks from several different directions at once and had survived. But there was much for the ageing and ailing king to ponder, not least the fact that the recent attacks had been supported by Vikings from East Anglia and Northumbria. As long as these remained occupied territories, they continued to pose a threat. Steps had to be taken to bring them into line, but this would have to be done by his successors. And so it was, for on 26 October 899 Alfred died, worn out by his monumental exertions. His son Edward took his place on the throne. He was young, and after a twenty-eight-year reign Alfred's people must have been nervous about what might come next.

Alfred – the Man and the Legend

Alfred was a clever man. He was also extremely pious, and this piety seems to have been completely sincere. Yet this was a complex age, one of transition from old gods to new, when fate still seemed a fickle arbiter and glory in battle continued to be supremely important. One truth remained above others, as eloquently described in *Beowulf*, that great work of transition: however outstanding a man might be, all must in the end die or, to quote an immortal phrase, 'so every man must yield the leasehold of his days'.[34] Alfred gave up the ghost in 899 having performed his role as king and nation builder magnificently. Whilst he did not live to see a united England, he laid its foundations. This despite the fact that according to Asser he had struggled with illness for most of his adult life.

Alfred's will survives and gives fascinating details of some of the wealth available to him, suggesting that despite the Viking attacks and the general decline in international trade in the period he was by contemporary standards a rich man. Approximately sixty estates across Wessex were left to various members of his family and this number would not include royal property, which was attached to the Crown permanently rather than him personally. The monks of Winchester also received legacies, and a sword went to his son-in-law Æthelred of Mercia. In an age when the only coin in everyday circulation was the silver penny, of which there were 240 to the pound, monetary legacies were left amounting to £2,000. During his lifetime he also made generous donations to the Church, two foundations – the monastery at Athelney and the nunnery at Shaftesbury, both of which he had established – receiving particular attention. Gifts were regularly given to his leading secular supporters, his noble thegns, as well as the jewellers and other craftsmen who served him. An Anglo-Saxon king was expected to be successful in battle and easy with his patronage, a 'ring-giver' in the language of *Beowulf*. Given the turbulent situation he inherited, Alfred had achieved more than anyone would have dared to hope.[35]

Whilst Alfred did not become king of England, he became an icon for a nation which was still gestating. In the twelfth-century *History of the Church of Durham* Simeon tells how Alfred, after hiding out in the 'marshes of Glastonbury' for nearly three years, was inspired to fight by a vision of Cuthbert, who became England's foremost saint. This suggests that slightly later commentators wished to make a direct link between a major spiritual English figure on the one hand and a prominent secular equivalent on the other. Simeon further has Alfred receiving assurances that 'he and his sons shall possess the kingdom of Britain', much as in the Bible figures like Moses are given promises by God concerning the future of their descendants. Clearly this is being wise after the event, but it helps to explain how the legend of Alfred developed over time.[36]

It is impossible to consider the life of Alfred without some mention of his culinary deficiencies regarding the baking of cakes. The story goes that, whilst on Athelney, 'surrounded on all sides by vast salt marshes and sustained by some level ground in the middle', Alfred was so absorbed with his mounting difficulties that he failed to watch some baking cakes that a local woman, the wife of a swineherd, had left in his care. They burned, leaving the king to be berated by someone who was by far his social inferior. She turned on him angrily: 'You hesitate to turn the loaves which you see to be burning, yet you're quite happy to eat them when they come warm from the oven!' It was a story demonstrating how far the mighty had fallen, but it was also an allegory which reminded the king that he should always be on watch, something he had failed to do in the earlier part of his reign. It is an iconic tale, sharing features with Robert Bruce and his arachnid housemate or Cnut and his vain efforts to turn back the tide. It is not contemporary, though, only appearing in a *Life of St Neot*, a relatively obscure Cornish saint who appeared later in the tenth century. Subsequent versions of the story added further detail in a series of twists and turns.[37]

The slow-burning development of the legend of Alfred can be seen in him being awarded the title 'the Great', which did not happen until the sixteenth century. This contrasts with Charlemagne, the Frankish emperor, who was referred to as 'the Great' in the first half of the ninth century, more or less contemporary with his lifetime, though initially this was as 'Carolus Magnus'; only two centuries later would he be referred to as 'Charlemagne'.[38] But Alfred's impact was clear to many of his near-contemporaries, not least because of his literary legacy as the translations from his reign continued to be used in the tenth and eleventh centuries. That said, Asser's biography of his life never achieved the wide popularity of Einhard's *Life of Charlemagne*. Another detail that provides insight into Alfred's relative popularity is that the later king Æthelred II, whose reign spanned the late tenth and early eleventh centuries, had several sons and named them after other rulers like Æthelstan and Edgar before finally using Alfred for the eighth and youngest of them. The famous homilist Ælfric of Cerne regarded three Anglo-Saxon kings as being of outstanding merit – Alfred, Æthelstan and Edgar – but to him Edgar was 'the strongest of all kings over the English nation'. This may be a case of recency bias as Ælfric was writing at the end of the tenth century, not long after Edgar's reign, but it is an interesting insight into where Alfred stood in the 'pecking order' in his own period.

Chroniclers such as Asser and the writers of the *ASC* were hugely biased in favour of their subject, and one view expressed by modern historians is that 'we hold that Alfred was a great and glorious king in part because he tells us he was'.[39] But only over many centuries would Alfred come to be seen as the greatest of all Anglo-Saxon kings; and for this to happen the reputations of Æthelstan and Edgar would have to decline to leave a space for Alfred. By the eighteenth century he had started to assume the dominant position in the public consciousness that he still largely retains, and it is perhaps fitting that one of the most famous of Britain's national songs, 'Rule Britannia', was part of a production of that period known as *Alfred: a Masque*. His singular status was firmly cemented in the reign of Victoria, which by helpful coincidence was removed from his own by a millennium. Statues and public monuments to him made their appearance and it was even suggested by some that the actual date of his death was 901, precisely 1,000 years before that of Victoria. This was skewing the facts to support the legend, but it is hardly the only example in history of such a thing taking place. An early nineteenth-century essayist William Hazlitt once wrote, 'No man is truly great only in his lifetime. The test of greatness is the page of history.' By Hazlitt's benchmark Alfred surely deserves many of the accolades directed at him, even if like all mortals he had his own demons to exorcise.

Alfred was first buried in the Old Minster at Winchester. His New Minster was not yet complete, but when it was finished his remains were transferred there. Both buildings were destroyed when the Norman cathedral in the city was erected, and Alfred's remains were then buried in nearby Hyde Abbey.[40] Eventually Alfred's remains disappeared, and despite several assertions that some bone fragments found on the site of Hyde Abbey may be his, no one has convincingly proved that they have ever been rediscovered. The most that can be said is that a pelvic bone fragment found on the site has been shown by scientists to date to between 895 and 1017 and was probably male. This is a long way from finding the complete skeleton of Richard III in a Leicester car park.[41]

Perhaps the most enduring image of Alfred's reign is the famous Alfred Jewel, which was found in 1693 at North Petherton in Somerset just a few miles from Athelney. It is probably an *æstel*, a kind of book marker and pointer, and it is an exquisite item. Just under 2.5 inches long and about 1.5 inches across at its greatest width, it is adorned with a figure who is widely thought to be Christ though there are other interpretations. The jewel is surrounded with magnificent goldwork, the king having been renowned for his sponsorship of goldsmiths. A wonderfully carved beast's head at the foot of the jewel provided an opening in which the pointer was probably placed, though it is now lost. The jewel is adorned with four words: *AELFRED MEC HEHT GEWYRCAN* – 'Alfred ordered me to be made'. The style of the script has been interpreted as being Mercian in origin. It is an important reminder that here was a man who was king both of Wessex and of Mercia, someone who had started to expand his kingdom during his lifetime. It is a powerful symbolic reminder of how, during his reign, the England we know had begun to be forged in the fires of war. But it is not just for this that Alfred should be remembered. His sponsorship of literacy was also a major development, laying the ground for a last hurrah of Anglo-Saxon England in the tenth century, one last Indian summer before the lights went out forever.[42]

6

Edward and Æthelflæd

English silver is not so softly won; first iron & edge shall make
arbitrement, harsh war-trial, ere we yield tribute.

'The Battle of Maldon'

The Men Who Would Be King

Alfred had laid the foundations on which England would be built. Yet
before a united country could emerge, Wessex had to deal with its own
internal issues. Alfred and Ælswith produced five children who survived
the ravages of infant mortality. Æthelflæd, the eldest, married Æthelred
of Mercia. The oldest son was Edward, who had been groomed to
succeed Alfred on his death. Æthelgifu, 'devoted to God through her
holy virginity',[1] had been given the prestigious position of the abbess of
Shaftesbury. The youngest child, Æthelweard, was renowned, according
to Asser, for his studious habits and love of reading: two of his sons
would die on the field of battle at Brunanburh decades later. The other
daughter, Ælfthryth, married the count of Flanders at some point in
the last years of Alfred's life, performing a useful role in forging closer
relations with an important power on the continent. There was even a
specific Anglo-Saxon term for such alliance-building wives: *frithuwebbe*
('peace-weaver').

We know something of Edward's early education, which is unusual for
Anglo-Saxon times when surviving records of such matters are scarce.
Edward's sister Ælfthryth appears to have received a similar education,
with Asser writing that both were taught by male and female tutors. They
learned to read works both sacred and secular in Anglo-Saxon, as would

be expected given their father's example. The Psalms and Anglo-Saxon poems were particular subjects for their lessons. Being at court, they would have been close to their father and Edward could observe Alfred in action from his early days. This contrasted with the upbringing of other nobles and some of Edward's siblings who were educated in a *schola*, a separate educational establishment away from the court, possibly at Glastonbury.[2] Edward and Ælfthryth were clearly being groomed for great things, in Edward's case the succession.

During the latter years of his reign, Alfred seems to have increasingly if subtly strengthened his grip over what we might call English Mercia. No doubt the marriage of Æthelflæd to Æthelred helped. It is noticeable that the formal treaty with Guthrum made in 885 stated that Alfred was supported by the *witan* of the *Angelcynn*, the English. The preface to Alfred's translation of Pope Gregory's *Pastoral Care* also used this phrase. How happy the proudly independent Mercians were with this suggestive phraseology is a moot point; perhaps they felt that being under the control of a king of Wessex was better than being host to a Viking colony. The role that would be played by Æthelflæd as 'Lady of the Mercians' and her share in the triumphs of the opening decades of the tenth century perhaps papered over the cracks regarding any resentment felt by the Mercians towards the acquisitive West Saxon royal dynasty. If so, then her untimely death would expose Mercia to a whole new reality around the *realpolitik* of the situation.

In Anglo-Saxon times there was no system of primogeniture as far as the succession was concerned. Rather than inheriting the throne, a man would be declared king because he had the strongest level of support amongst those who mattered in his kingdom (though royal blood was undoubtedly crucial and a would-be successor was expected to be an *ætheling*). A prince often did succeed his father if he had the right qualities, but sometimes not for many years. For example, in 675 Wulfhere of Mercia died and his son Coenred only became king twenty-nine years later. Now, on the death of Alfred, his son Edward did eventually succeed but found he had a rival in the shape of the late king's nephew Æthelwold. In 871, when Æthelred I of Wessex had died, he had not been replaced by his sons Æthelhelm or Æthelwold, who were too young, but by his brother Alfred. Now Æthelwold believed it was high time to reassert his right to rule. Back in 871, passing over the claims of Æthelred's young sons had seemed not only the right thing to do but the only thing to do. However, the decision would create a fissure in the dynasty, carving a wound that would never truly heal.

Anglo-Saxon succession was sometimes decided by bloodshed, which had a certain grim logic to it in that the man who won out in a trial of strength was likely to prove himself a strong king. In Æthelwold's case, his timing was always out. If Alfred had died a decade before he did, Edward would have been too young to succeed and Æthelwold's claim to the throne might well have been upheld. All that was hypothetical now. But his resistance to Edward's claims did not represent treason against a country called England, for it did not exist in a form that we would recognise; it was little more than an idea, and one that not everybody supported. Anglo-Saxon politics was driven primarily by family rather than nationalism, at this time a rather fanciful concept.

Whilst the Anglo-Saxon succession process was designed to ensure that a strongman was in charge, it created some inherent risks too. The process of becoming king involved a great deal of horse-trading as influential councillors with a role in deciding the succession jostled for position, seeking maximum personal advantage from the situation. This sometimes took a long time to resolve, meaning that there was inherent instability until the situation was resolved. This was apparently the case now, even though the late king had taken steps to secure his son's succession. For example, there are six surviving charters attested by Edward in the last seven years of Alfred's reign against one attested by Æthelwold. This was significant as it implies that Edward was accompanying Alfred frequently whereas Æthelwold was not. Even more significantly, a charter from Kent in 898 calls Edward *rex*. This might mean that Alfred had followed earlier precedent in giving his son a taste of rule in a sub-kingdom whilst he was still alive.[3]

Edward was also named Alfred's heir in his will, a blatant attempt to secure the succession for his eldest son. This went against the conventions of West Saxon kingship as previously practised. For example when Æthelwulf, Alfred's father, had succeeded Ecgberht, it was the first time for two centuries that a son had succeeded directly from his father. Alfred might argue with some justification that this was an attempt to secure stability in troubled times. It also however helped advance the interests of his own dynasty, something that Alfred was rather good at throughout his reign. Despite these efforts, when Alfred died in October 899 it was not until June of the following year that Edward was formally recognised as his successor in Winchester. The crowning ceremony subsequently took place in Kingston-on-Thames, right on the borders of Mercia and Wessex. It was the first time Kingston had been used for such an occasion, but it created a precedent that other kings would follow for a while. The crown had duly passed to Edward, subsequently given the moniker 'the Elder', but his position was far from secure.

Alfred seems to have built up support for his son's succession from within the *witan* by placing his supporters on it whenever a vacancy arose. This proved decisive. Edward was formally consecrated king at Whitsun in 900. A new coronation *ordo* was crafted for the occasion, designed for a king with two peoples, the West Saxons and the Mercians.[4] It was a splendid ceremony with the royal regalia – ring, crown, sceptre, rod and sword – bestowed on the king.[5] Old Testament greats were beseeched to provide Edward with their qualities: the faithfulness of Abraham, the meekness of Moses, the fortitude of Joshua, the humility of King David and the wisdom of Solomon. The ceremony was modelled, presumably consciously, on the rites that had been used for the crowning of Carolingian rulers in Francia.

Edward's crowning, however, was not a universally popular decision. Æthelwold clearly believed that his claim was equally strong, or at least equally persuasive, to that of Edward. After all, if a system of primogeniture had been in place, then Alfred's branch of the family in reality had an inferior claim to the throne. There were also other indications in his favour. His mother Wulfthryth was given the title *regina* in some surviving documents, an unusual awarding of regal status in West Saxon circles to a royal wife (the honour was not given to Edward's mother, Ælswith, for example).[6] It may be that Æthelwold also felt his branch of the dynasty was superior for these reasons too. He therefore determined to stake a claim for the throne. He might have been fired to do so in part by Alfred's will. Asser mentions that Alfred entered into an arrangement with his late brother Æthelred that whoever died first would pass all their property to the other, except for that which was directly bequeathed to his children. As a result, when Alfred died his will effectively disposed of both his own property and much of that which had belonged to Æthelred previously.

Unsurprisingly, most of Alfred's personal properties were passed to his children. Nearly twenty property bequests were made to Edward and a similar number went to Alfred's youngest son, Æthelweard. A kinsman of Alfred called Osferth, whose exact relationship to the late king is uncertain, was given seven different properties. Eight more were left to Æthelhelm (who may well have been dead by now as he disappears from view in the 890s) but only three to Æthelwold, his younger brother, at Godalming, Guildford and Steyning.[7] Possibly Æthelwold resented this, and his frustration soon boiled over. This might have been particularly acute as even during Alfred's reign there are hints that he was given high status. A charter tentatively dated to the 890s for a lease of land in Wiltshire has Æthelwold appearing in the witness list above Edward.[8]

A conflagration was ignited at Wimborne in Dorset where Æthelwold staked his own claim to the throne. The location was probably no coincidence. Wimborne was closely linked with Æthelred I, Æthelwold's father, who was buried there. It is furthermore likely that bitterness lingered over Alfred's decision to found what was in effect a rival nunnery at Shaftesbury, just 20 miles off. The adjacent *burh* of Twynham (Christchurch), 12 miles away, was also taken by Æthelwold. It is possible that this strategically important town, at the mouth of the Avon and the Stour (which also flowed past Wimborne), came out voluntarily in support of Æthelwold rather than being captured by him. The ASC state that Æthelwold 'seized' both places, but it must be borne in mind that the notion of treachery amongst any portion of the people of Wessex would not fit with its propagandist agenda.

To protect Edward's position, Æthelwold's rebellion had to be crushed in the bud. He therefore led his army towards Wimborne. As well as the *burhs*, Anglo-Saxon military strategy sometimes took advantage of old Iron Age hill forts as temporary strongholds. Later in the period temporary mints would be set up at Cissbury in Sussex, Old Sarum in Wiltshire and South Cadbury in Somerset for example. There was a substantial hill fort near Wimborne, Badbury Rings, known to the Romans as *Vindocladia*. Edward moved his army here, just a couple of miles from Wimborne, determined to assert his authority over the man he saw as a usurper.

Clearly Æthelwold felt outmatched by the army that Edward brought against him, for he fled. Instead of choosing 'to live or die there' as the chronicler asserts was his original intention, he fled in the night, allegedly in the company of a nun. Her identity is a mystery, but it should be remembered that being a nun was not always a matter of vocation in Anglo-Saxon times and it is possible that she had been forced to become one, perhaps because of who she was. It was also the case that, whilst having a relationship with a nun seems rather strange to the modern mind, in the Anglo-Saxon period it was not unheard of in England. Pope John VIII had indeed written specifically to Burgred of Mercia to criticise such goings-on in 874. Just a few years later the same pontiff was writing to Æthelred, archbishop of Canterbury, complaining of the English practice of taking a second wife whilst a first was still alive. In other words, English marital conventions back then were very different than they are now and were even controversial to contemporary observers.[9]

It has been plausibly speculated that this nun was probably of royal blood, either West Saxon or Mercian. One suggestion, intriguing but not supported by any conclusive evidence, was that it may even have been Æthelwold's cousin Æthelgifu, Alfred's daughter and abbess of nearby Shaftesbury.[10] Given the nature of marital politics at the time it is highly unlikely that this was a case of mere lust on Æthelwold's part. The nun's 'abduction', forced or voluntary, was at the time a criminal offence meriting a fine of 120 shillings.[11] Any impropriety with a nun was frowned upon. One of Alfred's laws stated that 'if anyone in lewd fashion seizes a nun either by her clothes or by her breast without her leave' the compensation to be paid was double that payable if a lay woman was involved.[12] Men were duly sent after Æthelwold. They failed to catch him, though the nun was taken. It is interesting that the once great double monastery at Wimborne now disappears into the shadows. Local opinion in some quarters is that it was destroyed in a great Viking raid – it was in the line of fire several times at the end of the tenth and beginning of the eleventh century – but so far there is no documentary or archaeological evidence found to support this theory. It is equally possible that, starved of royal support and perhaps punished for its contrary stance in the year 900, it withered on the vine. In the reign of Edward the Confessor in the middle of the eleventh century, what was by then in effect a 'derelict and deserted monastery' was planted with a new religious community on the orders of the king.[13]

It is what Æthelwold did next that was possibly most significant. The north was now firmly in Viking hands. Whilst initially they were prepared to let puppet kings rule in York, by 895 they appear to have taken direct control. Coin evidence from the period reveals the name of two kings with Viking names: Siefrid and Cnut. It is not necessarily the case that one succeeded the other; there are references in this period to many different Viking kings and it might be that the concept of kingship meant something different to them than it does to us. The coins carry Christian messages and motifs such as 'The Lord God is King'. This may well be because the long-lived archbishop of York, Wulfhere, who remarkably held his post for nearly half a century (854–900), had managed to exert influence over the Vikings. Wulfhere was a born survivor and had outlasted several regime changes. This was either because of extreme good luck or a well-developed charismatic or Machiavellian skillset. We can imagine him persuading the Viking leadership that adopting Christian symbolism, even superficially, was a smart political move. Certainly, it was a tactic other Viking leaders adopted.

Æthelwold now made his way north where it seems he received a warm welcome from men who saw an opportunity in the divisions amongst the

Saxons of the south. Coins from York bearing the name ALVALDUS have been attributed to Æthelwold.[14] Yet the ruling regime in Jorvik was about to be turned on its head. A chain reaction of events began across the Irish Sea in Dublin when, in 902, the ruling Viking elite was ejected and forced to flee to the north of England. Here they staked a claim to the throne of Northumbria, and the ripples of this disturbance would continue for the next half a century. It was a period when Jorvik became something of a Viking boom-town, as evidenced by the remarkable archaeological finds unearthed at 16–22 Coppergate. There are signs of increasingly intense industrialization, with the objects found indicating the presence of textile manufacturing, woodturning, ferrous and non-ferrous metal working, leather working, bone and antler working and a variety of other types of manufacture. Widespread finds of foreign objects also suggest a thriving international trade in the city.[15]

Possibly Æthelwold now found himself to be *persona non grata* in Jorvik for we next hear of him in the east of England, where he arrived with a fleet and 'enticed the raiding army in East Anglia into hostility'.[16] Alliances between important local leaders and Vikings were by no means unheard of. In Francia and Ireland there are many examples of unscrupulous individuals collaborating with Vikings in order to advance their own interests. In return, Viking warriors often recognised the opportunities offered by a disunited opponent. This occasion was no exception. The raiding army crossed into Mercia, attacking Cricklade before traversing the Thames, raiding further and then heading homewards. It was a challenge that, as a new king, Edward simply could not ignore. A sign of weakness now could bring the whole edifice of his kingdom crashing down around him. He summoned his army and set out in vigorous pursuit, ignoring the boundaries that had been agreed between Alfred and Guthrum nearly two decades before – after all, so had the raiders. He pushed into East Anglia, crossing the earthworks known as the Devil's Dyke and Fleam Dyke in Cambridgeshire. The location is significant as it was close to the Icknield Way, suggesting that the old Roman road network remained important even if it was well past its peak by now.

Having reached the Wissey, which rises in Norfolk and eventually flows into the Ouse, Edward decided that discretion should be the better part of valour, possibly because he felt his lines were overextended in hostile territory. He ordered the army to retreat. But for reasons that remain unclear, the Kentishmen with him ignored his commands on no less than seven occasions. The kingdoms were only newly united, and evidently indiscipline was still a problem. It was a fatal mistake by the men from Kent, who were surrounded and attacked by the enemy at what became known as the Battle at the Holme. Æthelweard suggests that it was fought five days after the feast of the Holy Mother, which would probably make it 13 December. He says that 'they clashed shields, brandished swords, and in either hand the spear was much shaken'. Many men fell on the Kentish side. Amongst the dead was one Abbot Cenwulf, another example of a fighting churchman in the best traditions of Heahmund, bishop of Sherborne, who had perished at Meretun in 871. Sigewulf, ealdorman of Kent, also perished as did ealdorman Sigehelm, whose daughter would later marry Edward. Among the many casualties were other men of note, described by Æthelweard as 'a part of the Kentish gentry nearly all-inclusive'.[17]

Despite appearances, this battle would prove to be a pyrrhic victory for the Vikings. While they too suffered notable losses, including a king called Eohric, most noteworthy was the demise of Æthelwold, removing Edward's rival from the stage. Others who were lost included a man named Beorthsige, son of the ætheling Beornoth. It has been plausibly suggested that the name of this man might identify him as a member of a rival branch of the Mercian royal family – these rival branches have been identified by the very prosaic detail that their names began with a 'B' for one branch and 'C' for another.[18] If true, perhaps it was not just Æthelwold who was unhappy at the way in which the succession had turned out. This outcome showed that Edward enjoyed something that all rulers need to succeed: luck. It was a momentous year for the new king in other ways, as he also suffered the death of his mother, Ælswith.

There are other hints at disunity. Early in his reign Edward made a grant of land near the River Wylye in Wiltshire to a man called Æthelwulf. Edward was seemingly not a man much given to handing out land throughout his reign, and there are only a few charters surviving from this specific period, so this is already significant. But more important than this is the detailed information it contains. The land had previously belonged to an ealdorman named Wulfhere and was taken 'when he deserted without permission both his lord King Alfred and his country in spite of the oath which he had sworn to the king and all his leading men. Then also by the judgment of all the councillors of the Gewisse and of the Mercians he lost the control and inheritance of his lands.' Clearly all was not well in the upper echelons of the state. It is also significant that this grant was made at around the time of Æthelwold's rebellion, being given to Æthelwulf 'on account of his pleasing obedience', implying that he had stayed loyal during these difficult days unlike Wulfhere. A man by this name was prominent in King Æthelred's time; Æthelred was Æthelwold's father. Perhaps Wulfhere had been linked to the latter during Alfred's reign.[19]

The first few years of Edward's reign were turbulent, then. Æthelwold's campaign gives us some insight into the man who would be king before he met his death at the Holme. The fact that he was able to obtain support from both Scandinavians and Anglo-Saxons suggest that he was a man of some quality. It is easy to buy into the stereotype of a troublemaker who sought to upset the rightful line of succession, though in the context of the time he had a strong claim to the throne. It is also worth remembering that most of the chroniclers who wrote about his uprising were supporters of the West Saxon Alfredian dynasty, and unlikely therefore to be disinterested and objective observers. After all, history is written by the victors. It is telling that Æthelweard kept back some important details about these events, and although he mentions a battle against 'the eastern enemy' at the Holme[20] he never refers to Æthelwold by name. The chronicler was writing an account of Anglo-Saxon history for a kinswoman in Germany many decades after the event. As a descendant of Æthelwold's line (the chronicler tells us that he was the great-great-grandson of King Æthelred I, Æthelwold's father, but unfortunately omits to mention the generations in between), it is as if he would rather forget that these events had ever happened.

Wessex and Mercia – the Burgeoning Alliance

Edward had already expanded Alfred's dynasty by fathering a son. Æthelstan was his name, and he was about five years old when Alfred died. According to William of Malmesbury he had been singled out at a young age for special honour in a ceremony where he was effectively knighted by Alfred and given a scarlet cloak, a belt studded with diamonds and a magnificent sword with a gold scabbard. It was not a 'knighting' in the sense that William understood it but it was a ceremony that echoes the story of the Pope recognising a young Alfred in Rome, and we should be careful about accepting either account at face value. This is not to say that Æthelstan's early 'knighting' was a complete fabrication; Alfred's health was already suspect when it took place, and it would not be unusual for an ageing patriarch to proudly display his grandson – and possibly ultimate successor – to the world in such a way.[21]

However, such public recognition could be potentially controversial for, again according to William, Edward had not been married to Æthelstan's mother. The chronicler has the good grace to note when he relates the tale of Æthelstan's conception that he is drawing his information from 'old ballads' (he is writing several hundred years after the supposed events) rather than reputable historical records. But the story is an intriguing if sordid one. William writes that Edward was passing through a village where his former wetnurse lived when he met a beautiful shepherd's daughter whom she had fostered. Edward was smitten by this young woman and, after what was effectively a one-night stand, fathered Æthelstan. Yet there was an element of the supernatural to this story, almost a parody of the Virgin's Immaculate Conception. Years before, the shepherd girl, named Ecgwynn, had a vision in which 'the moon shone from her womb, and all England was illuminated by the light'. It was because of this augury that the former wetnurse had taken in Ecgwynn and dressed her as befitted a woman of noble upbringing.[22]

It is worth reflecting on what was meant by 'marriage' at the time. The modern view of the concept has been shaped by centuries of development under the spiritual direction of the Church, though it has changed over time and views about subjects like divorce have evolved radically over the centuries. But in Anglo-Saxon times, the Church had not yet reached the hugely powerful position that it eventually would. It certainly already had enormous influence, but secular men and women still regularly pushed the boundaries. This was particularly so regarding the relationship between the Church (especially but not only the papacy) and secular kings. The two parties were jostling for position and tensions could arise from time to time, accumulating and exploding spectacularly in the Investiture Conflict in the final decades of the eleventh century. Early medieval kings could be stubbornly independent regarding matters that affected them personally.

Whilst England came under a lot of fire from popes of the time concerning marriage practices, some controversial approaches were also practised elsewhere. Historians have noted a development in Francia in the second half of the ninth century which amounted to a 'trial marriage'. It typically involved a young man and woman entering into what was in most conventional respects a marriage and something more than concubinage. The big difference, though, was that one party (normally the man) could later repudiate the marriage and enter into another marital relationship which, for want of a better phrase, we might call a 'formal marriage'. The male in such an arrangement normally enjoyed the senior social status in terms of family origin, which reinforced this imbalance. In such situations an individual might later exit the 'trial marriage' for political and dynastic purposes, and it may well be that this is what happened in the case of Edward and Ecgwynn.[23]

When Edward later remarried, Æthelstan was taken to be brought up in the court of his uncle and aunt, Æthelred and Æthelflæd. This story is given some credibility from a much later charter dating to 1304 in which it is noted that Æthelstan had given land to St Oswald's Priory in Gloucester in an act of 'paternal piety' as if he regarded Æthelred (who was buried there) as a stepfather.[24] Whatever the truth of the tale, Edward's relationship with Ecgwynn would not stand the test of time as, early in his reign, he married Æthelwold's niece Ælfflæd, perhaps in an attempt to placate him. It is possible that Ecgwynn had not been discarded but had died by the time of this second marriage, but it would not have been that unusual for her to have been a concubine.[25] In any case, Ecgwynn had also given Edward a daughter, who would have the dubious honour of being married off to a Viking warlord in adulthood.

Young Æthelstan's removal to Mercia makes sense; the boy's presence at Edward's court would have been extremely awkward after the king's marriage to Ælfflæd, whose father was likely the Æthelhelm of Wiltshire who had bested Hæsten. The marriage to Ælfflæd would be a fruitful one, producing two sons – Ælfweard and Edwin – and six daughters. However, it seems that Æthelstan's move to Mercia did not completely remove him from the Wessex scene for he appears as a witness on several charters at Winchester alongside his young half-brother Ælfweard in 901. It is notable that he appears lower down the list of witnesses than Ælfweard despite being the older brother. Such things mattered in Anglo-Saxon royal politics.[26]

The relationship between Mercia and Wessex had changed. There are unmistakable signs of this in a charter to the Mercian bishop Wærferth made in the last decade of Alfred's reign. It concerned the establishment of a *burh* at Worcester, showing that even in Alfred's reign *burh*-building was underway in Mercia. Another fascinating element of the charter is that it not only mentioned the fortifications at Worcester but also trading rights there, which were to be shared between the bishopric and the rulers of the Mercian kingdom. These rights were granted by Æthelred and Æthelflæd as if they were joint rulers, an intriguing picture that is completed as the charter records on several occasions that the acts are witnessed by King Alfred himself. This is a clear sign that the king of Wessex was in the driving seat regarding this important transaction and probably regarding others too. Other records state that fees collected from the salt mines at nearby Droitwich are to go to the king, 'as they always have done'. Only one king is mentioned in the charter and that is Alfred, not Æthelred. By implication, then, Alfred is regarded as king of Mercia.[27]

But it is probably over-simplifying matters to see this as a total West Saxon takeover of Mercia. Æthelred of Mercia appears to have ruled with a good deal of autonomy, as would his wife Æthelflæd when she later succeeded him. And there were important Mercians serving in Edward's administration too, not least the remarkable Plegmund, who would serve as archbishop of Canterbury until his death in 923. It was probably under Plegmund's direction that the dioceses of Wessex were completely revamped. He was a great reformer, and his efforts paved the way for a major change of direction in the monastic movement in England later in the tenth century.

Soon after the deaths of bishops Asser of Sherborne and Denewulf of Winchester, the western part of Wessex was carved up for ecclesiastical purposes.[28] The diocese of Winchester was divided into two with the Wiltshire element now holding its own bishopric at Ramsbury. Asser's old see of Sherborne suffered the most, now merely responsible for Dorset whilst Devon and Cornwall had a new bishopric centred on Crediton and Somerset had one at Wells. These 'demotions' may be calculated snubs by the king against the two bishoprics that lost out. Relations between Denewulf of Winchester and Edward appeared to be difficult on occasion during his reign, and perhaps the part played by Sherborne in the rebellion against Æthelwulf half a century before still rankled in family circles.

The issues between the bishop of Winchester and Edward are well documented. They were evidenced in the building of the New Minster in the city. The land for the New Minster was obtained in part from some already owned by the bishop of Winchester and some by secular individuals. That procured from the bishop seems to have come about as a result of regal pressure from Edward. The New Minster dwarfed the Old Minster that stood right next door. So close were the two that when the choirs of each sang at the same time there was sometimes a discordant clash, which sounds like an apposite metaphor for the situation between king and bishop. The adjacent buildings were not complementary, then, but rivals.

Neither was this the only occasion when king and bishop were involved in difficult conversations. A lease document, not precisely datable but from sometime between 899 and 908, concerned land owned by the bishop in Beddington, Surrey. This seemingly dry and dusty document contains several elements of intriguing information. One is the statement that Beddington had recently been devastated, 'stripped bare by heathen men' (Vikings). Another is a list of the 'moveable property' that had just survived what was a harsh winter: 9 oxen, 114 full-grown pigs, 50 wethers (castrated rams), 110 sheep and 7 slaves. There were also 90 acres of corn.

Perhaps most interesting of all is the closing paragraph of the document, which reads like a heartfelt plea to the king: 'The bishop and the community at Winchester beg that in charity for the love of God and for the holy church you desire no more of that community's land, for it seems to them an uncalled-for demand.' The document went on to close with a thinly veiled injunction that God himself would be unhappy if further transactions of this type were to be cajoled out of the Winchester community in the future.[29] No wonder that a near-contemporary draughtsman at the Old Minster noted in the margins of one document that Edward was a *rex avidus* (loosely translated as 'greedy king').[30]

Though Mercians like Plegmund played a prominent role in Edward's government, the autonomy of Æthelred and Æthelflæd had its limits. In 903, in the presence of both, Edward issued charters granting land in the Mercian territories of Oxford and London. He also issued other grants concerning Mercian possessions after this.[31] Whilst Æthelred and Æthelflæd could issue charters in Mercia in their own names, it was Edward whose head adorned the coinage there. If the relationship between Wessex and Mercia was really an alliance, it was an unequal one.

In the meantime, the fortification of Mercia continued. Other *burhs* followed in Mercia including at Gloucester, a place that would assume special significance during the coming years. Gloucester had been home to a Roman fortress and again some of the remains from that period were used in the defences that were now constructed. This was not just a defensive base though. An old bridge was restored, and communications improved as a way of facilitating trade. A new street network was established inside the walls. As well as this, a minster church was built to replace one that had been defunct since the eighth century. Gloucester is an excellent example of how the function of a *burh* was partly military, partly commercial and partly religious.

The borders of Mercia were soon under threat when Vikings ejected from Dublin in 902 sought refuge in the region of Chester. The city was by now a pale reflection of what it had been during the Roman period, although substantial parts of the walls had survived. Chester had already been briefly occupied by the Vikings in their abortive campaigns of 893. According to an Irish source, the *Fragmentary Annals of Ireland*, negotiations with them were led by Æthelflæd in person, her husband being ill. The refugees' leader, Ingimund, asked 'for land in which he would settle, and on which he would build barns and dwellings, for he was tired of war at that time'.[32] Æthelflæd agreed to allow the refugees to take up residence in the Wirral, though Chester remained in Anglo-Saxon hands.

Æthelflæd may have come to regret that act of diplomacy. Just a few years later the settlers were on the attack. They had established themselves close to Chester and had seen first-hand how prosperous it was. Envy quickly followed. Our sources tell us that they were not acting alone but were working in concert with other peoples of Scandinavian origin, probably either men from Northumbria or East Anglia. A Viking force soon laid siege to Chester. The *Fragmentary Annals*, our source for these events, is a dubious source: amongst other things the annals claim that the defenders drove the Vikings off by the unusual expedient of hurling beehives and boiling beer over the walls. Welsh sources say that the raiders had previously tried to establish a base in 'Mons' (Anglesey) and fought a battle at Rhos Meilon.[33] The *Fragmentary Annals* corroborates this to some extent by stating that 'the Britons assembled against them and gave them hard and strong battle, and they were driven by force out of British territory'.[34]

The defenders of Chester sent out to Æthelflæd, asking her and her husband what they should do. The message came back that they should sally out from the city, attack the besiegers and then retreat, taking care to ensure that the gates could be quickly secured once they were back inside. This they did, trapping many pursuing Vikings inside the walls and subjecting them to 'frightful slaughter'. The hardy besiegers responded by digging tunnels under the walls but were subjected to heavy counterattacks with rocks and beams of wood thrown down on their heads whilst a rain of spears and arrows also took a toll. The siege was later raised, and Chester remained in Mercian hands. In 907, the defences of Chester were restored. It had been a tough period for the Vikings for at about the same time they had suffered a heavy defeat against the men of Alba in Fortriu, an old Pictish kingdom in Scotland.[35]

It is generally thought that this is the period in which somebody buried one of the most fantastic of all Viking treasure troves ever found in England. This was the Cuerdale Hoard, discovered in 1840 on the banks of the Ribble near Preston. The collection was broken up after discovery though a substantial portion of it is still on public display in the British Museum. It is estimated that when complete it contained about 7,500 coins from fifty-nine different mints. There was a large amount of silver bullion too. The total estimated weight of the silver in the hoard is around 40 kilograms. About 5,000 coins are of Viking issue, originating in Northumbria and East Anglia. There were about 1,000 Anglo-Saxon coins, mainly from Alfred's reign but with a few from Edward's. There were also about 1,000 coins of continental origin, mainly from Francia. A few are from even further afield and of Islamic origin, some from Cordoba in Spain but with others from thousands of miles away in the Hindu Kush. There are also arm rings and penannular and 'thistle' brooches of Hiberno-Norse origin, evidence of the cultural mix between indigenous and Scandinavian elements that had taken root in Ireland. In other words, the hoard was not only enormous but cosmopolitan.

What makes the Cuerdale Hoard even more remarkable was that it is one of a series of such finds dating from the same general period. Eleven major hoards from the time have been identified, all from the north of England. This is totally out of kilter with any other period before or after, and together the troves provide evidence of interaction between the Viking kingdoms based on Jorvik and Dublin. Whilst it is notoriously difficult to state with confidence why these valuable items were buried and not subsequently recovered, it seems likely that the deposition of so many of them is linked to a period of intense uncertainty in what was in effect a frontier zone. In the years between 902 and 918, increasing instability would manifest itself on the north-west frontier of the Anglo-Saxon kingdom, brought about by increasingly aggressive moves by the Mercians under Æthelred and Æthelflæd as well as the forces of King Edward. This is the context underlying the burial of so many hoards.[36]

In 906 Edward agreed a treaty with the East Anglian and Northumbrian Vikings at Tiddingford in Buckinghamshire. The different versions of the *ASC* imply various dynamics for these discussions, with some suggesting that Edward held the dominant hand in negotiations whilst others state that this was more a meeting of equals where a period of peace suited both parties. In 909 the *ASC* record that the sacred remains of St Oswald were brought back from Bardney in Lindsey to Mercia. They were transferred to Gloucester, where the priory was originally dedicated to St Peter. It had been constructed in part of recycled Roman stonework. Now a new minster was built, dedicated to Oswald, which may well have been the last resting place of both Æthelflæd and her husband Æthelred. It is not clear whether Oswald's remains were taken as part of a raid or were recovered peacefully – Lindsey was firmly in Viking territory.

But then peace was shattered. Edward had sent an army to ravage Northumbria in 909, and the next year a Viking raiding army stormed over the border, presumably in retaliation. They pushed deep into Mercia, almost reaching the frontier with Wessex on the Avon. This suggests that the Mercians were unprepared for the thrust. The raiders, buoyed by their success, then crossed the Severn into Wales. Here they enjoyed further triumphs. Weighed down with their plunder, they recrossed the Severn at Bridgnorth. But the Mercians and West Saxons had used the break to combine their forces. On 5 August, the two sides met at the place called Wednesfield. Named after Odin, who amongst other things was the Norse god of battle, there could not have been a more appropriate place for a fight. The battle, sometimes referred to as taking place at nearby Tettenhall, ended in a crushing Anglo-Saxon victory. Amongst the many dead were several Viking kings including Halfdan and Eowils, offering another example of multiple Viking 'kings' at the same time and suggesting that the title was given to any powerful warlord with a large retinue rather than the unique title of an undisputed ruler of a tract of land. Another king, with the iconic Viking name of Inwær (Ivarr), also 'hastened to the hall of the infernal one'. Other senior Vikings perished on the field but their names are not remembered. It was a signal triumph for the combined forces of Wessex and Mercia.[37] It would not be their last.

Myrcna Hlæfdige

Ealdorman Æthelred of Mercia died in 911. By some accounts he had been ill for a while, but it is not impossible that he was wounded at Tettenhall. He is in the unusual position for the period of being overshadowed by his warrior wife, Æthelflæd, not to mention his illustrious father-in-law. As such he has been somewhat airbrushed from the bigger picture, not least because of what happened following his death. For the Mercians now did something very rare for the time, not just in England but also in the wider contemporary world: they chose his widow as their ruler. Æthelflæd became *myrcna hlæfdige*, 'The Lady of the Mercians'. The assumption of a position of power by a woman in Anglo-Saxon society was highly unusual though not unique. The *ASC* record that when the seventh-century West Saxon king Cenwalh died he was initially replaced by his widow Seaxburh. And when there was a revolt in Wessex against the *Bretwalda* King Ine, it was his wife Æthelburh who led an army against the rebels based at Taunton.[38]

It helped that Æthelflæd had Mercian blood flowing through her veins via her mother. It has been suggested that she may even have been a great-granddaughter of the mighty Offa.[39] The eldest of Alfred's children, she was probably born around 869. If so, she had married Æthelred when she was approximately seventeen years of age. On the whole,

Mercia had been more open to giving women a degree of power in the past than Wessex had. Offa's wife Cynethryth had witnessed charters and her image had even been minted on coins. Her example, as far as witnessing charters was concerned, was followed by most Mercian queens in the ninth century. In contrast, as we have seen, the wives of the more recent kings of Wessex were not even called queens and rarely witnessed charters, although they had played a more prominent role in the kingdom in earlier centuries.[40]

Despite the victory of Tettenhall, the Viking threat was far from over. Edward and Æthelflæd were well aware of this. *Burh*-building continued, further north than had typically been the case in Alfred's reign. Edward constructed one at Hertford on the northern bank of the River Lea in 911. It was no coincidence that this was right on the frontier between the independent Anglo-Saxon kingdoms and what became known as the Danelaw. They were set up in Mercia too, sometimes at locations whose identity has since been lost such as Bremesbyrig, Brycge (possibly Bridgnorth) and Scergeat. We are more certain about the construction of a *burh* at Stafford by Æthelflæd, who also founded a church dedicated to the local saint Beorhthelm (alternatively known as Bertelin). Stafford was in a marshy area and little evidence has been found of any earlier Anglo-Saxon activity there, so these events marked the effective founding of what would become an important town.[41]

The *burhs* served several purposes in a military sense. They of course had a defensive use but could also be important gathering points in support of forward movements into Viking territory. It was for the first of these military purposes that the *burhs* were most useful in 913, a year in which more incursions were made by Vikings from Northampton and Leicester. They moved into the north of Oxfordshire before clashing with an Anglo-Saxon force at Hook Norton, and many English soldiers fell in the battle. The Vikings returned homeward, laden with booty. They met and joined forces with another raiding party moving towards Luton but soon after were confronted by an English force. This time they were beaten and much of the booty they had seized was recovered. The raid subsequently fizzled out.

With the threat receding for the moment, Æthelflæd turned her attentions to constructing a *burh* at the ancient Mercian settlement of Tamworth. Once a key royal centre, it had probably been in Viking hands for a while. Now was the time for it to regain its lost status. It had a proud Mercian heritage, known in an earlier time as *Tomtun*, founded according to tradition by Creoda, grandfather of the notorious Penda for whom it appears to have been a favoured location. Offa later had a palace there, a claim backed up by the discovery of the footprint of a large wooden hall. Archaeological discoveries suggest several phases in the construction of fortifications, the simpler initial phase possibly taking place a century and more before Æthelflæd. The tenth-century building scheme included a substantial ditch behind which was a timber palisade on top of a rampart up to 8 metres wide. There was a wooden walkway on top of the rampart which connected towers at the corners. Tamworth seems to have been pillaged in a Viking raid in 874, during Mercia's dark period when it was divided up by its conquerors. Its re-emergence in 913 was a statement of defiance against the unwelcome Viking neighbours.

In 914, there was a raid from Brittany which bore many of the characteristics of a classic Viking attack of earlier times. It was led by two jarls, Ottar and Hroald. In the previous year they had devastated Brittany, sacking the great monastery of Saint Winwaloe at Landevennec. They now made for the Severn, attacking the region of Archenfield, a Mercian frontier zone around Herefordshire. They captured a Welsh bishop, Cyfeiliog of Llandaff, whom Edward ransomed for £40. Important men such as the bishop were more valuable to the Vikings alive than dead. This might not fit very well with the stereotype of the Vikings as slayers of bishops and holy men (though they undoubtedly sometimes were), but kidnapping clergymen was good business.

This was a good start for the raiders, but it was not a portent of things to come. Buoyed by their early success, they attacked Archenfield again. This time, the attack ended catastrophically for them. Hroald was killed, as was a brother of Ottar along with many other men amongst the raiders. They took cover behind the walls of an old earthwork but were soon under siege. Forced to hand over hostages, they agreed to leave; not for the first time, their promises meant little. They made the short crossing over the Bristol Channel, attacking the north coast of Wessex at Watchet and Porlock. Several times they raided ashore under cover of darkness, and on each occasion they were repulsed. Edward seemingly had little faith in Viking promises as watching stations had been set up between Cornwall and Avonmouth to guard against infractions of the agreement. The Vikings then took up residence on the lonely island outpost of Steep Holm.[42] Here their troubles were far from over, as there was insufficient food available, the ASC claiming that some of them died of starvation. Soon, gnawed at by the pangs of hunger, the dejected raiders sailed off to Ireland to try their luck there, making their way over from Dyfed in south-west Wales. In the end, the raid had been an unmitigated disaster. They seem to have stayed in Ireland for a few years, causing havoc, before the *Annals of Ulster* notes that in 918 'Ottir' and a confederate called Graggaba sailed off to Scotland to make further predations there.

The resurgence of Wessex and Mercia was a worrying portent for the Vikings in England, whose troubles were compounded by divisions. This period in history was characterised by frequent flare-ups between different Viking groups in Ireland which spilled over into England and indeed into Wales and Scotland too. Soon after the raiders from Brittany had been sent on their way, there was a major battle between two Viking groups off the Isle of Man. The victor of this fight was a man named Ragnall (or in Old Norse Rognvaldr). The chronicles name him as *ua Ímair* ('of the family of Ivarr'), which may link him to a famous ancestor in Ivarr the Boneless. The ruling Viking regime had been ejected from Dublin in 902 and had since set up bases in north-west England, Galloway in south-west Scotland and on the Isle of Man. On the losing side in this battle off Man was Bardr Ottarsson, probably the son of that Ottar who had recently been driven from England.

Following these events, Edward seems to have decided to up the ante with the inhabitants of the Danelaw. Frequent raids from across Watling Street may have convinced him that those living there were too much of a threat to be left undisturbed. The response seems to have been a coordinated one involving both Edward and Æthelflæd. Again, the construction of *burhs* was a key part of the strategy. One of them was at Buckingham, which was close to the frontier between the Anglo-Saxon state in the south and the Danelaw. Edward moved on it before Martinmas (11 November) 914, spending four weeks there building fortifications on either side of the Great Ouse. Without defensive work the river had the potential to be a 140-mile highway for the Viking longships, starting in Northamptonshire and eventually flowing out into the Wash.

The construction of forts either side of the river again echoed earlier Frankish attempts to neutralise the Viking river-borne threat, cutting off an important link between East Anglia and the Danelaw to the north. If the move was meant to intimidate the Viking settlers it seems to have worked. Bedford and Northampton were well inside the Danelaw but men from both now recognised Edward as their lord. Amongst them was the jarl Thurcytel. Two years later we read that the same Thurcytel left England for Francia, apparently with King Edward's active support. Francia had of course been a frequent port of call for Viking raiders in the past, but Charlemagne's empire was by now a shadow of its former self and had indeed been divided for many decades between competing factions, all of whom seemed incapable of forging a united kingdom or at least hanging on to it. In 911, Charles the Simple, king of West Francia, had even given lands to a Viking adventurer in return for protection. This man became Count Rollo of Normandy. Perhaps to men like Thurcytel Francia now looked an easier option than England.

In early summer 914 a *burh* was constructed at Eddisbury in Cheshire, and another went up later that year at Warwick (Wæringwik). Both were close to old Roman roads, suggesting that the legacy of the legions continued to play a part. Warwick was near the Fosse Way, which centuries before had linked Lincoln to Exeter. With Lincoln now a powerful Viking base, it was important to block any moves from raiders from that direction. A *burh* was therefore constructed there, probably on the site where the later Norman castle now stands.

The Vikings had by now firmly established themselves in lands to the north-east of the famous Roman thoroughfare known as Watling Street. Towns had grown up, particularly in the 'Five Boroughs' of Nottingham, Leicester, Derby, Stamford and Lincoln. Derby's name, with the Norse -by suffix, showed it to be a core part of the Danelaw, but it had once been Northworthy in the land of the North Mercians, a territory swallowed up by hungry kings who gave shape to a greater Mercia. That too had gone, gorged on by Vikings, but it was now being reborn, or perhaps more accurately reincarnated, for it was about to be incorporated into an emerging nation-state: England. This new kingdom was being given form by a fearsome sibling double-act, the king of Wessex and the Lady of the Mercians.

The measures that Edward took at Buckingham were clearly a precursor to more ambitious plans. In 915, the king moved on Bedford. Many of the more prominent citizens of that place had already recognised him as their overlord; he was in effect making a reality of what had already been the case in theory. At Bedford, the king mirrored the steps he had taken at Buckingham by building a fort on one side of the Great Ouse to complement the one that already stood opposite. Again, the river would be dominated, preventing the passage of Viking ships. The southern part of the Danelaw was being slowly strangled. Æthelflæd took similar steps in Mercia, adding several other *burhs* to those that had already been constructed in the kingdom. Perhaps one of the most strategically significant was at Runcorn (Rumcofan), which overlooks the Mersey. This was close to where Viking refugees from Ireland had taken up residence. In recent years they had been a source of threat to Mercia, and the Lady of the Mercians was clearly determined to put that genie firmly back into the bottle.

Some 11 miles from the probable site of the *burh* at Eddisbury, the fortifications at Runcorn formed part of a front line for the Anglo-Saxons;

again, it was both a defensive stronghold and a useful jumping-off point for any offensive action they might choose to initiate by pushing north. It helped protect the newly important site at Chester, now enjoying something of a revival after centuries of decline. A church was, by tradition, erected at Runcorn, again dedicated to St Beorhthelm who seems to have been a personal favourite of Æthelflæd. It is noteworthy that these *burhs* were much closer together than they were further south in Wessex; this was frontier country, after all.

But Mercia was not just looking north – it also had to address the threat on its western borders. On 16 June 916, an English abbot called Ecgberht was killed by the Welsh. Although we do not know a great deal about him, he may well have been the man of that name who witnessed a charter at a place called Weardwyrig in the previous year, suggesting he was well connected. The response from the Lady of the Mercians was decisive and brutal. Just three days later, a Mercian army marched into the Welsh kingdom of Brycheiniog and launched a *blitzkrieg* against a royal site at Llangorse Lake. This was a *crannog*, a settlement built in the lake and connected to the land by a wooden causeway. It was extremely vulnerable, hard to hold against a confident Mercian army and only large enough to accommodate a small garrison. The king of Brycheiniog was not present but his wife was. She was taken back to Mercia along with thirty-four other captives, a powerful lesson to the Welshmen. This brief but decisive campaign may also form part of a wider context, reasserting Mercian hegemony over Brycheiniog in the way that Æthelflæd's father Alfred had previously done with several Welsh kingdoms. It is also a useful reminder that building England meant dealing with more than just the Vikings.

In the same year Edward erected a *burh* at Maldon in Essex, a place which less than a century later would resonate in Anglo-Saxon history as the site of a battle which would inspire one of the great works of early English poetry. An advance on Towcester, another old Roman town, in 917 was a significant symbolic move. It was right on Watling Street, which defined part of the border between the Danelaw and Anglo-Saxon England. It was also on the edge of Edward and Æthelflæd's respective spheres of influence. It was Edward who according to the ASC took the lead in constructing a *burh* there. This may have been seen as an incendiary act by those on the other side of the border, for a Viking force mostly drawn from Leicester and Northampton soon moved on Towcester. The words of the ASC succinctly describe what happened. The raiders 'broke the peace and went to Towcester and fought against the stronghold all day, and thought that they would be able to break it down. However, the people who were inside there defended it until more help came to them; and then they left the stronghold and went away.' The *burh* system had proved its worth in a crucible of fire.

The border was now in turmoil as Viking and Anglo-Saxon jostled for supremacy along it. The men of the Danelaw almost seemed to have sensed a decisive push coming and tried to pre-empt it by returning to the old ways and going on the offensive. Like some heavyweight pugilist trying to land a knock-out blow, they swung left and right hooks against their opponent. But the opponent had perfected a strong defence and took their blows before delivering a counterpunch. It was as if the Anglo-Saxons were sapping the energy from the men of the Danelaw, waiting for the right moment.

The *ASC* record several determined raids into English territory by men from the Danelaw. There were attacks by raiders in Buckinghamshire in the region of Aylesbury, an important monastic establishment of the time. These were successful in seizing both men and property. Other raids were launched from Huntingdon and East Anglia. A Viking fortress was set up at Tempsford, from which they thought that they would be able to 'reach more of the land again with war and with hostility'. They attacked Bedford, where there was a hard fight. At the end of this, the Viking raiders were put to flight and many of them killed. Another attack was launched on a newly erected fort at Wigingamere.[43] Its precise location has not been discovered but it had only been constructed on Edward's orders a year or two previously. Presumably it was somewhere along the border in the east of England. The fight lasted all day, and cattle grazing outside the fort were seized. However, the attack on the fort itself was resisted.

Recent fighting had seen Edward on the defensive, but he now decided to attack. An initial target was the newly constructed Viking base at Tempsford, which seems to have taken the place of Huntingdon. Its construction was in some ways taking a leaf out of Edward's book. In no mood to let the challenge go unanswered, the king ordered an army to lay siege to the new base. These attackers broke in, wreaking havoc in the process. Amongst the dead were an unnamed Viking king and two jarls, Toglos and his son Manna.

This was just part of a wider strike across the frontier. Another army composed of men from Kent, Surrey and Essex was assembled. Their target was further east, in the southern part of Viking East Anglia, specifically Colchester. The ancient town had once, as Camulodunum, been the main town of Roman Britain and as such had been ransacked by Boudicca's army. Its walls still stood reasonably strong nearly nine centuries after that epic event. It is likely that the fight was hard, but in

Above: Church Ope Cove, Portland, a candidate for the first recorded Viking raid on Britain.

Below: Lindisfarne: the raid on the monastery here in 793 shocked England to the core.

The fortress at Bamburgh played a crucial role in the fortunes of Bernicia, part of Northumbria.

An Irish manuscript: Irish and British culture suffered badly at the hands of the Vikings.

Burrow Mump, Somerset, a prominent point in the landscape close to Alfred's island sanctuary at Athelney.

Carhampton, Somerset: the royal estate here suffered from several Viking raids.

Edington Priory, built on part of one of Alfred's estates and close to the scene of his greatest victory.

The White Horse adjacent to Bratton Castle, epicentre of the Battle of Edington.

A Victorian view of Alfred from his famous statue in Winchester.

Above: Portchester, a Roman site which in common with several others was repurposed as an Anglo-Saxon *burh*.

Below: The Somerset Levels, which provided strong watery defences for Alfred at a moment of great danger.

King Doniert's Cross on the edge of Bodmin Moor, possibly commemorating the death of the last Cornish king at the hands of West Saxon invaders.

Badbury Rings just outside Wimborne, where Edward the Elder assembled his forces against his rival claimant Æthelwold.

Simple graffiti showing a Viking ship.

The little-known church of St Edwold in Dorset, a spot where Edmund of East Anglia established a hermitage.

Burghead in Moray, site of a Pictish stronghold: the Picts found themselves squeezed between Scots, Anglo-Saxons and Vikings.

The remains of a Viking ship salvaged from Roskilde Fiord in Denmark.

Viking scales: silver was a prime commodity for Viking traders, its value measured by its weight and quality.

This neck-collar for a slave is a disturbing reminder of the brutality of the Viking Age in Britain and Ireland.

Right: Æthelstan presents a volume to St Cuthbert in the first known picture of an English king.

Below: The dramatic site of Dunottar far to the north in Scotland, besieged by Æthelstan's army in 934.

Durham which became a key part of later Anglo-Saxon Northumbria.

The tomb chest allegedly containing the mortal remains of King Eadred in Winchester Cathedral, on the site of a mausoleum for Alfred's dynasty.

Malmesbury Abbey, last resting place of King Æthelstan.

A reconstructed Viking longhouse in Trelleborg, Denmark, a possible barracks for Viking armies invading England.

Inside a reconstructed Viking longhouse in Stong, Denmark.

The hilltop at Corfe where, by tradition Edward, King and Saint, met his violent end.

Lydford, Devon, a *burh* attacked by Vikings in the late tenth century.

Warriors, possibly Vikings, on the march as carved on a stone at Lindisfarne.

The bay at Watchet, Somerset, in some ways an archetypal landing site for Viking ships.

Odda's Chapel in Gloucestershire, an Anglo-Saxon church of eleventh-century vintage.

the end the English forces were triumphant. Many Vikings fled for their lives over the walls; many more were slain.

Despite these advances, the north remained outside the control of the rulers of southern England. Place-name evidence indicates the growing strength of Scandinavian influence in this part of the country. There are some 860 place names ending in -by in the country (e.g. Derby, Kirby, Selby). This is the Danish word for farm, the equivalent of the Old English -tun or -ton (e.g. Kingston, Beeston). Some 220 of these -by names are in Lincolnshire and 210 in Yorkshire. Then there is -thorp (e.g. Scunthorpe), which is associated with a secondary settlement. There are 155 of these identified in Yorkshire and 109 in Derbyshire, Nottinghamshire, Lincolnshire and Leicestershire. There are also, perhaps most intriguingly of all, what are known as 'Grimston hybrids', with a Scandinavian name followed by the Old English -tun or -ton. There are many Grimstons and Grimstones but also names like Scampton and Wiggington, especially in Derbyshire, Leicestershire, Lincolnshire, Nottinghamshire and Yorkshire.[44] Combined with increasingly large numbers of finds (to which the oft-maligned metal detectorist community has contributed) showing widespread use of Scandinavian fashions, there is increasing confidence that Viking influence in the north and east of England came through mass settlement. This goes against the findings of the influential twentieth-century historian Peter Sawyer, who argued that the scale of Viking settlement had been greatly exaggerated.[45]

Indeed, it is now argued that the contribution of Scandinavian settlers to the emergence of urban life in England has been much underplayed. In the opinion of some historians, urban life went into substantial decline after the departure of the Roman legions. But during this period, it started to re-establish itself in England. By the end of the ninth century Viking-controlled mints in Lincoln appear to have been issuing coins in imitation of Anglo-Saxon designs. By 1066 it has been estimated that as many as 12,000 people lived in Lincoln, worshipping in thirty different churches. Other places, now small in comparison, assumed some importance at the time. Large-scale pottery manufacture in Torksey fed markets throughout Lincolnshire and Yorkshire. It seems that the one-time Viking winter camp had become a much more significant and longer-term settlement.[46]

The campaign of 917 took place across a wide front. Further west, Æthelflæd's sights were trained on the important Viking town of Djúrabý (Derby), which she attacked before Lammas (1 August) 917. It was a ferocious fight, in which the Lady of the Mercians lost four highly regarded thegns. Derby had been in Scandinavian hands for nearly half a century; for many of the defenders it was therefore not a temporary base but a home, perhaps the only one that they had ever known. This explains the tenacity with which they fought, though in the end they lost the fight. Derby and its environs fell to the all-conquering Lady of the Mercians. Yet most versions of the *ASC* make no mention of this signal triumph, a record of it only appearing in what is known as the Mercian Register. There are few better examples of the pro-Wessex bias of most chroniclers.

Early in 918, another important Viking town, Leicester, also submitted to Æthelflæd. There is no record of a fight. It appears that the reputation of the Lady of the Mercians had gone before her. All that was needed to make Leicester fall into her hands was the threat of an army marching on it. Neither had Edward been idle in the interim. After gaining the submission of Colchester, he fortified Towcester. At Passenham, a delegation from the Danes of Northampton came to offer their submission to him. They were led by a man called Jarl Thurferth who swore an oath of allegiance to Edward. Thurferth decided to remain in Britain where he continued in an important position and was allowed to keep his estates. It was not just the art of war in play on the part of the Anglo-Saxon leaders here, it was the art of politics too.

It appeared that the star of Æthelflæd could rise no higher in the sky, but this was not the case. The Vikings of Jorvik had been without a king for some time, possibly since the disastrous reverse they had suffered at Tettenhall. They now approached Æthelflæd, offering their submission. This remarkable turn of events was possibly brought about by a decline in the overall position of Viking Northumbria. In recent years lands around the Solway Firth had been lost to the Strathclyde Britons. Bernicia, often a stubbornly independent region, had broken away too. Viking refugees from Dublin had possibly destabilised the position to the west of Northumbria, on the eastern coast of what is now the Irish Sea. It may have seemed that the protection of Æthelflæd and her Mercians was much the lesser of several evils.

Annals from Ireland also suggest that she formed an alliance with the Scots to the north and the Strathclyde Britons in an effort to counteract the Viking menace in the north-west of England. The few details that have survived the passage of time suggest a vigorous response by the Vikings to this arrangement. However, despite determined attacks on Strathclyde and widespread plundering in the area, they were unable to break the alliance. Some historians are sceptical of this account, which is found in the *Fragmentary Annals of Ireland*. This source is particularly controversial and cannot be relied on without some serious reservations.

Nevertheless, some kind of deal between the Mercians on the one hand and the Scots and Strathclyde Britons on the other makes a lot of strategic sense for all parties concerned. The king of the Scots at the time was Constantin. It is not certain who was king of the Strathclyde Britons, though it may have been a man called Owain, son of Dfynwal.[47] This was an age of uncertain and changing alliances. Just two decades later, the Scots and the Strathclyde Britons were united alongside a Viking ally, fighting for their lives against an increasingly assertive Anglo-Saxon Kingdom of England.

But fame and fortune are fickle mistresses. Out of the blue, on 12 June 918, Æthelflæd died in her palace at Tamworth. Her remains were taken to Gloucester to be buried in the church she had co-founded with her husband. Even the design of the building spoke of her extraordinary personality. It was in many ways an old-fashioned design that would not have been out of place two centuries before. On the other hand, the addition of a western apse was unusual in England but not so in Francia, emphasising how the Carolingian dynasty had become an example for all monarchies in Western Europe to follow. In other words, the church was an amalgam of very traditional values and innovation. Æthelflæd was probably around fifty years of age when she died. There are many references to her life and death in annals from countries outside of England. One chronicler described her as 'a woman of extraordinary talent, skill, and exalted justice and virtue', adding that she had been responsible for 'a vigorous and upright rule' when she governed the Mercians on her own.[48]

The death of the Lady of the Mercians was a massive blow to the Anglo-Saxon cause, and an even greater one to Mercia itself. Whilst she had been alive, she and her people had acted, if not on an equal footing with Edward, at least in a semi-autonomous way. With her death that situation was turned rapidly on its head. Edward's campaigns against the Vikings were paused as he worked to fully assimilate Mercia into his kingdom as its undisputed monarch and sole ruler.

Edward Rules Alone

Edward had moved further into Viking territory. In 918, the people of the important town of Stamford 'sought to have him as their lord', though whether they truly had any say in the matter is a moot point. Lead-glazed pottery, similar in style to examples found in Francia, was a Stamford specialty, the lead perhaps coming from the mines of Derbyshire. The town may well have hosted another Viking mint, with examples of coins dating back to the 890s. When Edward took the town, he erected a fort on the other side of the river, continuing the approach he had recently employed at other places.[49]

It was whilst he was at Stamford that Edward heard of the death of his sister. Æthelflæd and Æthelred had a daughter, Ælfwynn. There are no records of other children, though it is possible that there had been some who did not survive infancy. Writing several centuries later, William of Malmesbury suggested that the act of childbirth had been such a painful experience for Æthelflæd that she resolved to abstain from sexual relations with Æthelred from that point on. There is limited charter evidence from Mercia surviving from the time but one surviving document includes Ælfwynn as the second witness after Æthelflæd. The example of her mother proved that gender was no obstacle to a woman being a successful ruler – or should have done at least.

The details of what happened next are unclear, but the final outcome is not: by the end of the year, Edward was the sole ruler of Mercia. However, the implications of what is said in the Mercian Register, which is no more than a short set of annals giving a different slant from the pro-Wessex bias of most of the chroniclers of the time, are on this occasion suggestive. The cursory remarks in the 'A' (Winchester) version of the *ASC* give the impression that as soon as he heard of his sister's death, Edward simply walked in and was accepted at once by the Mercians. However, the Mercian Register states that 'here was also the daughter of Æthelred, Lord of the Mercians, deprived of all authority in Mercia, and she was taken to Wessex three weeks before midwinter'.[50]

So, according to the Mercian Register, Ælfwynn was deposed. It is possible of course that her own people had instigated her overthrow. Perhaps she lacked the force of personality of her mother. But the most likely scenario is that, with his powerful sister no longer on the scene, Edward felt it was time to bring Mercia into his kingdom definitively without any middleman (or in this case woman). Ælfwynn was taken back to Wessex where in all likelihood she lived out her life comfortably but safely ensconced in a convent, with Shaftesbury, Winchester or Wilton suggested as possible locations, all of them having royal connections.[51] There is a tantalising reference in a charter of 948, three decades later, to a 'religious woman' named Ælfwynn. She was given land at Wickhambreaux near Canterbury. The grant was made by the then king Eadred, son and eventual successor of Edward. It was given at the behest of his mother, Edward's widow and third wife Eadgifu. Perhaps this was a peace offering, or at least one to salve a few consciences. It has been suggested that as Eadgifu was also a benefactor of Wilton that it was here that Ælfwynn lived out her days.[52] Honourable 'retirement' in a religious establishment was a tried and tested way of moving an important female figure away from the public spotlight; after becoming a widow, Eadgifu herself would become a lay associate at Shaftesbury.

Edward was also strengthening his position in Wales, a traditional opponent of the Mercians for centuries. Three Welsh kings submitted to him: Hywel Dda, Clydog and Idwal ap Anarawd, the first two brothers from the south of Wales and the last from Gwynedd in the north. Edward's father Alfred had also been successful in securing the allegiance of a number of Welsh kings during his lifetime. Possibly they considered the Anglo-Saxons a safer bet than Viking raiders. Joint operations against Ottar and his raiders just a few years before had proved that the Anglo-Saxons and the Welsh could work together in the face of a common threat.

Family matters were very much on Edward's mind at the time. In 917 or 918 he put aside his wife Ælfflæd and placed her in a nunnery. The reasons for this are obscure but he soon took another wife, this time in the shape of the above-mentioned Eadgifu, daughter of the ealdorman of Kent. As was almost invariably the case, this was again probably a political move designed to strengthen Edward's position in Kent. There is no sign of trouble from this direction but Edward perhaps wished to ensure the continued support of Kent whilst he pushed further north in his attempt to subdue the Viking Midlands. Political marriages were an important part of contemporary diplomacy, as can be seen by the marriage of Edward's daughter, another Eadgifu, to Charles the Simple in 919. As well as confirming links between the English and Frankish royal houses, this may have been prompted by a flare-up in Viking activity in Brittany which could have negative consequences on both sides of the Channel. Continental records tell how 'the Northmen devastated all of Brittany, defeating, killing or exiling the Bretons'. It was the start of seventeen years of Viking domination in the region.[53]

Edward, like other Anglo-Saxon rulers, took full advantage of the opportunities available to use religious establishments for his own and his family's interests, as his actions with his second wife demonstrated. Several of his daughters were also to find residence in them. Eadburh entered the establishment at Nunnaminster in Winchester. Another daughter, Eadflæd, and her sister Æthelhild both took up places at Wilton, the latter as a lay sister. This emulated long-established traditions such as when King Ine's sister Cuthburga was put in charge of the new nunnery at Wimborne at the beginning of the eighth century, or more recently when Alfred had established Shaftesbury with his daughter as the first abbess. Edward was prolific as a father. There were a son and daughter from his first marriage with Ecgwynn, eight children from his second marriage to Ælfflæd and there would be three (possibly four) more from his last match with Eadgifu. As these children grew up, tensions between them would increase from time to time.

In the meantime, Edward continued his advance into the Danelaw where he took another important town, Nottingham. Here he took the surprising step of merging his own men with the existing Danish garrison after taking over. This is perhaps a sign that the Scandinavian settlers in Nottingham had started to change their stance regarding the Anglo-Saxons. They had begun to eke out a settled life for themselves in the country, one which perhaps contrasted with the rather more unstable situation in Viking Northumbria. Maybe a strong Anglo-Saxon king had started to seem preferable to a volatile Viking warlord as their ruler. That said, we should not overplay this because events in the next few years were to suggest that there was still a long way to go before the east Mercian lands that had fallen under Viking control would fully accept the overlordship of an Anglo-Saxon king.

For 918, the *ASC* note that 'all the people that were settled in the land of Mercia, both Danish and English, turned to him [Edward] as their king'. This suggests that in the eyes of the chroniclers Mercia had now become fully integrated into Edward's expanding kingdom. If so, two peoples who had previously been masters of their own destiny – on the one hand the Angles of Mercia and on the other the Scandinavian settlers with their Viking heritage – had accepted that they should be ruled by a monarch from the West Saxon royal family. Perhaps for the Mercians it was not so bad. After all, Edward was the son of a Mercian mother. For the Scandinavian settlers their obeisance may have been more to do with pragmatism than any natural affinity with the king. In any event, it was a remarkable achievement on Edward's part.

The following year, towards the end of the harvest season, Edward pushed on to Thelwall, a site beside the Mersey close to Warrington. Here he constructed a *burh*. He then made a leap forward, crossing into Northumbria and setting up a fortification at Manchester. In 920 he returned to Nottingham with his army and again ordered a fort to be constructed on the opposite side of the Trent from the existing defences. A bridge was built between the two, once more emulating Frankish practice. He was tightening the screw and strengthening his control in this potentially fragile frontier region. He was also effectively closing off the Trent as a means of access into Mercia. By building *burhs*, Edward did not just have military considerations in mind. He was also making a powerful statement about consolidating royal authority in the places where they were constructed.

The king then moved on to Bakewell in Derbyshire, where he ordered the construction of further defences. Soon after, a remarkable conference was held, possibly at Bakewell. It involved Edward, the kings of Strathclyde and the Scots, and Ragnall, the new Viking ruler of Jorvik. Following the death of Æthelflæd, the Vikings of Jorvik had changed their stance. Her demise was not the only thing that had altered the political landscape, however. Ragnall had only recently appeared on the scene, staking a claim for Viking Northumbria and taking on the Scots in battle at Corbridge. The records concerning the outcome of that battle are far from definitive in what they tell us but the implication we can draw is that Ragnall won a victory which, if not decisive, was enough to secure his claim to Jorvik. He was a probable grandson of Ivarr the Boneless, and he may well have been ejected from Dublin when the ruling regime there was thrown out in 902. The return to power of this regime was affirmed not only by Ragnall taking Jorvik but also by his long-term confidante and possible brother Sihtric recapturing Dublin at around the same time. This came after a decade of raiding by both men across a swathe of territory which included Ireland, northern England and Scotland. Another attendee at the conference was Ældred, the independent ruler of Bamburgh, who had sided with Constantin, king of the Scots, at Corbridge – Ragnall had seized some of his lands in 914.

The *ASC* assert that at the conference the Scots, the Strathclyde British, the English in Northumbria and Ragnall chose Edward as 'father and lord'. This is hard to accept at face value. Edward had done little to stake a claim for overlordship of any of them, and it is not obvious why they should meekly submit to such an arrangement without compelling reasons to do so. This has not stopped more recent historians interpreting this along nationalist lines whereby England established a hegemony over Scotland (and Scottish historians have sometimes been arguing the contrary). Such views are depressingly predictable and totally anachronistic. As much as England did not exist at the time, neither in its modern political sense did Scotland.[54]

More likely this was a conference where a truce was arranged. Edward may have wished to consolidate his recent gains in Mercia and would therefore be keen to avoid raids from Northumbria. Ragnall was new in his post and would welcome a period of stability to establish himself in Jorvik. The Scots, the Strathclyde British and the English of Northumbria would be anxious to avoid further attacks by Ragnall's men. In other words, it was in everybody's interests to arrange a ceasefire. It would in fact prove to be little more than an affirmation of the *status quo*, but as the conference had been held on his territory it would have brought considerable political kudos to Edward.

With Æthelflæd gone, Edward was increasingly proactive in the far corners of Mercia. In 921, he ordered the construction of a *burh* at Cledemutha, possibly Rhuddlan on the north-eastern borders of Wales. Its position meant that it served a dual purpose. Not only could an eye be kept on the Welsh, but it also served as a guardhouse against Viking raiders coming from the north-west of England or from across the Irish Sea, perhaps a greater risk now that the grandsons of Ivarr had re-established themselves in Dublin. Rhuddlan would later develop into an important medieval town and the site of an impressive castle which may well have been built in the footprint of the older *burh*.

The need to strengthen defences in this region was emphasised shortly after when there was trouble again from Chester. The whole area had been an Achilles' heel for the Anglo-Saxons since the Vikings had been ejected from Dublin in 902 and made the short hop over the Irish Sea. However, it is too glib to blame the Vikings for every outbreak of violence in the region so it must be acknowledged that Chester was also right on the border of Wales. In addition, the local residents who were 'English' probably had no real affection for or attachment to a distant monarch from the West Saxon dynasty. According to William of Malmesbury, in 924 Edward was forced to lead his army north to subdue the 'contumacy' of Chester. It was one of his last acts. A few days later, Edward breathed his last at the nearby royal estate at Farndon on 17 June. His body was taken back to Winchester to be buried alongside his parents in the New Minster there.

The site of Edward's tomb in its own way neatly marked out his reign. The New Minster was the brainchild of Alfred, but he had not seen it, having only purchased the land on which it was built before he died. Therefore, one of the first acts of Edward's reign was to finish the construction of what would in effect become a mausoleum for Alfred's dynasty. It was a great symbolic gesture, a statement of intent. Alfred had effectively set in chain a sequence of events that presaged nothing less than a new kingdom which we might call England. This great event needed a monumental pantheon for the mighty dynasty that would emerge. By ordering the construction of such a building Edward was affirming that not only would he pick up the baton laid down by his father, but he would take it further still.

Edward's achievements had been immense. Alfred's reign had seen Wessex (and England) on the front foot, but Edward and his sister had taken this to another level. The construction of *burhs* as a key part of Edward's strategy was another idea he had inherited from his father. It was probably at some time during Edward's reign that the document known as the *Burghal Hidage* was prepared, though the surviving version is a sixteenth-century copy of the original. It lists thirty-three *burhs* across Wessex (excluding Kent, Cornwall and London, though Southwark is included) and their hidage (a hide being a unit of land measurement which, rather than being based on area, was related to the tax drawn from it). Whilst the semi-autonomous nature of Cornwall makes its omission understandable, and London may have been governed from Mercia in strict legal terms, the fact that Kent is missing is mysterious. The *Burghal Hidage* also gives us an insight into the size of garrisons and the dimensions of the *burhs*. The basic equation underlying the garrison strength was that one hide was needed to support one man, so Winchester with a hidage of 2,400 hides would be supporting a garrison of 2,400 men. Further, four men were needed for every pole (5.5 yards) of wall, meaning that the walls of the city were about 3,300 yards (or 2 miles) long. These relationships are largely supported by recent archaeology discoveries in some of the *burhs*.[55]

The *Burghal Hidage* provides concrete evidence for the achievements of Edward's reign. As William of Malmesbury commented, this had been a time of 'noble exploits, both in war and in peace'.[56] It had indeed, and not the least of these exploits was the pushing north of what we might now start to think of as 'England'. As a man, Edward was of course not perfect. His takeover of Mercia, and the shunting aside of his niece there, demonstrated an unmistakable ruthless streak. But his reputation has been overshadowed by that of his illustrious father and in recent times by the interest in his sister, a rare example in the public imagination of a successful female leader from the period. While Æthelflæd's death was referred to by Welsh and Irish commentators, they made no mention of Edward's passing. The events of Alfred's reign filled twelve pages in Æthelweard's chronicle whilst Edward's rule was discussed in little more than two. More recently, Edward's contribution to building England has been better recognised, a fully deserved increase in his status and one that hopefully will continue. But historians writing in the early Norman period such as William of Malmesbury and Florence of Worcester painted a picture of Edward as inferior to Alfred in learning, equal in dignity and power, and superior in glory and conquest.[57]

Yet the process of building England was far from over. There are occasional hints in surviving sources that Mercia still contained restless elements, some of whom did not buy in to being ruled by a West Saxon king. More obviously, much of Northumbria for the time being remained in Viking hands. Ragnall, the ruler of Jorvik, had died in late 920 or early 921 and had been replaced by his possible brother Sihtric, who had raided into Cheshire in 920 and was very much a chip off the old Viking block. It was likely that a confrontation between Viking Northumbria and the rising star of the Anglo-Saxon kingdom was not far off. It was no doubt a great relief to Sihtric that Edward was no longer on the scene. He could take advantage of the uncertain position of a new and inexperienced king and advance his own interests as a result.

Pagan Viking sorceresses were famed for their powers of prophecy, clairvoyance and divination. The most famous example of this was perhaps one such woman in the *Völuspá*, a poem of the *Poetic Edda*. She told Odin of the terrible fate awaiting the gods in the end times of Ragnarök. Then, the frozen age of Fimbulvetr (the Bitter Winter) and its three years of driven snow, fierce winds and severe cold would arrive. There would be cataclysmic battles in which father would fight son and brother would kill brother. Then the Midgard Serpent would spew over the earth a venom so foul that even Thor would succumb to it.[58] We do not know if Sihtric had such a sorceress in his entourage, but he would have been wise to seek her counsel if he did. She would have told him that a storm was coming, a hurricane that would overwhelm everything in its path.

7

Æthelstan

Nowhere, they said, north or south, between the two seas or under the
tall sky on the broad earth was there anyone better to raise a shield or
to rule a kingdom.

Beowulf

Rex totius Britanniae

Edward's death left an opening, but who would step into it? Æthelstan
was his eldest son but he was far away from Winchester in Mercia. He was
also the son of a woman who may have been regarded as inferior. It was
apparently not just William of Malmesbury who thought so. In about 930,
Eadgyth, Æthelstan's half-sister, was married to Otto I of Saxony. A few
decades later a German nun, Hrotsvitha, wrote a verse history of this Saxon
king, emphasising the reputable status of Eadgyth's bloodline, contrasting
it with that of Æthelstan's mother who was said to be an ignoble consort
of lesser descent.[1] However, given Edward's death at the north-western
extremities of Mercia, Æthelstan may well have been present when he
died. This would put him in an ideal position to stake his claim to the
throne. However, whilst this might work for the Mercian element of the
kingdom there was no saying what would happen in Wessex.

The *ætheling* closest to the centre of power in Winchester was
Ælfweard, a son from Edward's second marriage to Ælfflæd. Riders
galloped post haste across the land, bearing the shocking news that
Edward was dead, and the would-be successors jockeyed for position.
It has been suggested that Ælfweard, not Æthelstan, was Edward's
preferred choice, and he soon emerged as the favoured candidate in

Winchester – but not, significantly, in Mercia. In that kingdom, Æthelstan was promptly elected king. It is not difficult to understand why. Roughly thirty years old, he was in his prime and had military experience. He had been brought up in Mercia as the foster-son of the Lord and Lady of the Mercians. One historian remarked that 'having been brought up at his aunt's court ... Æthelstan was perhaps seen more as Æthelflæd's heir than Edward's'.[2] As far as the Mercians were concerned, he was one of their own.

Alfred and Edward's efforts to consolidate the two kingdoms already looked set to unravel. Whether either brother would be prepared to accept this division of the realm on a long-term basis remained to be seen. But no one would ever find out. Just sixteen days after Edward's death, Ælfweard also died. Perhaps he had gone to see his half-brother in an attempt to reach an accommodation. We shall never know. But his death left Æthelstan as the ruler of both Wessex and Mercia, of one combined Kingdom of the Anglo-Saxons. Quite how Ælfweard met his end is another thing we do not know, but its timing was certainly extremely convenient for Æthelstan.[3]

Like his father, Æthelstan was consecrated at Kingston though William of Malmesbury notes that one 'Elfred' did his best to stop the ceremony from going ahead. William tells how this man attempted to seize Æthelstan whilst he was in Winchester and blind him, a practice which was well known in Byzantine circles; contemporary thinking was that a man suffering from such a disability would be unfit to be king. In any event, Elfred's efforts were unsuccessful. When the plot was discovered, he was sent to Rome to defend himself before the Pope at St Peter's. But William says that as soon as he has sworn an oath that he had not been involved in this devious plot, he collapsed. He was carried to the English School, in an area of Rome which still exists around the church known as Santo Spirito in Sassia after its Saxon roots. Here Elfred died three days afterwards. As William would have it, God had clearly passed judgement on him.[4]

The coronation ceremony did not take place until 4 September 925, more than a year after Edward's death. Revealingly, the charters issued by Æthelstan in the year preceding his formal crowning are dominated by Mercian witnesses. The choice of Kingston as a location for the ceremony has often been remarked on by historians as being symbolically significant, lying as it does right on the border between Wessex and Mercia. However, it might also have been a place where the new king felt relatively safe. With seeming antipathy towards him in Winchester, his presence there may have ignited a spark that led to a major explosion. On being crowned, Æthelstan immediately made an important placatory gesture by restoring land in Thanet to the important abbey of St Augustine's, Canterbury. Notably, the signature of the bishop of Winchester was not one of those attached to the grant.

At the time of the coronation, Æthelstan made a powerful symbolic gesture when he released a slave named Eadhelm. This perhaps symbolised the new king's intention to act with justice but also with mercy, or to liberate those currently under foreign rule. On the other hand, it is also a timely reminder that slavery was not just an evil that was inflicted by Viking slave masters.

Not everybody was happy with the course of events. The scribes in Winchester mentioned Æthelstan in lukewarm terms if they mentioned him at all. Rumours that Æthelstan had plotted to take the crown continued to circulate for centuries. The Winchester version of the *ASC* took its normal brevity to new levels: there are no entries at all for the years 924 to 931. It was an early attempt to airbrush an unwanted king out of history. And to complicate Æthelstan's position still further there was another surviving brother of Ælfweard, Edwin, who remained on the scene, waiting in the wings should an opportunity present itself.

Whilst Æthelstan would show many of the qualities of his father and grandfather, he differed in one significant respect: he had no wife or heir. It has been suggested by some historians that this was the result of a deliberate policy on his part. The argument goes that, as his claim to the throne was contested, he chose to present himself as a caretaker king, holding the throne for when one of Edward's other sons was ready to take his place after his death. Certainly, he was a devotee of the renowned eighth-century saint Aldhelm, who wrote a famous work on the virtues of virginity, which might be regarded as supporting circumstantial evidence of this view. It is also possible that what must have been a traumatic childhood affected him. Æthelstan had been separated from his mother when young and had been brought up in Mercia. He had probably seen little of his father when growing up and may well have been conscious that his brothers from Edward's second marriage were taking precedence over him. This could have made him reticent to engage in close adult relationships.

Although Æthelstan did not marry, he saw the opportunities offered by marriage alliances. In 926, plans were made to marry his only full sister to Sihtric Cáech, the Viking ruler in Jorvik. Evidence of coins bearing Sihtric's name as far south as Lincoln suggest that he may even have reversed some of Edward's conquests in the Danelaw.[5] The later chronicler Roger of Wendover suggested that the sister's name was Eadgyth, though it is possible that he confused her with a half-sister of the same name. Harmony with a potentially troublesome northern neighbour made great strategic sense for Æthelstan, and the marriage brought advantages to both parties although the bride's feelings about it are perhaps a matter for speculation. Sihtric journeyed to Tamworth to seal the deal, and the marriage duly took place on 30 January 926.

This was not the only significant marital alliance made at this time. Whilst the court was at Abingdon, discussions took place with a view to marrying Æthelstan's half-sister Eadhild to a Frankish duke, Hugh. In return for this Æthelstan would receive generous amounts of gifts and relics. Some of them were of striking imperial provenance, including the Lance of Charlemagne (which had according to some accounts been the very same weapon that had pierced the side of Christ on the cross), the sword of Constantine the Great (which had a nail from the True Cross embedded in its hilt) and the banner of St Maurice.[6] These moves to forge marital alliances this early in his reign suggest that the new king had a very outward-looking focus. In some ways Æthelstan's many siblings and half-siblings gave him a wonderful opportunity to strengthen his position politically.

The many relics Æthelstan received give an insight into his personal priorities. He would show himself to be an avid relic collector during his reign, suggesting that he was personally extremely devout, a point of view that is reinforced by other actions such as the generous gifts he made to various monasteries and religious foundations. Indeed, even at the start of his reign he had already earned this reputation. The association of some of the relics with the Carolingian dynasty also added to their lustre and the vicarious increase in prestige that Æthelstan received as a result,[7] their imperial provenance adding substance to Æthelstan's own claims to be an emperor of Britain. Later in Æthelstan's reign official documents referred to him as *basileus*, a title usually given to Byzantine emperors. Clearly here was a king who wished to be noticed. This comes through loud and clear in many of his official documents, which from the early part of his reign were written by a clerk with a very distinctive style. This anonymous clerk has been given the nondescript title of 'Æthelstan A' by historians. The introductory comments to these documents – proems, to give them their formal title – are full of bombastic pronouncements extolling the virtues of the king and self-proclaimed emperor who presumably knew exactly what was being said in them and approved.

Whilst very few letters have survived from Æthelstan's reign, one sent by Radbold, the prior of St Samson's at Dol in Francia, which was delivered sometime between 924 and 926, discusses various relics that had been sent to the king. These included the bones of Saints Senator, Paternus and Scabillion. They are not well-known saints now but at the time Æthelstan would have delighted in receiving these relics. The letter came accompanied with a glowing if not sycophantic word-picture of the king as 'exalter of holy church, subduer of wicked barbarism, mirror of your kingdom, example of all goodness, disperser of enemies' and so on and so forth. Clearly Æthelstan was highly regarded even in the early days of his reign. William of Malmesbury mentions that the letter was later found by him in a shrine at Milton Abbas, a holy site founded by the king.[8]

The peaceful start to Æthelstan's reign was not an accurate precursor of what was to come. The year 927 would be momentous, in some respects possibly more so than any other in the entire Anglo-Saxon period. Indeed, it might even be suggested with some credibility that the events of that year would shape the Britain which exists today. The writer of the Worcester strand of the *ASC* recognised as much when he told how the year commenced with fiery rays appearing in the northern sky. Such cosmic phenomena are often employed as omens of dramatic and important events in the chronicles of the time. God was sending a message that something extraordinary was about to happen.

In 927, just a year after his marriage to Æthelstan's sister, Sihtric died. Roger of Wendover later suggested that the marriage had not been consummated.[9] Before the resulting vacuum could be filled by any other members of the Viking dynasty in Dublin, Æthelstan quickly stepped in and added Jorvik (now York) and the surrounding region to his territories. In the process, he pushed the borders of his kingdom farther north than any other member of Alfred's dynasty had done before him. It is not clear whether there was any resistance to this move but on the balance of the admittedly flimsy surviving evidence it appears likely that there was not. This was an epochal event, celebrated at the time by a poet named Petrus (possibly a man of continental origin) as a moment that saw 'this Saxon land now made whole'. The celebration of this event through poetry rather than prose was entirely appropriate: the king's court would become famous for his patronage of this particular art form. Æthelstan's activities in this respect were recognised by a renowned Viking *skald* by the name of Egil Skallagrimsson. It has even been suggested that the greatest epic of Anglo-Saxon literature, *Beowulf*, may have been written up in Æthelstan's reign, though this is probably never going to be proved one way or the other.[10]

Æthelstan had perhaps caught the authorities in York unprepared. Alternatively, possibly the people there were happier to accept the rule of a known quantity in the form of the Anglo-Saxon king rather than a member of the Dublin dynasty with whom they were unfamiliar. William of Malmesbury suggests that the king ordered the destruction of the fortifications that had been built by the Vikings around the city so that they could not be reused as the base for a future insurgency against his rule. He also says that copious amounts of riches were captured by the king, who gave them all away to the followers who were with him. William adds that this was in keeping with Æthelstan's general approach to earthly wealth.[11] By his taking of Viking Northumbria, Æthelstan gave himself a claim to be the first ruler of a country that approximates to the modern version of England. His position would be further strengthened by other contemporary events.

Shortly after, a remarkable meeting was held at Eamont near Penrith. According to the 'D' (Worcester) version of the *ASC*, Constantin, king of the Scots, Owain, king of Gwent (south Wales) and Hywel, king of the west Welsh, recognised the supremacy of Æthelstan over them. So too did Ealdred, son of Eadwulf, who ruled the northern (non-Viking) part of Northumbria centred around Bamburgh. The tantalising detail that those present agreed to forbid all devil worship in their respective realms is also included in this account. Whether this should be taken literally or rather as an oblique warning not to consult with pagan Vikings is a matter of interpretation.[12] Æthelstan soon followed this up by making his way to the borders of Wales, where an assembly of Welsh princes agreed to pay homage to him and hand over a sizeable tribute. Thus within two years of his becoming king, Æthelstan had dramatically increased the size of his territory to include not just England but in nominal terms Wales and parts of Alba too.

The submission to Æthelstan in 927 stands alone amongst similar events in the tenth century. Both the 'submissions' at Bakewell to Edward in 920 and that to Edgar later in the century in 973 fail to convince that they are quite as definitive as presented. That of 927 on the other hand has much stronger evidence to support it, including the numismatic evidence that Æthelstan claimed to be *'rex totius Britanniae'* or king of all Britain.[13] Yet if we were to rely exclusively on the 'A' (Winchester) version of the *ASC* for our knowledge of these events, we would know next to nothing. Apart from a note that in 927 Æthelstan drove out Gothfrith, a Viking who came over from Ireland and tried to replace Sihtric after his death, nothing is mentioned.[14] Neither does Æthelweard say anything of them, though he does have the good grace to recognise Æthelstan as 'a very mighty king' in the few paragraphs he devotes to discussing his reign.[15]

William of Malmesbury says somewhat more. He mentions a meeting at Dacre, on the River Eamont, where Constantine [*sic*], king of the Scots, and 'Eugenius', king of the Cumbrians, submitted to Æthelstan.[16] Assuming that by referring to the king of the Cumbrians William of Malmesbury means the kingdom of Strathclyde, the ruler of this territory at the time was a man called Owain rather than Eugenius. It is tempting to assume that when the *ASC* mention 'Owain, king of Gwent' it should actually refer to the man of the same name who was king of Strathclyde (a logical confusion given that the term 'Welsh' was used to refer to the people of Strathclyde and both kingdoms had a ruler called Owain). Given the location of the meeting near that very kingdom, the involvement of representatives from Strathclyde makes perfect sense. Although it is also claimed that there was a Welsh king there in the form of Hywel, this in unsurprising as he was a well-known ally of the Anglo-Saxon kingdom.

The submission of these various kingdoms can in some respects be easily understood. In just a short space of time, Æthelstan had proved his military credentials. It was in some ways a move of self-defence to enter into an agreement with him: nominal submission might be better than facing a military campaign against the Anglo-Saxon army. Furthermore, it offered a degree of protection against the Viking threat. With the Viking dynasty ejected from Northumbria, there was a danger that they would go back to their old rampaging ways. Should this be so, Scotland, Strathclyde and Wales might all be in the line of fire. There may also have been an element of threat underpinning this meeting too. William of Malmesbury suggests that Gothfrith, after he fled from York, sought sanctuary in Alba and Strathclyde. He claims that Æthelstan subsequently sent messages to the rulers of both these territories threatening to take aggressive action if they went along with the expelled Viking king's request for protection.[17] Discretion may well have been the better part of valour.

A New Kind of King

Anglo-Saxon kings always lived a peripatetic existence, making the modern notion of a capital somewhat irrelevant, though both Alfred and Edward spent significant chunks of time in Winchester. The king would move around, staying for a few days in one place before moving on to another, preceded by his officials who were required to check that everything was ready. He may have had a favourite spot, or perhaps a few favourite spots, but he and his court would travel far and wide in pursuit of good governance. However, Æthelstan seems to have taken things to a new level in the size and cosmopolitan nature of the entourage that moved around with him. He enjoyed the trappings of kingship, hosting lavish banquets in the best traditions of Anglo-Saxon hospitality. Surviving charter evidence reveals that important men travelled from across Britain to be at his court, including the rulers of Strathclyde and Alba. He also widened international relationships. This was a very different kind of court, and England had never seen its like before.

Unlike many other Anglo-Saxon kings, Æthelstan's court was increasingly dominated by men. In the absence of a wife or daughters, and as his large brood of sisters were progressively married off or entered the convent, these men came to monopolise the king's company. If nothing else, we know some of their names thanks to their witnessing of charters: Odda, Wulfsige, Wulfhelm, Ælfric, Eadmund and Wulfgar. These were powerful secular figures who would have been at the king's side in times of war. They likely would have enjoyed listening to poetry with the king. On other occasions they would be more serious, perhaps discussing the religious aspects of life which were also very dear to the king. Two men of this court, Æthelwold and Dunstan, would later unleash an earthquake that would shake the English Church to its very foundations.

We even have a description of what Æthelstan looks like, though we should perhaps be cautious in accepting it at face value. The description comes from the quill of William of Malmesbury. Æthelstan, he says, is 'of becoming stature, thin in person, his hair flaxen … and beautifully wreathed' with golden threads. As William was looking at the remains of the king rather than his life image, and he had by then been entombed for several centuries, this description may not be particularly accurate.[18]

Æthelstan had expanded the size of his kingdom to an extent that had not been witnessed before amongst the Anglo-Saxon kings. Despite this, he continued to spend most of his time in the south, mostly in Wessex although he avoided Winchester. He seemed to have a particular affinity for the western part of Wessex, especially Wiltshire. Early on in his reign there was the occasional move outside of the core territory of Wessex. For example, he was in Tamworth for the wedding between his sister and Sihtric in 926 and then in the following year took York before travelling to Eamont to accept the submission of other British rulers. Shortly afterwards he moved to Hereford to accept the submission of the Welsh and agree tribute from them. He then proceeded to Exeter, where he drove out the Cornish force that had taken the city, leaving it with impressive new defences against any future incursions.

Throughout Æthelstan's reign, his council would meet regularly at different places at Easter, Christmas and Whitsun (the latter an innovation of his own). There were men from both Wessex and Mercia, and after taking Northumbria the archbishops of Canterbury and York were regularly present. The list of witnesses became more intriguing as the reign went on. They would increasingly include Welsh sub-kings such as Hywel Dda, Idwal Foel, Morgan ap Owain and Tewdwr ap

Griffri. Æthelstan had campaigned in the Welsh kingdoms of Dyfed, Gwynedd, Morgannwg, Gwent and Brycheiniog in 927, forcing them to submission. This understandably rankled. A Welsh poet who wrote a work entitled *Armes Prydein Vawr* made a heartfelt prediction about the Anglo-Saxon occupier soon after: 'As an end to their taxes, they will know death.'[19] Later on, these sub-kings would sometimes be joined by Owain of Strathclyde and Constantin of Alba, though how much they really wanted to be there is a moot point. Men with Scandinavian names like Guthrum would also be present from time to time, attesting to the cosmopolitan nature of not just Æthelstan's court but also his realm.

Given his pious nature, Æthelstan also had strong links with the Church. This was particularly strongly marked in his positive interaction with Æthelhelm, archbishop of Canterbury. With the king adding the north of England to his domains, this also inevitably strengthened the position of Canterbury. Æthelstan also strengthened his own position by replacing deceased bishops with men of his own choosing. These often came from amongst the priests who had previously served in his own household.[20] Given the position of influence that the Church had in his day, this also strengthened Æthelstan's own grip on England. He supported this by munificent gifts to a range of establishments including Athelney, Malmesbury, Wilton, Shaftesbury, Sherborne, York and others. In fact he was so generous that he appears to have acted unwittingly as an inspiration for later forgers who manufactured false charters in favour of various other churches.

Æthelstan re-founded the minster at Exeter in 932, which later (in 1050) became the cathedral for the diocese of Devon and Cornwall, replacing Crediton in Devon and St Germans in Cornwall.[21] The king gained a reputation for exceptional piety and was an avid collector of relics, some of which he gifted to the church in Exeter. These were gestures that may well have been motivated by genuine spiritual emotion but certainly would not do him any harm politically in a strategically important part of his kingdom.

Churchmen played an important role at court in helping the king to draw up legal documents. They came from far and wide to visit him, either as part of diplomatic delegations from abroad or just out of general interest in studying at what would gain a reputation as one of the most enlightened courts in western Europe. There were churchmen from Wales, Ireland, Brittany, Francia and Germany known to have journeyed there. They came to England and brought with them books, relics and precious objects to be used in liturgical services. They also brought ideas. Given the integral linkage between learning and the Church back then, this had a major impact. Monastic reform was accelerating on the continent, driven by the spiritual powerhouse of Cluny in Francia, where major changes to the monastic shape of Europe were in train.

These overseas connections became particularly strong with states in Germany. Æthelstan was very much an internationalist. He sought to build links with what he may have regarded as the 'old country' in Saxony, and in return Germans visited England; some of them are recorded witnessing charters. Another prominent connection was with Brittany. There was what was in effect a Breton court in exile taking up residence in England whilst their home territory was occupied and pillaged by Vikings. Its presence is particularly marked at Winchester. Agreements of confraternity were entered into between England and overseas establishments, almost like 'twinning' arrangements. The depth of these relationships is sometimes evidenced in continental sources. For example, an entry in the records of the monastery of Reichenau begins with the statement, 'In the name of Christ, we commend king Æthelstan to your service.'[22] Æthelstan's outlook can be seen to be wide ranging, far removed from a 'Little Englander' mentality. His view was that his greatness and that of his country would be enhanced by playing a prominent role in wider western European affairs. His thirst for knowledge could only be satisfied by trying to attract the best scholars and the greatest minds to his court, regardless of their origins.

Æthelstan was also an enthusiastic lawgiver, with several law codes issued during his reign. The fact that written copies were sent to local officials is strong evidence of increasing levels of literacy. Alfred's reforms were clearly bearing fruit. Æthelstan's laws covered a number of different areas. He gave instructions that all *burhs* were to be repaired within a fortnight of Rogation days, which fell within forty days of Easter Sunday. This presumably was meant to coincide with the start of campaigning season, which fell in the May–June period. He was also disturbed at the number of minors being executed for trivial offences and changed the law to prevent these harsh penalties being inflicted on those under fifteen years of age. Church matters also figured highly, especially in his earlier legal codes where the need to pay the institution its dues such as tithes was strongly emphasised. In addition, the king's officials were required to make charitable donations from his estates to the poor. This was not entirely altruistic; by his Christian actions the king wished to secure the wellbeing of his immortal soul.

Later law codes from Æthelstan's reign give an insight into the social problems besetting his newly expanded kingdom. There was almost an obsession with preventing acts of thievery, suggesting that they were considered to be far too common. Harsh penalties were to be doled out to anyone who stole goods worth more than eight pence; these miscreants were 'not to be spared'. Those who harboured such offenders were also to be punished. Tenth-century kings have been regarded as operating 'a fearsome judicial system'.[23] These strict laws were issued at a council held at Grately, Hampshire; but the code issued subsequently at Exeter suggests that in the interim little progress had been made in dealing successfully with the problem. In frustration, Æthelstan (or at least the clerk who wrote on his behalf) bemoaned the fact that 'all the oaths, pledges and sureties that were given there [i.e. at Grately] have been disregarded and broken'. Good intentions had apparently come to nothing. Perhaps despairing that his efforts at Grately had achieved little, at Exeter a complete change of tack was adopted whereby an amnesty was offered to thieves who would confess their offences and pay compensation to their victims.

As well as being perhaps the greatest 'forgotten' monarch of Alfred's dynasty, Æthelstan is also its most enigmatic. As discussed above, his decision not to marry in an age when kings almost invariably did is striking. Perhaps, as Michael Wood has suggested, this was a way of presenting himself as a caretaker king given his seemingly disputed accession to the throne, a very public symbol that on his death the throne could revert to a possibly less controversial line of descent.[24] It is also striking, as the same historian pointed out, that the works of St Aldhelm, including those on virginity, feature prominently in Æthelstan's library. Before Aldhelm's time the virtue of 'chastity' was mostly associated with widows who gave up earthly pleasures to live a celibate life after the death of their spouse. Aldhelm reshaped the concept into something quite different, developing a category of the 'chaste' who renounced marriage to still-living husbands to enter religious institutions.[25] It is possible to see Æthelstan's single status as a particularly extreme version of this renunciation. Certainly, he admired Aldhelm. The verbose nature and florid language used in Æthelstan's charters closely mirror the complex rhetoric of Aldhelm, someone of whom it might be said that he would never use one word when two would do.[26]

As noted, Æthelstan was not averse to using his sisters as useful aids to building political alliances. In this respect he was lucky, with eight (by some counts nine) sisters who would make attractive royal wives. One, Eadgifu, had already been married to the Frankish king Charles the Simple in Edward's reign. Charles had subsequently been deposed and their son, Louis, was sent to live in Æthelstan's court for a while. Several other daughters of Edward had entered nunneries but there was still a clutch of marriageable princesses who could find powerful and politically useful royal husbands. Perhaps the most significant marriage took place in 929 or 930 when Eadgyth, a daughter of Edward and Ælfflæd, was married to Otto, the son of Henry the Fowler, the East Frankish king. This widened Æthelstan's sphere of influence significantly.

An interesting story was related by the chronicler Æthelweard, who wrote for the edification of his cousin Matilda some half a century later. In a prefatory letter Æthelweard told Matilda that when a delegation, replete with a generous array of gifts, was sent to Æthelstan's court seeking a wife for Otto, the king decided to send two of his sisters back to Germany so that Otto could choose which one he preferred. Eadgyth was selected to be his bride, which was significant given the fact that Matilda, the recipient of the letter, was her direct descendant. Eadgyth apparently made a perfect queen, being beautiful, charming and regal in her bearing.

Æthelstan also built relationships by acting as a foster father to the sons of several important men. As someone who had himself been fostered, he knew first-hand how important such relationships could be. Such arrangements were common at the time, an important symbolic gesture in terms of building political alliances and an alternative to intermarriage. But whilst the political aspects of fostering were undoubtedly important, we should not forget that Æthelstan was a human being as well as a king. Perhaps as someone who had personally benefited from fostering and the security, psychological and actual, that it could bring, he genuinely wished to help the sons of great rulers who were in one sense or another vulnerable and under threat.

It is easy to see why Æthelstan would want to help his young nephew Louis, whom he fostered at his court. Fostering a potential future Frankish ruler had clear political benefits for him but the family connection also gave Æthelstan personal reasons to offer his protection. However, this was not the only example of fostering that we know of from his reign. Another situation involved what on the surface appears to be an extremely unlikely scenario, involving no less than the fostering of the son of the king of Norway at his court. Harald Finehair is normally regarded as the first king of Norway. Before his time the country as we now know it did not exist in a political sense. There were a number of fragmented sub-kingdoms, in some ways not dissimilar to the position in the past in England, and from time to time there would be attempts to unite all of them under one ruler, but these would not come to anything sustainable. Harald, who reigned for about sixty years, changed all that. In the process he made enemies inside his own kingdom, men who would not take kindly to having another lording it over them.

Much of what we know of the Vikings is derived from later sagas, written in Iceland and elsewhere several centuries after the events they purport to describe. Of the saga writers, the greatest of them all was

Snorri Sturluson (1179–1241). Snorri was a man who lived life to the full and his story would not be out of place in one of the sagas that he penned about the great men and women of the Viking age. He wrote many important and influential sagas, but one of his greatest works is the *Heimskringla*, 'the Sagas of the Norse kings'. In it Snorri describes events concerning Harald and Æthelstan, calling them 'the Victorious' and 'the Faithful' respectively. Snorri tells us that Æthelstan sent a delegation to Harald that tricked the latter into giving his allegiance to the English king.

During the summer following the arrival of this delegation, Harald sent a ship to England carrying his son, Hákon, on board. Hákon became the English king's foster son. He was later baptised. Æthelstan gave Hákon a sword with a hilt and handle made of gold and a blade so strong that it could cut a millstone down the middle, which led to the weapon being called the Quernbiter.[27] William of Malmesbury adds additional information concerning the relationship between Harald and Æthelstan. He says that Harald sent the gift of a ship with a golden beak and purple sail, festooned with 'a compacted fence of gilded shields'. Two men, Helgrim and Offrid, were sent with it. They were received magnificently at York and given many gifts. This is an extraordinary tale concerning the presentation of a Viking ship to a king of England.[28]

There are some dubious elements in Snorri's account which contains some details which appear formulaic and typical of the kind of devices used in other sagas. Nevertheless, we should not overlook the possibility that the core of the story is true. Harald had many enemies and securing an alliance with Æthelstan would help protect him and his dynasty. According to Snorri, Harald was seventy years of age when he fathered Hákon which also makes it believable that he should seek the protection of a powerful ruler for his young son. There are obvious advantages for Æthelstan too, so it is by no means implausible that there is a germ of truth in this extraordinary tale.

A connected form of alliance building involved sponsorship through becoming a godfather. During Æthelstan's time Brittany was ravaged by Viking raiders. As a result of this, Matuedoi, count of Poher, found refuge at the English king's court. He brought his young son Alain with him, and Æthelstan stood as the boy's godfather. Alain subsequently grew up alongside Æthelstan's young half-brothers Edmund and Eadred. Known in adulthood as 'Barbetorte' ('Crooked Beard'), Alain thereby formed close links with the West Saxon dynasty and also with his fellow exile Louis, son of Charles the Simple and Eadgifu. Later, Æthelstan would give them both practical and military support as they sought to secure their respective domains. Æthelstan was showing himself to be a paragon of contemporary Christian rule.

And then in the year 933 there are suggestions of an event which could undermine the reputation of this paragon. The *ASC*, in this case the 'E' (Oxford) version, records that 'here the ætheling Edwin drowned at sea'. Edwin was another half-brother of Æthelstan, a son from Edward's second marriage to Ælfflæd and therefore a close rival. No further details are given in the *ASC* so we might on the surface assume that this was no more than a tragic accident, though it was yet another happy coincidence for Æthelstan and his security on the throne.

Writing several centuries later, William of Malmesbury adds some salacious details to this story. In his account, Edwin was falsely accused of treachery by the king's cupbearer. Æthelstan believed these accusations and forced Edwin into exile. However, Edwin was put in danger as he was compelled to board a vessel with a single attendant, no rower (nor even an oar) and with 'the bark crazy with age'. The ship took him far out to sea and the wind blew up to the extent that the sails could not endure it. Edwin, overcome with terror and desperation, threw himself into the sea and drowned. The attendant stayed on board and managed to recover the body, bringing it to land on the far side of the English Channel. Here, Edwin's body was given an honourable burial at the monastery of St Bertin.

William says that Æthelstan was overcome with grief when he heard of his brother's death and blamed himself. He undertook to perform seven years' penance to recompense for his actions, and his construction of a new monastery at Milton in Dorset might also have been a penitential act for a grievous sin. The relics of St Samson – an arm and some bones – which he received as a gift from Brittany were also donated to the monastery. As for the cupbearer who had accused Edwin of plotting against him, the king ordered him to be put to death. William is prudent enough to note that this story is based on gossip rather than verified history so it may not be true, though he suggests that it is extremely probable that it is.[29] His is not the only account of these events. Simeon of Durham is unambiguous in his succinct statement that 'King Ethelstan [*sic*] ordered his brother Edwin to be drowned in the sea'.[30] A history of the abbey of St Bertin written in 962 by Folcuin, the deacon there, relates that Edwin left England 'driven by some disturbance in his kingdom' (Folcuin wrongly thought Edwin was king there). Whilst crossing the Channel, a storm blew up, wrecking the ship and overwhelming it. Edwin's body was washed ashore where it was recovered by a relation, Count Adelolf, who took it to St Bertin for burial.

Whilst the gap between the events of 933 and the writings of these later chroniclers tell us to be cautious, we should not be too dismissive. The account of Folcuin was written just three decades later, when some of these events were still fresh in the minds of men who were still living. Looking at the accounts collectively, there is an unmistakable intimation of a plot against Æthelstan in which Edwin was implicated. It has been noted by some historians that the Irish would set a person out to sea in a boat if they had plotted against their sibling, the idea being that God would decide whether he should live or die by steering the ship to safety or letting it founder. In some ways this was a variation on the trial by ordeal, wherein God himself would decide whether a man was guilty of a crime and punish him accordingly.

So, both of Æthelstan's half-brothers from Edward's marriage to Ælfflæd were now dead. His two closest rivals for the throne – and, in the eyes of some factions in Winchester, the legitimate rulers of the Anglo-Saxon kingdom – were no longer a threat. This is notable when considering that Æthelstan was extremely close with his half-brothers from Edward's last marriage, to Eadgifu. The elder, Edmund, would fight at Æthelstan's side in the epochal battle of his reign and would take his place as king when he died. In all probability, he was being groomed for the succession during Æthelstan's reign. These two half-brothers were not a threat to Æthelstan. They were too young to be: when Edmund became king in 939, he was still only eighteen years of age. On the contrary, Æthelstan seems to have been actively protective of their interests.

The Storm Clouds Gather

So far, after the momentous events of 927, Æthelstan's reign had been mainly marked by peacetime developments. This is in some ways ironic as it is as a warrior that he is perhaps best remembered. It is true that some fighting probably occurred when Æthelstan seized Northumbria in 927; although the *ASC* does not mention any battles or military campaigns, other chroniclers such as Simeon of Durham, John of Worcester and William of Malmesbury do. Yet any fighting there had been followed by several years of peace. That same year had also seen the submission of Constantin of Alba and Owain of Strathclyde to Æthelstan. It seems that they had honoured this arrangement ever since, at least nominally – until now.

The later chronicler John of Worcester suggests that in 934, Constantin of Alba broke the peace. Simeon of Durham makes a similarly succinct reference to the events of 934; neither gives any reason. Whilst we cannot make too much of this scant information, it is not difficult to imagine that Constantin was starting to feel irked at being subservient to Æthelstan. In any case, John of Worcester and Simeon of Durham suggest that there had been some aggressive action by Constantin, something more than mere frustration, perhaps some of the border raiding that had characterised the frontier between England and Scotland for centuries. An alternative possibility is that Constantin had been attempting to interfere in Northumbrian affairs. Henry of Huntingdon, whilst not adding much more by way of detail, suggests that Æthelstan's actions were to bring the 'faithless Scots' to heel, again intimating some perceived treachery on their part. He also noted that the 'heathen Danes' were a target, and it is notable that the prominent Viking warlord Gothfrith had just died; perhaps Æthelstan was seeking to exploit a perceived power vacuum.[31]

The text of surviving charters enables us to trace something of Æthelstan's route as he set out on campaign. In May he was in Winchester, but by 7 June he was with his council at Nottingham, a long way from Wessex.[32] As he moved further north towards Alba, Æthelstan sought help from a higher authority in the form of England's foremost contemporary saint. St Cuthbert (or at least his mortal remains) had survived the apocalyptic attack on Lindisfarne which had announced the arrival of the Vikings in England in 793. The community there had hung on limpet-like for decades, but with the subjection of Northumbria by the Viking army in the latter decades of the ninth century they had decided enough was enough. They left their monastery but took the remains of the saint with them. For many years the monks had wandered around the north of England, going from place to place. They were now at Chester-le-Street, which is where Æthelstan headed.

Northumbria may have been notionally part of Æthelstan's kingdom, but it remained very loosely integrated. There is no surviving evidence of northerners witnessing Æthelstan's charters and no evidence that coins in his name were ever minted in Northumbria. Possibly Ealdred, son of Eadwulf, ruled with a considerable amount of autonomy there.[33] Whilst Æthelstan's primary aim was to sort out the problem of Alba, the journey north was also an opportunity to remind his Northumbrian subjects who ruled them. Appropriating their greatest saint would do no harm in this respect.

Simeon of Durham reminded his readers that Cuthbert had appeared to Alfred and promised him that 'the rule of the whole of Britain shall be placed at the disposal of your sons by my assistance'. According to Simeon, Edward the Elder had reminded Æthelstan of this on his deathbed, encouraging his son to prove himself a faithful follower of the saint. Æthelstan took these words to heart and apparently showed greater reverence to the church of St Cuthbert than any of his predecessors had done. According to Simeon, it was because of this that he was to enjoy such a glorious reign. He made extravagant offerings to the saint, confirming them in a testament that he left behind when he departed. This ended with a fierce malediction: 'If anyone steals anything there, let him be damned on the Day of Judgement with the traitor Judas and be thrust into everlasting fire which was prepared for the devil and his angels.'

Æthelstan's adoption of Cuthbert may have been completely sincere but it was also a smart political manoeuvre. It endeared him to the Northumbrians, as did his sponsorship of St Oswald who had also crossed regional boundaries as the favoured saint of his uncle and aunt, the Lord and Lady of Mercia. The West Saxon dynasty even claimed a highly dubious blood connection to Oswald.[34] It may not be coincidental that the first attribution of miraculous acts concerning Edmund, king of the East Anglians, was apparently made by an old man at Æthelstan's court. It was as if the king was targeting every major saint from the former kingdoms of England. Æthelstan donated no less than 12 vills to Cuthbert's church to support it. Simeon also noted that at the king's command the army with him made gifts amounting to more than 96 lbs of silver at Cuthbert's tomb. Going on his way, he asked that if he were to die on campaign his brother and probable heir Edmund should ensure that his body was taken to the church of the saint and buried there. However, he was not yet destined to meet his end.

Æthelstan's offering of gifts at the tomb of St Cuthbert led to a hugely symbolic artistic moment. The frontispiece to a manuscript now in the library of Corpus Christi College, Cambridge, shows the king offering Bede's *Lives of St Cuthbert* to the saint, juxtaposing two very famous Northumbrians. This is the earliest extant portrait of an English monarch.[35] The king bows, possibly in homage to England's greatest saint or perhaps contemplating the acts of devotion and spirituality contained in the book. He looks both deferential and learned as befitted his reputation – like his grandfather, Æthelstan was a great patron of learning. Æthelstan deposited some magnificent clerical vestments in Cuthbert's tomb which were still there when it was opened in 1827. They had apparently been initially commissioned by Ælfflæd, King Edward's second wife, for Frithustan, bishop of Winchester, but had not been completed before she was replaced by another consort. They had obviously been finished at a later stage. These were no doubt pious gestures from a devout king, but they also symbolically affirmed the approval of England's (and Northumbria's) foremost saint for a West Saxon king's right to rule over all the Anglo-Saxon peoples.[36]

The army that had set out from Wessex had accumulated extra men from Mercia and recruits from friendly elements in the Danelaw too. A charter dated 7 June 934 whilst the army was marching towards Alba is revealing. It concerns land in Amounderness in the north of Lancashire, which had been in Viking hands since their arrival from Dublin earlier in the century but was now transferred to the church of York. The witness list was also significant. Both archbishops, Wulfhelm of Canterbury and Wulfstan of York, were on the list, second and third after Æthelstan. There were many bishops too, including those from Lichfield, London, Selsey, Wells, Ramsbury, Sherborne, Winchester and Worcester. Most intriguingly of all, amongst the earls witnessing were some with clearly Scandinavian names: Ragnald, Ivar, Scule, Thurferth and Halfden, for example.[37]

Æthelstan's force now represented a sizeable threat to Constantin. Whatever he had done, the king of Alba had stirred up a hornet's nest. So too, according to Simeon of Durham, had 'Owin [*sic*] king of the Cumbrians'.[38] In response, the extent of Æthelstan's counter had reached sledgehammer proportions. Not only was there a large land army marching on Alba, there was also a substantial fleet sailing up the North Sea too. So striking was this fact that it even shook the *ASC*'s writers out of their normal vow of silence concerning Æthelstan to comment on the fact.

This massive thrust from the south of England represented a campaign that was breath-taking in its scope. Given the range which it covered in a short period of time, arguably nothing like it had been seen in Britain before. The army came crashing over the border and deep into the heart of Alba. Simeon of Durham gives more details than other accounts, telling us that there were large cavalry forces with Æthelstan. Whilst current evidence suggests that Anglo-Saxons did not use cavalry much on the battlefield, they were excellent horsemen. Horses allowed men to move rapidly, and it is probable that Æthelstan used this manoeuvrability to exhaust Constantin's defensive forces, pulling them this way and that until they were on the point of collapse.

Simeon also tells us how far this juggernaut of a force reached. Perched on the edge of the North Sea in what is now Aberdeenshire, Dunnottar is a spectacular place where history has been made repeatedly. A king of Alba, Domnall, had died fighting a Viking army there as recently as 900. It is 500 miles from Winchester, illustrating starkly the extent of Æthelstan's ambitions. Its jagged remains still stand on precarious cliffs, accessible only by a climb up a rocky staircase at the foot of a steep ravine caressed by a crescent-moon bay. Its promontory site seems to make it impregnable; yet it is an illusion. Its isolation means that it can be cut off, especially if an opponent has control of the sea, as Æthelstan had here.

The army marched beyond Dunnottar to the mountains of Fortriu. Exactly where the latter place was remains unclear, but it is often associated with an ancient Pictish kingdom thought to be centred around the Moray Firth. It has been suggested that it could loosely refer to the mountains of the Mounth which shield the northernmost parts of Scotland from unwelcome interlopers from the south.[39] The navy would go further still, pushing up as far as Caithness, possibly part of a move to catch the Scots in a pincer movement. It is probable that the fleet was working in close support of the land army, enabling a reliable source of supply for the latter, much needed given the sparseness of provisions in the area. Caithness was in the backyard of the Viking earls of Orkney and as such this might be interpreted as an act of defiance against the supposed masters of the sea. It was not only Constantin who was in danger of being taught a lesson here.

By all accounts the campaign was devastating. Simeon says that the land was 'depopulated' after the campaign whilst John of Worcester tells how the English king's army 'ravaged a great part of the country'.[40] The earth of Alba was metaphorically and perhaps in some cases literally scorched. The Irish *Annals of Clonmacnoise* states that there was no great Anglo-Saxon victory, but this might be little more than semantics. Whilst no mighty battle had been fought, the devastation unleashed during the campaign had succeeded in bringing Alba to heel.

Constantin had paid dearly for his temerity, whatever form it had taken. Æthelstan marched his triumphant army back southwards, and by 13 September he was witnessing a charter in Buckingham. In his train was Constantin's son, taken to England as a hostage. Even more remarkably, Constantin himself was there as well; he would not remain for long, however. He witnessed the charter at Buckingham, relating to land in Wiltshire, and was recorded as *sub regulus* ('sub king'), a title that presumably would not have pleased him. Æthelstan perhaps thought that this conclusive rebuff had been enough to put Constantin in his place – that is, at the king's feet.

Sometime in 935, an important meeting was held at Cirencester. Constantin was there, as were Owain of Strathclyde and three Welsh sub-kings. The setting was appropriate. Cirencester was a venerable town of Roman heritage and its ancient amphitheatre probably still cut an impressive dash. It appears that Constantin returned to Scotland shortly after. Æthelstan was at Frome in Somerset in December, and Constantin was not. However, when the group from Cirencester assembled again at Dorchester in Dorset that Christmas, Owain was still present. It has been noted that the foremost Scottish source for these years, *The Chronicles of the Kings of Alba*, is unsurprisingly deafeningly silent about these events.[41]

The problem in the north had been put to bed as far as Æthelstan was concerned. He was now confident enough to turn his attentions elsewhere. Two years later he was supporting the exiled Bretons in a successful attempt to displace the Vikings who had taken over their lands. They were led by Alain 'Barbetorte', Æthelstan's godson. In that very same year, Louis, son of Charles the Simple, was also summoned back from exile to take up his rule in Francia. Æthelstan's influence was spreading far beyond the shores of England. But he had taken his eye off the ball. Even whilst he gloried in the successes he had enjoyed, a cloud was appearing in the distance. At first a small, misty wisp on the horizon, it would grow in intensity and energy as time passed. Before long, it would become a storm cloud so intense that it threatened to overwhelm not just Æthelstan but also the country that he and his forefathers had built.

The Great War

The events of 934 would have cut both Constantin of Alba and Owain of Strathclyde to the quick. These were proud men, leaders of proud peoples, and they had been humiliated. They had seen their lands invaded, their independence obliterated, their peoples overrun. They had then been forced to travel around Æthelstan's realm like reluctant camp followers. They had been treated with a degree of respect – Constantin and Owain had been the second and third names to be included on the list of witnesses on Æthelstan's charters after only the king of England himself, and above the Welsh sub-kings on the list – but this was little compensation. However respectful their treatment might have been, they were being exhibited as conquests. It might have been better than a triumph marching up the Appian Way and into Rome – they were not at least in chains – but the end result was similar.

Their peoples had seen all this too, and this fact was most dangerous. A warrior-king of the period was expected to be successful; if he failed, he could be fatally undermined. Constantin's position was particularly vulnerable. He had been king for nearly four decades, and he was getting old by the standards of the time. He had become king after the death of Domnall at Dunnottar in 900. A few years later, a ceremony was held at

Scone in Perthshire to recognise what was in effect a contract between Constantin and the Church. It was not his coronation – he had already been ruler for some years – but it was the first time that Scone had been mentioned as a place of such importance. A mound there dubbed the Hill of Belief, which was integral to the ceremonies, may have been the very spot where later Scottish monarchs were enthroned. Constantin's people had always needed to be resilient. In the face of regular Viking attacks, not to mention the struggle for supremacy with the vanished Picts, there had always been ups and downs. Yet to be an ageing king, and moreover one who was unsuccessful in battle, was a dangerous combination. If Constantin wanted to survive, he had better right the wrong done to him. And he had better do it quickly.

But the pertinent question was *how*. The resources controlled by Æthelstan had already proved superior to those available to Constantin and Owain. Additional resources would be needed to supplement those already available to them. The solution arrived at was difficult but not unique. Nearly a century earlier, Viking leaders and Cinéad mac Alpin, often regarded as the first king of Scotland, had carved up the country between them.[42] Not only the Scots and the Strathclyde Welsh had been humiliated by the king of England; so too had the Viking rulers of Northumbria, who had been ejected from a region they saw as home. It was a classic case of my enemy's enemy becoming my friend.

The vacuum in Ireland left by the death of Gothfrith in 934 had now been filled. His place had been taken by his son Óláfr, whose first task was to secure his position in Ireland. He did this soon after by attacking the main royal sites in Brega, north of Dublin. In 936 he sacked the sacred site of Clonmacnoise to the west. This was enough to remove any immediate opposition in Ireland. It is probable that he also had influence in Galloway and the Isle of Man as well as the north-west of England. This put him in an ideal position to cooperate with the kings of Alba and Strathclyde should he choose to do so. The prize on offer to him – the rulership of Northumbria – was an attractive one. He only had to take it from Æthelstan.

We do not know who was the main driving force behind this alliance, but there was one last piece of business that Óláfr needed to attend to before leaving Ireland. The Vikings never completely occupied the island and were located in a ring of coastal bases dotted around the periphery: places like Waterford, Wexford, Dublin and Limerick. These were not all ruled by the same regime and were often at odds with each other. Limerick, in the south-west corner of the island, often had its own ruler stirring up trouble. Before sailing east across the Irish Sea, Óláfr had to subdue his namesake, Óláfr Ceincarrech, the ruler of Limerick, which he did on Lough Ree in the Irish midlands in August 937. Now he felt confident enough to activate the alliance with Constantin and Owain.

Æthelstan had been caught off guard by this turn of events, and the size of the threat now facing him was so great that it could have had fatal consequences. Even if he knew of the alliance – and there is no reason to think that he did – it was now late in the year, and he would not have expected an attack in the autumn. William of Malmesbury is critical of the king, saying that 'he languished in sluggish leisure'. The invading army marched into the north of England, burning crops as they went – a clue that it may well have been harvest time, sometime in mid to late September. The timing was perfect: Æthelstan was unprepared, his men were in the fields harvesting crops or at least supervising the exercise, and any army he sent to deal with the threat would be deprived of critical supplies.

We now enter the realm of informed speculation. Having made the short hop across the Irish Sea, Óláfr and his men joined forces with the Scots and the Strathclyde Welsh. This combined force set about pillaging the north. Confirmation of the attack on Northumbria comes from an unlikely source. Egil Skallagrimsson was a larger-than-life character from a Viking culture that produced more than its fair share of such individuals. He was a renowned poet but also a warrior. *Egil's Saga*, probably written up by Snorri Sturluson, covers a number of dramatic episodes including its eponymous hero's involvement in the campaign of 937. It tells of a great battle in Northumbria between Óláfr's men and those of the alliance on the one side and two earls, Godric and Alfgeir, on the other. Godric was killed and Alfgeir fled to Æthelstan with the terrible news that the north of England had been overrun. Egil and his brother Thorolf had sailed to England to offer their services to Æthelstan, hearing that he needed men. They arrived there in the autumn, in time for the forthcoming campaign.[43]

The route taken by this combined force of Æthelstan's opponents is also a matter of speculation. The most likely road to follow was the old Roman highway from Carlisle down to Manchester from where it would eventually link up with Watling Street. John of Worcester suggested that the fleet from Dublin sailed into the Humber, but this makes little sense. Why sail hundreds of miles round the north of Scotland, a notoriously difficult passage, when a short hop across the Irish Sea would suffice? It may be that John is confusing the later invasion of England by Harald Hardrada, who came over from Norway and entered the Humber; given where he was coming from, that would make a lot more sense. Considering the presence of Viking elements already in the north-west of England and the probability that they would welcome Óláfr, this would be a very logical place to go. Óláfr could have headed straight there and waited for the men of Alba and Strathclyde to join him (or moved out to meet them). Alternatively, he could have made his way further north, for instance to Galloway, and marched his men down. His fleet could have sailed on to the Mersey or the Dee to meet him there later.

If there was an initial battle against local Anglo-Saxon forces which the alliance won then that would likely have led to more men joining them, especially from settlers of Scandinavian extraction in the region. The opposite would be true for the Anglo-Saxons; this was a formidable force arrayed against them, and those who could probably fled, a stream of refugees pouring south. Given Æthelstan's alleged initial dithering over his response, it is easy to assume that he was in danger of being overwhelmed by events. But perhaps he genuinely did not know the alliance's main target. Was it York? This was a logical assumption given its connection to a long-established Viking ruling dynasty. But if he moved there, would he expose his forces to a flanking move into Mercia, cutting him off? It was a difficult decision to make given the high stakes. Æthelstan's defeat and death might bring the whole dynasty crashing to the ground and the fledgling English nation state with it.

This multinational alliance posed an enormous threat, and whilst it came as a surprise to Æthelstan it had been earnestly hoped for by others. A prophetic poem expressed this hope eloquently, of 'courageous men in battle' who 'will bring about rejoicing after devastation and reconciliation of the Cymry [the Welsh] and the men of Dublin. The Irish of Ireland, Anglesey, and Scotland, the Cornish and the men of Strathclyde will be welcomed among us.' Certainly many of those mentioned had reason to feel threatened by Æthelstan, and the poet clearly anticipated with glee the moment when the hated Saxons would be expelled from Britain by this cosmopolitan alliance, forced to wander the earth, vainly seeking somewhere to call home. The irony was that the poet was Welsh, and in the looming campaign his people are conspicuous by their absence. Several Welsh under-kings had recognised the supremacy of Æthelstan, but they may have felt compelled to do so. The frequent summonses to Æthelstan's court may have been irksome, an irritating reminder of their subservience. It would not be a surprise if they stayed on the side-lines in 937, possibly secretly hoping that Æthelstan would be overthrown but anxious not to show their hand in case he was not.

We do not know where Æthelstan was when the deeply disturbing news of the invasion arrived. But above the old religious establishment at Milton Abbey in Dorset stands St Catherine's Chapel, where tradition asserts that Æthelstan experienced a vision before the looming epochal battle was fought.[44] The decision could be put off no longer. Æthelstan would have to gather his own forces together and march them off to his appointment with destiny.

The king set out northwards, picking up men as he went. There must have been a great deal of nervousness amongst his troops given the scale of the threat. Eventually they found themselves closing in on the combined force. The scene was set for the greatest battle of the Anglo-Saxon era before Hastings in 1066. It would be fought at a place called Brunanburh. There have been many suggestions about where this was, but increasingly historians feel it was likely at a place called Bromborough on the Wirral. Finds from that town announced in 2019 led the famous literary figure Bernard Cornwell to proclaim that 'the search for Brunanburh is over'.[45] A number of early medieval battlefield implements have been found there, consistent with the Viking period, including broken blades and axe- and spearheads. Although further research is needed, it is a firm step in the right direction as far as identifying the battlefield is concerned. (Such issues are contentious; it was rather alarming to read that a historian who has written on the Bromborough site reported that he had 'received more hate-mail for arguing this conclusion than I have for the rest of my academic work put together'. Clearly such things matter to some people, perhaps in some cases a little too much.[46])

Of the fight itself, we have much more detail than usual. However, some of the main sources are problematic. One of them is the *ASC*. Departing from their characteristic curtness, they contain in several surviving versions a poetic description of the battle that would not be out of place in *Beowulf*. It begins in dramatic fashion: 'Here King Athelstan [*sic*], lord of earls, ring-giver of men, and his brother also, Prince Edmund, age-long glory won in strife with swords' edges near Brunanburh.' So here we learn that Æthelstan was not alone and his half-brother fought alongside him. The action is described in Beowulfian terms: 'They split the shield wall, hewed the battle-wood with hammer-beaten blades ... Their enemies perished. The men of the Scots and the men of the seas, fated, they fell.' This is totally different in character from other references to Æthelstan's reign, and the reference to Edmund may well indicate that it was written up when the latter had become king.[47]

According to this account, the fight lasted all day: 'The field darkened with the blood of men, from the rising of the sun in the morningtime, when that glorious light glided over the ground, bright candle of God, of the eternal Lord, until that noble creation sank to rest.' The list of the dead was long. 'Five lay still on that battlefield – young kings by swords put to sleep – and seven also of Anlaf's [Óláfr's] earls, countless of the army, of sailors and Scotsmen.' Many warriors lay dead, and the triumphant West Saxons and their Mercian comrades-in-arms pursued their fleeing enemy with an energy fired by bloodlust. Óláfr made it back to his ships, where he and some of his men managed to sail back to safety in Ireland. Sixty-something Constantin, 'that hoary-haired warrior', also escaped. His son did not. He fell 'on the field of slaughter, with wounds ground to pieces'. The king may well have been a broken man. A few years later he abdicated, living out his last days in a monastery.

It was a monumental triumph – though not, despite its seeming totality, completely decisive in the short term. Even so, it was a seminal event in the foundation of England and practically saved the country and Alfred's dynasty from disintegration. Arguably it had an even greater symbolic effect as part of the foundation legend of England, when West Saxon and Mercian had fought and died side by side against a common foe and triumphed. Half a century later the chronicler Æthelweard noted that people still referred to Brunanburh as 'the great war'.

As Æthelstan and Edmund headed back south with their tired but ecstatic troops, they left behind a scene of devastation described by the chronicler with words that would not have been out of place in the greatest of Viking sagas:

> They left behind to divide the corpses
> the dark-coated one, the black raven,
> the horn-beaked one, and the dark-coated one;
> the white-tailed eagle, to enjoy the carrion,
> that greedy war-hawk, and that gray beast,
> the wolf of the wood. Never was there more slaughter
> on this island, never as many
> folk felled before this
> by the swords' edges, as those books tell us,
> old authorities, since here from the east
> the Angles and Saxons came ashore.[48]

Egil's Saga also discusses the battle in some detail as Egil claims he was there. Sagas are always a difficult source to approach. Most of them were written centuries after the period concerned. *Egil's Saga*, for example, was written up three centuries after its main protagonist lived.[49] They are also full of highly dubious material, including magic and dragons. Some historians claim that this makes them of little value in terms of understanding real-life events. Others however suggest that we should not dismiss them out of hand and that they provide useful clues as to what happened in history, although of course they should be handled with care.

In Egil's account Æthelstan initially made an offer to try and buy off Óláfr, but the invaders held out for more. Eventually Óláfr accepted, on condition that the king hand over Northumbria. However, the negotiations had merely been a way to buy time whilst Æthelstan gathered more men. With a greater force now assembled, Æthelstan changed his stance completely. He would allow Óláfr and his men to leave, but only if they made reparation for the damage that they had caused and gave him their allegiance. This sudden *volte face* made a fight inevitable. However, rather than wait for a set-piece battle, some of the combined force decided to launch a surprise attack on the Anglo-Saxon army. Marching through the night, they attacked at daybreak. They collided with an advanced force led by the two brothers, Thorolf and Egil. This was richly ironic, an allied force including many of the men of Dublin being resisted by a group of Viking mercenaries.

Thorolf fought like a man possessed. He 'began fighting so furiously that he threw his shield over his back, grabbed his spear with both hands and charged forward, hacking and thrusting to either side. Men leapt out of the way all around, but he killed many of them.' Approaching one of the leaders of the enemy force, Earl Hring, he killed the man's standard-bearer and smashed into pieces the pole on which the standard had been placed. Then he killed the earl too, driving his spear into his chest and through his body until it came out between his shoulder blades. He lifted the writhing earl into the air and placed the other end of the spear into the ground so that he hung there, impaled like a flailing animal. This understandably shattered the spirits of Hring's men, many of whom fled. Large numbers of Scots and Vikings perished, and the attack was abandoned.

But this was just an overture. The next day, Æthelstan and Óláfr moved up with their men. Thorolf was again at the front, his standard flapping in the breeze as his men advanced along the side of a forest. They may have been trying to surprise their enemy. But instead it was they who were ambushed, and Thorolf was brought down under a flurry of blows. Egil, who was elsewhere, sensed that something was wrong. He hurried up with his men. Hacking and slashing with his sword, Adder, he killed many enemy warriors before bringing down an earl. The enemy now broke and ran, pursued hard by Egil and his men. Egil, perhaps unsurprisingly, suggests that this action was the turning point in a hard-fought battle. Æthelstan now urged his own men forward and they carried all before them, killing Óláfr (other accounts say that he escaped back to Ireland) and most of his men.

There is much about this account which does not ring true, and the role of Egil, the hero of the saga, is probably significantly exaggerated.

But this vignette is revealing in its suggestion that 'Vikings' fought on Æthelstan's side. Whatever the truth, in one respect the account chimes with all others: this was a glorious victory for Æthelstan. The invasion force was decimated. Egil, whose greatest fame was as a poet, spoke eloquently of the ultimate outcome of the battle: 'Even the highland deer's paths belong to mighty Athelstan [*sic*] now.'

Yet Æthelstan would have little time to glory in his triumph. On 27 October 939, at around the age of forty-five, he died at Gloucester. He was buried in Malmesbury Abbey. It was the last resting place of one of his favourite saints, Aldhelm, and also the burial site of two of his cousins who had fallen on the glorious field of Brunanburh. But this act also served to set him apart from Alfred's dynasty. No other king was buried there; the regal mausoleum was most definitely in Winchester. Perhaps Æthelstan had deliberately chosen to rest right on the borders of Wessex and Mercia. But possibly he had no wish to spend eternity in a place where he did not feel welcome. A splendid tomb was erected at Malmesbury, and a memorial was later composed:

> Here lies one honoured by the world and grieved by his land;
> Path of rectitude, thunderbolt of justice, model of purity.
> His spirit has gone to Heaven its covering of flesh dissolved;
> an urn receives these triumphant relics.
> The sun had lit up Scorpio with its twelfth dawn
> when he struck down the king with his tail.

It has been suggested that William of Malmesbury himself may have been the author.[50]

Perhaps the last word on this extraordinary ruler should go to the same man, a distant beneficiary of Æthelstan's patronage through the king's support of the monastic establishment of Malmesbury. William summed him up in words that were succinct but eloquent: 'His years, though few, were full of glory.'[51] It was a fitting epitaph. Alfred's dynasty had more than its share of great men and women; but, however much some of the family may have resented him, Æthelstan, the first king of England, was by many measures the greatest of them all.

8

The Age of Edgar

I do not believe earthly estate is everlasting.
'The Seafarer', Anglo-Saxon poem

Edmund – The Accession of the Heir Apparent

Although only about eighteen years old when he became king, Edmund had already experienced two major campaigns. He had been with Æthelstan on his Scottish campaign of 934 and had also fought at the battle of Brunanburh. He was going to need every ounce of that experience in the days ahead. If Æthelstan had indeed groomed Edmund to succeed him, his masterplan seems to have worked to perfection. There is no mention of any succession dispute, which was certainly not routinely the case in the Anglo-Saxon period.

But trouble was not slow to reveal itself. News may not have travelled fast back then but it reached Óláfr in Ireland quickly enough. Presumably reasoning that with a new and young king on the throne York might fall into his hands again, he crossed the Irish Sea. His gambit was entirely successful. The speed with which York became Viking once more suggests that the relatively recent addition of Northumbria to England was not yet established on firm foundations. Óláfr was helped significantly by the support of Wulfstan, the archbishop of York. To some this might have seemed a betrayal; but a betrayal of whom? Whilst the concept of England was not new, the actuality of it was. The archbishop may have felt that his first loyalty was to Northumbria and not to some newly established West Saxon dynasty that wished to rule all it surveyed. Wulfstan proved himself to be a born survivor, able to change his political skin like a chameleon. Not that the *ASC*'s scribes were impressed. The 'D' (Worcester) version states unequivocally that 'the Northumbrians belied their pledges and chose Anlaf [Óláfr] from Ireland as their king'.

And that was not the end of it. Óláfr crossed the border into Mercia (now an actual border again) and moved on Northampton, where he was driven off. He then attacked Tamworth, a symbolic move which would have profoundly shaken confidence. His army took away a great deal of plunder with them along with a lucrative hostage in the shape of a high-ranking Mercian noblewoman named Wulfrun. She may be forgotten now, but the town named after her, Wolverhampton ('Wulfrun's homestead'), lives on. The traditional heartlands of the Danelaw, the renowned Five Boroughs (Lincoln, Leicester, Nottingham, Stamford and Derby), also fell to this Viking onslaught from the north. The façade of England was in danger of cracking asunder.

But young though he was, Edmund also had the warrior instincts of his forefathers. He got his army together and marched it up to Leicester where he confronted Óláfr. The looming fight was avoided after negotiations led by the two archbishops, Wulfstan of York on the one hand and Wulfhelm of Canterbury on the other. However, this was not a bargaining of equals and Edmund was forced to hand back the Five Boroughs to Óláfr. Wales was also problematic. Idwal Foel, king of Gwynedd, allied himself with Óláfr and no doubt revelled in this turn of events, although he would be killed the following year in battle against the English.

Óláfr also pushed north, sacking the ancient religious establishment at Tyninghame near Dunbar.[1] However, his time was running out. He died in 941, leaving the way open for Edmund to launch a vigorous counterattack which succeeded in recapturing the Five Boroughs, an act that was celebrated with another rare example of poetry in the *ASC*. One intimation in this poem is particularly interesting as it suggests that Edmund rescued the Christian Danes in the Danelaw from persecution by pagan Northumbrians. Not that we should think of the Northumbrians as being pro-English or pro-West Saxon; matters were not that simple. Óláfr' was married to the daughter of the powerful Northumbrian earl Orm. This is undoubtedly a Norse name, but the daughter had the decidedly Anglo-Saxon name Aldgyth. And the moneyers in York were men with Anglo-Saxon names like Æthelferth and Rathulf, though they seem to have adapted very easily to the frequent regime changes.[2]

A new Viking king in York, also named Óláfr (Sihtricsson), took over in 943. However, his rule was not uncontested. He had two rivals in the city,

Ragnall and Sihtric. They all issued coins of the same design, which might suggest that they exercised some kind of joint rule. Óláfr was sponsored by Edmund at his baptism in 943 and given splendid gifts. Sometime later, Edmund was also present at the confirmation of Ragnall and adopted him as his son.[3] But the year after, he moved on York and took it with the aid of Archbishop Wulfstan and Æthelmund, the ealdorman of Mercia. Both Óláfr and Ragnall are reported to have fled, though no mention is made of Sihtric, the third part of the old triumvirate, who had presumably either been deposed or had died in the interim.[4]

Henry of Huntingdon suggests that the attack on York was in retaliation for raids that Óláfr and Ragnall had recently launched against Edmund's kingdom.[5] These events reveal that Northumbria was still far from properly assimilated into this new country called England. Edmund determined to safeguard his northern borders by a strike against Strathclyde, implying that the Viking attackers of York may have had support from that direction. The campaign was brutal. Two sons of the king of Strathclyde were blinded, and Edmund then handed the kingdom to Malcolm, who had succeeded to the Scottish throne after Brunanburh, on condition that the Scottish king would be 'his co-operator both on sea and on land'.[6] It was said that this was because 'he was unable permanently to subjugate the people of that province, a treacherous and lawless people'.[7]

During Edmund's reign, several men of influence rose to power. The most prominent of them was Æthelstan, known as Half-King, an East Anglian ealdorman. Although his territory was in East Anglia, his family's antecedents were in Mercia and Wessex. Yet the area he governed was far bigger than that traditionally associated with East Anglia, hence his nickname. He had already been an ealdorman since 932 but in Edmund's reign two of his brothers, Æthelwold and Eadric, also became ealdormen in southern England. The eldest brother, Ælfstan, had also been an ealdorman but had not survived for long. It has been suggested that he may have died on King Æthelstan's Scottish campaign of 934.[8]

The Half-King's territories included a number that had only recently been part of the Danelaw. King Æthelstan had wanted a strongman ruling in these newly acquired lands, and clearly the ealdorman fitted the bill. Some historians have suggested that by putting so much power in the hands of one family Edmund made a rod for his own back or, more accurately perhaps, for the rulers who came after him. The complicated relationship between the family of the Half-King and another, that of ealdorman Ælfhere, created significant problems in the years ahead. Edmund's mother Eadgifu also re-emerged from the shadows and appears to have been an important influence on the king. That said, the former territories of the Danelaw remained largely trouble-free when the Half-King was in charge, something which allowed Edmund to recover the territories he had lost as well as subduing Strathclyde. This would not have been possible without the ealdorman's strong government.

The Half-King was also a strong supporter of several emerging Church reformers. The most famous of them was Dunstan, who would become a colossus of the English Church across several decades. It was during Edmund's reign that he was made abbot of Glastonbury, which was to become a powerhouse of the reform movement. However, Edmund and Dunstan did not always see eye to eye. There had been a major falling-out between them at Cheddar when 'Edmund in a great rage ordered him to be stripped of every office and also deprived of every honour'. Dunstan had prepared to go into exile, not for the first nor the last time in his life. But then Edmund's life was saved by a miracle. He was out hunting when he lost control of his horse, which threatened to go tumbling over the steep cliffs of Cheddar Gorge before pulling up at the very last moment. Edmund took this as a sign to repair damaged relations with Dunstan and therefore, instead of facing exile, the churchman was installed at Glastonbury. He would be joined there by Æthelwold, another notable reformer of the future.

Church reform was in the air but had not yet fully taken root in England. In 944 Edmund granted refuge to some monks from St Bertin's who were fleeing from a stricter form of monasticism in Europe and were granted an establishment in Bath. It is likely that Edmund was well disposed to monks from St Bertin's given that they had treated the body of his half-brother, the drowned Edwin, with such honour. Dunstan had some powerful friends in his reforming efforts: Æthelstan Half-King and his brothers would be particularly generous benefactors of his establishment at Glastonbury.

With his spectacular turnround in fortunes, Edmund could look further afield. Emulating his half-brother Æthelstan, he fostered important relationships with major continental powers. Louis IV, who had grown up in exile in England at Æthelstan's court, had now returned to mainland Europe and become king of West Francia. He had been captured in a raid by the Danish prince Harald – later King Harald Bluetooth – and then held captive by Hugh, a Frankish duke. Edmund intervened on Louis's behalf along with his brother-in-law Otto, the king of East Francia. Louis was eventually released, though only after handing over the important town of Laon.

It had been a remarkable start to the reign. After a shaky beginning Edmund had quickly restored the dynasty's fortunes, offering great promise for the years ahead. He issued three legal codes in just a few years, carrying forward the traditions of Æthelstan's time. Clearly the late king had been an excellent mentor for his younger half-brother. Penalties against non-celibate churchmen were introduced, including depriving them of burial in consecrated ground. There was also an interesting emphasis on sorcery and idolatry and a prohibition on the use of magical drugs. The law codes also provide further compelling evidence that these were times of significant violence and lawbreaking (though there are intimations that levels of theft were at least dropping). Cattle rustling appears to have been a significant issue. Slaves were to be particularly harshly punished if they were involved in thieving. If there was a group involved, the leader should be hanged whilst the rest should be scourged three times, scalped and have their little finger mutilated as a permanent reminder of their crime.

Feuds were to be prohibited provided that suitable *wergild* (a form of compensation, the values of which were linked to a victim's social status) was handed over. The well-known twentieth-century historian Dorothy Whitelock suggested that this was partly due to the influx of Viking settlers, as feuding was a core part of Scandinavian life at the time. Murderers were forbidden from coming into the king's presence unless they had done penance. Indeed, murder was to be seen as an offence against the king's person. It was an impressive set of laws and Edmund would be later regarded as a wise lawmaker.

In 945, Edmund visited the shrine of Cuthbert at Chester-le-Street, emulating Æthelstan by making generous gifts there. He left two gold bracelets for the saint and two lengths of costly Greek cloth. William of Malmesbury suggests that he brought relics of the Northumbrian saint Aidan to Glastonbury. Edmund also exhibited the same love of learning that Æthelstan and Alfred had formerly shown. The Canterbury school of Archbishop Oda, a man who appeared to be of Danish descent and therefore a symbol of the emerging nation of England, won widespread praise for its standards of learning. Oda was also an example of something else, a holy man who was also a warrior – according to some interpretations he may have even fought at Brunanburh.[9] As an archbishop whose period in office would span three successive reigns, he was part of the cement that would help to hold together the fledgling English nation. Oda's background powerfully demonstrates the folly of viewing the Vikings in England as one coherent group. Those who were largely of Danish descent in Mercia and East Anglia may have assimilated more easily into the new country than those of Hiberno-Norse (and originally Norwegian) stock in Northumbria.

Edmund also did his part in propagating the dynasty. His first wife, Ælfgifu, was mother to two sons and later kings, Eadwig (often referred to as 'Edwy') and Edgar. She died in 944 and was buried in Shaftesbury Abbey, of which she was a benefactor. She later became a saint. Edmund married again to Æthelflæd of Damerham, daughter of ealdorman Ælfgar. The king was now in his mid-twenties, in the prime of life, and his people looked forward to a long and successful reign.

But then the applecart was upset in the most dramatic fashion. Edmund was holding court at Pucklechurch in Gloucestershire on 26 May 946. It was the feast day of Augustine, the apostle to England back in 597. A known troublemaker called Leofa was present, and he had an altercation with Edmund's steward. The steward appeared to be getting the worst of it, so Edmund intervened. It was a fatal move. There was a flurry of blows, and a knife was drawn. Leofa struck out against the king, who fell to the ground mortally wounded. Leofa was 'shortly torn limb from limb by the attendants who rushed in, though he wounded some of them ere they could accomplish their purpose'.[10] In the end, this promising young king had been struck down in a common brawl (though some historians have claimed that this was a planned political assassination). He was buried at Glastonbury, further suggesting a reconciliation between the king and Dunstan after their troubles earlier in his reign. The abbot apparently knew in advance that Edmund was dead, having been taunted by a devil with the news whilst he had been out riding.

Eadred – The Last of the Sons of Edward

The sudden and unexpected demise of Edmund came as a shock, particularly given the tawdry way in which it happened. The late king had sons, but their tender years meant that they were unsuitable candidates to succeed him. Fortunately, King Edward's prodigious virility meant that there was a ready-made successor in the shape of Eadred, his last surviving son. According to the *ASC* he was quick to stamp his mark on the kingdom, subduing Northumbria and persuading the Scots by one means or another to renew their oaths with England.[11]

In 947, Eadred met the leading men of Northumbria at Tanshelf, near Pontefract in the West Riding of Yorkshire. They were led by Wulfstan, the archbishop of York, who had demonstrated well-developed Machiavellian characteristics over the years. He was about to do so again. Although he and other leading Northumbrian councillors swore pledges of allegiance to Eadred, subsequent events showed such promises to be largely worthless. A new Viking candidate had emerged as a potential king of Northumbria in the form of Erik, often associated with a larger-than-life character known as Erik Bloodaxe.

It should be said that not all historians accept that Erik, king of Jorvik, is the same man as Erik Bloodaxe. Erik Bloodaxe was the son of the famous early Norwegian king, Harald Finehair. The 'E' (Peterborough) version of the *ASC* refers to Erik as being the son of a man named Harald, so this is good circumstantial evidence.[12] However, opponents of the theory that the Northumbrian Erik was of the Bloodaxe variety suggest that too much is being made of much later sagas that argued in favour of it.[13] If indeed this was Erik Bloodaxe, then he had enjoyed a dramatic career. On the death of Harald Finehair, Erik seemed to be in pole position to take his place in Norway. But he was outwitted by the teenage Hákon, the young boy who had been fostered at the court of Æthelstan. Forced to flee Norway, Erik sailed west, raiding in Orkney and mainland Scotland before arriving in Northumbria.

Eadred reacted to this news in the manner expected of a grandson of Alfred. He descended on Northumbria in 948 like an avenging angel, an appropriate metaphor given that Erik most likely remained a pagan Viking warrior and warlord like some of the great men of old. Devastation followed in Eadred's wake. Whilst details are scant, the few that survive give the impression of a calculated reign of terror. The later chronicler John of Wallingford tells of 'burned down towns, razed fortifications, slaughtered opposition and arrested suspects'. William of Malmesbury says that he '[laid] waste the whole province with sword and famine'.[14] Perhaps most shockingly of all, Ripon, associated with Wilfrid, one of the giants of the early Anglo-Saxon church, was burned. Clearly its venerable heritage was not sufficient to protect it from the retribution Eadred felt Northumbria deserved given the treachery of its leaders. It is quite possible that Wilfrid had become something of an icon of Northumbrian separatism; he was renowned for his supreme self-confidence which to some observers suggested that he was answerable to nobody except for God, and this may have inspired emulation by the people of the region.

The church was a splendid building originally built in the seventh century along the lines of an Italian basilica (the crypt still remains). However, intriguingly, relatively recent archaeological finds suggest a strong contemporary Scandinavian impact on the tenth-century building, with carved heads of Norse images such as Sigurd the Dragon-Slayer and Fafnir, the beast he killed. Perhaps some zealots in the Anglo-Saxon army – including the king himself – felt that the Northumbrians had sold their soul to the devil. Oda, the archbishop of Canterbury, helped himself to the relics of St Wilfrid and took them back to Kent. This may have been to protect them, as he himself suggested, but equally it removed a focal point for those of a Northumbrian separatist persuasion.

Northumbrian sensibilities were outraged by this act. As the Anglo-Saxon army moved back south, probably laden down with booty, it crossed over the Aire at Castleford, a strategically important place since Roman times at least. Before the rearguard could make the crossing, it was ambushed and suffered heavy losses. This infuriated Eadred who resolved to move north again and unleash even greater devastation on the region. There was a ferocity about his manner that deeply disturbed the Northumbrian leadership. They abandoned Erik and sued for peace, being required to pay significant compensation for their attempted desertion of Eadred.[15] Later garbled Norwegian accounts mention that Erik took himself off to Spain. Contemporary accounts of visitors to Iberia at the time mention large numbers of European slaves, including soldiers in the armies of the local emirs who ruled there as well as women for their harems. This was part of a vast slave-trading network flowing through Sweden, with Scandinavian traders travelling as far away as Bokhara and Samarkand to sell their human wares. It is very likely that if Erik did go to Spain for a time this was the brutal commerce with which he busied himself.

In truth, Northumbria was far from subdued. Erik had been driven out but not decisively finished. Neither was he the only Viking candidate to be king in York. According to the Peterborough version of the *ASC*, in 949 a familiar figure in the shape of Óláfr Sihtricsson took over in the city. Clearly, however crushing Eadred's campaign of the previous year might have seemed to be, it was insufficient to ensure that Northumbria had been irrevocably incorporated into England. Óláfr held on to power until 952, and when he was ousted it was not Eadred who succeeded him but the previously exiled Erik. Alternatively, perhaps Óláfr had acted as a pliant puppet king, recognising Eadred's ultimate overlordship in a role reversal from previous times when Viking rulers had been the masters.

According to the saga writers, during his time in Northumbria Erik came into contact with that self-proclaimed hero at Brunanburh, the warrior-poet Egil Skallagrimsson. The two men detested each other. Egil had been disgusted at some of Erik's actions and at one stage erected a scorn-pole, a mark of disdain topped by a horse's head, as a token of his disrespect. Unfortunately for him, his ship later ran aground in the mouth of the Humber Estuary. He therefore found himself at the far-from-tender mercies of his archenemy. Erik's wife Gunnhild wanted Egil killed at once, but Erik delayed. He was persuaded to let Egil plead for his life through the medium of poetry. Egil – now the *skald* rather than the soldier – came up with moving words which he delivered with passion and skill. It is indeed a masterpiece of *skaldic* verse, full of colourful descriptions of battle:

> The web of spears
> did not stray from their course
> above the king's
> bright row of shield.
> The shore groaned,
> pounded by the flood
> of blood, resounded
> under the banners' march.

He went on to say how:

> Ravens flocked
> to the reddened sword,
> spears plucked lives
> and gory shafts sped.
> The scourge of Scots
> fed the wolves that trolls ride,
> Loki's daughter, Hel,
> trod the eagle's food.

The poem and its delivery saved Egil's head. The incident may be of unlikely historical veracity but is worth retelling for the descriptive brilliance of the verse alone.[16]

It was not until 954 that Erik was driven out of Northumbria for good. In this year, according to Roger of Wendover, 'King Eric [*sic*] was treacherously killed by Earl Maccus in a certain lonely spot which is called Stainmore, with his son Haeric and his brother Ragnald, betrayed by Earl Oswulf' (the latter being the lord of Bamburgh).[17] Stainmore is to be found in the remote recesses of Edendale between Catterick and Carlisle – wild, inhospitable border country back then. Maccus is a name with Scandinavian origins. Treachery, death at the hands of a fellow Viking, a major bloodletting of Erik's dynasty, falling in battle in a remote spot; all of this was a suitably dramatic end for a larger-than-life Viking. As is so often the case, the details of his demise are confused by a number of colourful and often contradictory elements in later sagas. One such saga was devoted to Erik, known as the *Eiriksmal*. It describes how

Erik, after his death, was welcomed by the gods into Valhalla with the following words: 'Hail to you Erik, be welcome here and come into the hall, gallant king!'[18]

Yet there is a paradox here. There are other records of how Erik, emulating Æthelstan and Edmund, journeyed to Chester-le-Street where he offered up gifts at the sacred tomb of Cuthbert. This reflected the reality that Viking culture was at something of a crossroads. Christianity had started to impress itself noticeably in the latter years of the ninth century. The trend had accelerated in the tenth century but there are many signs that ostensible converts to the new religion continued to hedge their bets by retaining vestiges of their previous beliefs. Perhaps Erik echoed this to some extent by having a foot in both worlds, the old and the new.

The ultimate demise of Erik may owe something to Archbishop Wulfstan's absence from York in these crucial days. He had made the mistake of journeying south at a time when many who were living there believed that he was behind the semi-permanent state of unrest in Northumbria. It is easy to believe that, given what we know of him and his personality, he saw himself as a kingmaker and acted accordingly. Certainly, many in Wessex and Mercia seemed to think so. Once Wulfstan arrived in the south, he could not be allowed to go back to Northumbria again. He was placed well out of harm's way at a place called Iudanbyrig, which some believe to be Bradwell-on-Sea. On a salty promontory in Essex, it was a long way from any major thoroughfare. Short of locking up the archbishop in a dungeon, it would be difficult to think of a place where Wulfstan would be more isolated from the mainstream.

Another candidate for Wulfstan's place of exile is Jedburgh in the border country between England and Scotland.[19] In any case, he would eventually be released to live out his days as the bishop of Dorchester-on-Thames in Oxfordshire. He would die an exile, in emulation of his possibly subconscious role model Wilfrid. He passed away on 16 December 956 and was buried at Oundle near Peterborough. His episcopal role in York was effectively assumed by Oskytel, a relative of Oda, archbishop of Canterbury, and another man with Scandinavian antecedents. He was a close ally of Dunstan, the abbot of Glastonbury, and would remain as archbishop of York until 972. It was a very sensible appointment given that many of the peoples of the areas for which he was responsible in Northumbria and the Danelaw were, like him, of Scandinavian descent.

Eadred also helped advance the career of another religious reformer in the shape of Æthelwold, who was put in charge of the re-founded establishment at Abingdon. Although he was a close friend of Dunstan,

Æthelwold appears to have been the more ascetic of the two, desiring a simple monastic life based on the model of Fleury in Francia which in turn had emulated the powerhouse at Cluny. The king took a close personal interest in rebuilding Abingdon's monastery; sources mention one occasion when he visited with a party of Northumbrians, including the titillating detail that they partook of a rather extravagant drinking session involving copious amounts of mead.[20]

That this was still not a fully united country was evidenced in 952 when Eadred ransacked Thetford in revenge for the killing of an abbot named Eadhelm. Thetford was in East Anglia, which had of course been under Viking rule for a time. Eadred clearly wanted to send a strong signal that he would not tolerate insubordination from his subjects. By 955, his scribes felt confident enough to start using the title of 'ruler of the whole of Britain' on his charters, an epithet which had not been in common use since the glory days of Æthelstan.[21] But his reign came to an early end in November 955 when he died at Frome in Somerset after a sustained period of illness. It was said of him that 'he endured with patience his frequent bodily pains', suggesting that he had not enjoyed good health for a while.[22] Several sources hint at a chronic stomach condition.[23]

Eadred had been a good friend to Dunstan, the abbot of Glastonbury, who presided over the late king's burial in the Old Minster at Winchester. His premature demise in his early thirties was part of an increasingly worrying trend where English kings were dying before their time. Sadly for the English, the trend was to continue. Eadred was unmarried and therefore left no immediate heirs. Henry of Huntingdon wrote that he was 'an exemplary and powerful king'.[24] Certainly, he gave promise that he might have indeed become one, but his reign was marked by unfulfilled potential through no fault of his own. He bequeathed £1,600 to his bishops, to be used either to help his people in the event of famine or to resist a 'heathen army' if required – a revealing insight into the challenges of the period.[25] Whilst the Viking threat had been overcome for the time being, there were clearly fears that it had not completely disappeared.

Divided and Reunited

Two sons of Edmund and Ælfgifu were available as prospective kings: Eadwig, the eldest, and Edgar. Though both young (no older than their mid-teens when Eadred died), by the standards of the time they were roughly old enough to rule. The crown was passed to Eadwig, but his inexperience would soon reveal itself. Edgar, the younger brother, seems to have possessed the greater intellect or at least the greater political acumen. He would soon be seen as a preferable alternative to his older brother in many quarters. Eadwig's reign, which would be brief, also saw a changing of the guard. Not only did Archbishop Wulfstan die, so too did Æthelstan Half-King who would withdraw from the world and live out his days as a monk at Glastonbury. He would be replaced as ealdorman of East Anglia by his son Æthelwold. Three other ealdormen would emerge to play prominent roles for some time to come: Byrhtnoth of Essex, Ælfhere of Mercia and Ælfheah of Hampshire. The ageing Queen Eadgifu was also deprived of power, though she would later return to some semblance of it during the later reign of Edgar. She would never completely reverse her change in fortune, but she would still be witnessing charters as late as 966.

Soon after Eadwig became king, there was a major falling-out between him and Dunstan. Some accounts state that Dunstan was sent into exile by 'Edwy, king of the Angles'. Dunstan went to a place known as Blandunum, which is St Pierre de Gand in Ghent, Flanders, a foundation that would subsequently be generously supported by Edgar. It was a Benedictine monastery at a time when church reform was in full swing. Views on key religious practices were changing rapidly, involving matters such as who was and was not appropriate to marry. The monastery had been generously supported by Arnulf, count of Flanders, who was a grandson of Alfred through his daughter Ælfthryth and an enthusiastic backer of the reform movement.

There are several possible reasons behind Dunstan's exile. One account says that at his coronation feast Eadwig absented himself from the festivities for some time. He was found in incriminating circumstances with a young noblewoman, Ælfgifu, and her mother Æthelgifu. According to some accounts, Eadwig was attracted to both women; Roger of Wendover said 'both of whom it is reported, though horrible to repeat, he in turn made the subject of his base passions'. Supposedly this *menage a trois* was discovered and Dunstan did not hold back in his criticism of the king's inappropriate behaviour. This is not surprising if he had indeed, as recorded, walked in on the threesome to find the crown unceremoniously flung on the floor and 'the king wallowing in filthiness between the two women'.[26] Æthelgifu was particularly vocal in her response to his criticisms, but an early biographer of Dunstan asserts that she was later lynched at Gloucester.[27]

This at least is one version of the events that led to Dunstan's exile. A less salacious interpretation is that a young sixteen-year-old like Eadwig did not like being bossed around by a strongly opinionated churchman. After all, Dunstan had a track record of falling out with kings. The late king's support of Dunstan in the last part of his reign may also have generated a degree of resentment in some quarters. However, Dunstan would have the last laugh. Eadwig later married Ælfgifu but the marriage did not last long. In 958 they were divorced by Archbishop Oda on the grounds that they were too closely related.[28] That, at least, is one explanation; another, offered by Simeon of Durham, is that they were never actually married at all but that Eadwig 'loved her wantonly under the character of a wife'. In the latter case no divorce would be needed. But the fact that she was related to the *ætheling* Æthelwold, who had died half a century before whilst trying to displace Alfred's son Edward, may not have helped either as members of the opposing faction may have had long memories. All things considered, the fact that the church was able to insist that the king lived apart from his chosen partner, wife or not, suggests a degree of weakness in Eadwig's rule. During the latter part of his life, Archbishop Oda seems to have absented himself from court in another visible mark of his disapproval.[29]

According to Simeon of Durham, the rift with Dunstan also helped create a split in the government of England, with only Wessex remaining in Eadwig's hands. Mercia and Northumbria opted to support Edgar, who was quick to recall Dunstan from exile once he came to power in these regions. Charters from the period refer to Edgar as being 'king of the Mercians, the Northumbrians and the British' – that is, everywhere except Wessex. Soon after, when the bishopric of Worcester was up for grabs after the death of the current incumbent, Ceonwald, Archbishop Oda placed Dunstan in the role. Yet the division of the kingdom between the two brothers was maybe not quite as antagonistic as some chroniclers make out. Although there are a number of charters issued in Edgar's name after the division, he seems not to have issued coinage in his own right, which would have been an important mark of kingly independence at the time. Maybe this was an agreed division, with Edgar as a junior partner.[30] After all, there were precedents from earlier in Anglo-Saxon history.

Eadwig appointed his own men into positions of authority as they became vacant. One of them, Byrhtnoth, became an ealdorman in East Anglia, though he may have been descended from the Mercian royal family. Men with similar names who rose to senior positions may have come from the same family group, for example those called Byrhthelm, one of whom briefly became archbishop of Canterbury and another bishop of Winchester.[31] Such naming conventions, whereby family members were given similar names, is a regular feature of Anglo-Saxon culture. Byrhtnoth proved to have real staying power, being near the top of the tree for the best part of four decades. He would become an Anglo-

Saxon hero by his loyalty and later death at the epic battle of Maldon at a time when the Viking threat began to grow again. Another man who first emerged during Eadwig's reign was the chronicler Æthelweard, who was related to Ælfgifu, possibly her brother. There was also a newly appointed ealdorman, Ælfhere, whose arrival was sudden, with few mentions of him before Eadwig became king. This could be interpreted as a king faced with serious opposition attempting to build his support base by appointing men who owed their position to him.

One notable aspect of Eadwig's reign was his generous granting of lands. Eighty-five surviving charters from his reign have been found, though some of them are now believed to be forgeries. No less than twenty-four (again with some probable fakes included) were to churches. These included grants to Shaftesbury, Wilton, Bath, Abingdon, and the New Minster at Winchester. Archbishop Oda was also given extensive lands around Ely, which had become part of the king's patrimony after the reconquest of East Anglia from the Vikings. Sixty of these charters were issued in the first year of his reign. Giving away so much so early can be seen as a mark of political naiveite on the young king's part. It could also be indicative of a king whose position was weak and who desperately needed to secure allies.[32]

Then, in 958, Oda died. The chronicler noted that he 'was a man of truly distinguished talent and renowned virtue and abounding in the spirit of prophecy ... he departed from worldly affairs, and was carried by the hands of angels to paradise'.[33] It is a remarkable epitaph for a man who was the son of a Viking invader. Within a generation, someone who might formerly have been attacking England had become part of the mainstream establishment governing it. He was succeeded as head of the English church by Ælfsige, who was opposed to the reform movement. Supporters of the latter may have thought it quite appropriate that he froze to death soon after when crossing the Alps to pick up his pallium, a band of white wool symbolically bestowed on a new archbishop by the Pope in Rome. Some accounts suggest that he tried to save himself by thrusting his feet into the belly of a dead horse but that these desperate measures were in vain.

Eadwig himself died on 1 October 959, marking the end of another short reign and reinforcing a worrying pattern. Buried in the New Minster at Winchester, he was succeeded by Edgar. It is possible that his death may have not come through natural causes; the chronicler Æthelweard, who was related to the discarded Ælfgifu, glosses over Eadwig's short reign with perfunctory brevity which may be born of a degree of embarrassment. He simply notes that he was known as 'the All Fair' for his great beauty. It takes him just two sentences to breeze through the events of those times, the second of which states 'he held the kingdom continuously for four years, and deserved to be loved'.[34] It was a positive comment but not an unsurprising one if the chronicler owed his advancement to Eadwig. That said, Æthelweard appears to have been a born survivor. His importance increased when Edgar replaced Eadwig as king despite the tensions there had been between the two factions supporting either side. In the future, when Edgar was succeeded by his son Edward (later 'saint and martyr'), Æthelweard would become ealdorman of the Western Shires despite there being other candidates for the role.

His is a very different point of view than that of other contemporary commentators. England's divisions at the time were revealing themselves as much on parchment as they were on the ground. Roger of Wendover, writing centuries after the event, took a very different view in his unequivocal analysis of Eadwig: 'After oppressing the English during a lascivious and tyrannical reign of four years, he died by the just judgement of God, and was interred in the new Minster at Winchester.' 'Florence' of Worcester adopts a similar approach, saying that the Mercians and Northumbrians threw off the rule of Eadwig because they were 'disgusted at the folly of his government'. William of Malmesbury also pulled no punches, calling him a 'lascivious boy'. He has a further axe to grind regarding the fate of his own abbey at Malmesbury, which Eadwig turned 'into a sty for secular canons' though he redeemed himself in the chronicler's eyes to some extent by erecting an elaborate shrine there to St Aldhelm. Despite this positive caveat, his true feelings about Eadwig are barely concealed, putting his deficiencies down to 'the giddiness of youth, and the pernicious counsel of his concubine, who was perpetually poisoning his uninformed mind'.

It is perhaps unsurprising that a king who had been bold enough to exile a Christian paragon like Dunstan, whether justified or not, earned the opprobrium of some commentators.[35] Others mention him only briefly and suggest that he would have made a good king had he lived longer. Henry of Huntingdon stated that 'the king wore the diadem not unworthily; but after a prosperous and becoming commencement of his reign, its happy promise was cut short by a premature death'.[36] We are at the mercy of our surviving sources, and these are scant indeed for Eadwig's reign. But there is sufficient evidence to suggest that his reign was divisive. It is worth remembering the old maxim that history is written by the victors, and ultimately it was Edgar who emerged victorious in the confrontation with his older brother (if such it was) by the mere fact of his survival. Subsequent commentators who were favourable to Edgar would find it difficult to be objective about Eadwig, particularly as Edgar was a champion of the church reform movement, which was closely associated with some of the chroniclers. A story later grew up that Edgar had seen the ruins of Abingdon Abbey before he became king and resolved that if he were ever to come to the throne he would restore the battered glories of the English church.

Edgar was sixteen when he became sole king, and his reign would set a benchmark for all rulers to follow. The chronicler in version 'E' (Peterborough) of the *ASC* noted that 'he became greatly honoured wide throughout the land of the nation, for he readily honoured God's name ... and counselled all his nation wisely'. One of his early acts after becoming sole ruler seems to have been to remove some of Eadwig's men from power or at least from influence. Ealdorman Ælfric, probably responsible for Kent and Sussex, only appeared in 957 and disappears abruptly from charter lists after Edgar became king. Other prominent men from Eadwig's time slip down the order of priority on the witness list, typically reflecting a diminution in importance. Conversely, gifts made to known supporters of Edgar from his time in Mercia after his succession to the whole kingdom represent the opposite side of the coin.[37]

Viking raids had more or less disappeared off the radar by this stage, but there is one intriguing reference to an event in 962 when King Sigferth 'fell upon himself and his body lies at Wimborne'. The identity of this man is uncertain, though the name is not uncommon amongst Northumbrian Vikings. Somebody of the name attests a charter in Eadred's reign in 955.[38] Perhaps he was a hostage or a prisoner; his suicide does not suggest a happy time for him in Wimborne in any case. That same year saw a major pestilence and a large fire in London that destroyed St Paul's minster.

With war for the time being not on the agenda, religious reform moved up the list. On 29 November 962, Æthelwold was made bishop of Winchester. He was consecrated by Dunstan, now archbishop of Canterbury. In fact, a powerful triumvirate of reforming monks soon occupied key positions in the shape of the archbishop of Canterbury (Dunstan) and the bishops of Winchester (Æthelwold) and Worcester (Oswald, who would later become archbishop of York whilst continuing to hold on to Worcester at the same time).[39]

It did not take Æthelwold long to make his mark. The religious reform movement was about to sweep across England, and he seemed to be the most austere and fundamentalist of all the reformers then in the country. The church at Winchester was run by clerics, not monks, but Æthelwold ordered them to observe monastic rules or get out. He then approached Edgar and asked for permission to restore some of the monastic establishments that had been destroyed in Viking raids. Edgar fully supported him and secular canons were ejected not just from the Old and New Minsters in Winchester but also from Chertsey Abbey in Surrey and Milton Abbey in Dorset. Just a few decades later, in the 990s, Bryhtferth, abbot of Ramsey in East Anglia, would estimate that the king was behind the establishment of more than forty monasteries in his reign (including his own, which was planted with some monks transferred from Westbury in Wiltshire and had Æthelwine, son of Æthelstan Half-King, as a founder and benefactor).[40]

Æthelwold then focussed his attention on Ely. Having set up a monastery there, he appointed a brother called Byrhtnoth to be its head. He did the same at Peterborough, another victim of Viking raids, and 'found nothing there but old walls and wild woods'. Ealdwulf was installed as the abbot at the restored foundation that he caused to be set up there. The *ASC* for 963 in the Peterborough version gives a very detailed list of the lands and privileges granted by the king to the new St Peter's monastery, a lengthy exposition which is understandable given the vested interest that this particular chronicler had in the matter. When Oswald, archbishop of York, died later, Ealdwulf took his place.

We can get some idea of who Edgar relied on for counsel from charter witnesses where documentation has survived the ravages of time. One interesting aspect to this is that there is a notable absence of Scottish and Welsh kings acting as charter witnesses in contrast to Æthelstan's reign. One significant inclusion as a witness to Edgar's charter was his third wife, Ælfthryth (often Latinised as 'Elfrida'). After their marriage in 964, Ælfthryth and Edgar soon had a son of their own, Edmund. In a charter dated to 966 he is referred to as *clito legitimus*, 'legitimate prince', and his name appears above that of his older half-brother Edward. Such things mattered in Anglo-Saxon times. It implied that Edmund was seen to have a superior status to Edward, which could be significant when it came to the time to consider the succession. This particular chicken would come home to roost in spectacular fashion. A younger son, Æthelred, would later arrive and would be named specifically in Edgar's will along with Edmund. In the event, Edmund died in 971 and was buried in Romsey Abbey so he would not be alive to stake a claim. Any reference to Edward in Edgar's will, however, was pointedly omitted.[41]

It was not unknown in Anglo-Saxon times for a woman to act as a charter witness, but it was unusual and it reflects the powerful personality of Ælfthryth, her senior status and the impact that she made on the king. She was the daughter of ealdorman Ordgar of Devon and the widow of

Æthelwold, son of Æthelstan Half-King, who was Edgar's foster brother. Edgar, who had lost his mother at a very young age, had been brought up in the Half-King's home which Æthelstan shared with his wife Ælfwynn. It has even been speculated that Ælfwynn might have been the daughter of Æthelred of Mercia and his wife Æthelflæd, the Lady of the Mercians, who had been ejected from her kingdom by King Edward.[42] Theirs was a very suitable household in which to bring up a future king.

There is a hint of scandal here, supplied by William of Malmesbury. In a tale that would do Hollywood proud, he relates that Ælfthryth was a woman of great beauty and that Edgar had heard of this before her previous marriage. He sent Æthelwold to report back to him about her qualities as a prospective wife and, as soon as the ealdorman saw her, he desired her for himself. He subsequently told Edgar that her beauty had been exaggerated, causing the king to lose interest, then married her. When later Edgar personally met her and observed her exquisite beauty he was enraged at the ealdorman's subterfuge. When he was out hunting soon after with Æthelwold at Wherwell in Hampshire, he 'ran him through with a javelin'.[43]

Edgar married Ælfthryth in 965. She would formally become his queen, atypical for West Saxon and latterly English consorts. He had been involved in two previous liaisons, both resulting in children. From the first with Æthelflæd a son, Edward, was born. From the second with Wulfthryth there was a daughter who would grow up to be St Edith of Wilton, a prominent religious figure of the period. There is an interesting story behind the second marriage. There were two sisters, Wulfhild and Wulfthryth, who were ancestors of King Æthelred I. Marriage to one of them would help strengthen Edgar's position given the instability of recent times. Edgar first tried his luck with Wulfhild but there was a problem: she was being educated at Wilton Abbey. This did not necessarily mean that she meant to become a nun, but she was not interested in the marriage proposal. She was locked in a room when visiting her grandmother and attempts were made to cajole her into the match. Instead she escaped from the house by climbing out through the sewers. Such determination convinced Edgar that he should try elsewhere, and he ended up marrying the other sister instead.[44] After the birth of Edith, Wulfthryth would take the veil and become abbess at Wilton, suggesting that her heart might not have been in the match from the outset. These events were not hushed up – indeed, Wulfthryth was escorted to Wilton in great ceremony with Edgar prominent. She was allowed to take her daughter with her. She was later reported to be very rich, Edgar presumably having paid her off extravagantly.

The Indian Summer

By 970 an interesting trend was emerging in Edgar's reign. As ealdormen grew old and died, Edgar was reluctant to replace them. He may have reasoned that the factions within his court, headed by ealdorman Ælfhere on the one hand and the sons of Æthelstan Half-King on the other, were threats to stability. This perhaps is one dynastic consideration behind his marriage to the daughter of Ordgar, ealdorman of Devon. By introducing a new dynastic element to the mix, he was potentially reducing the power of the two main blocs that already existed. The latter years of his reign appear to be characterised by a greater presence of men from the West Country at his court, a phenomenon that would be consistent with such a strategy.[45]

In the 970s Æthelwold wrote a treatise on the Old English Rule of St Benedict, clearly in support of the monastic reform that he was spearheading. In it, he also referred to Edgar as an example to be praised for the huge part he had played in bringing peace and security to his country.[46] The support of the most powerful members of the church in England, such as Æthelwold and Dunstan, gave Edgar legitimacy; and he was able to protect them and nurture the interests of the reform movement in return. It was an arrangement that was mutually advantageous.

A seminal event of Edgar's reign was his so-called 'coronation' at Bath in May 973. The long delay between the start of his rule and this event has historically been seen as a punishment for his sexual promiscuity with Wulfthryth, whom some accounts claim was a nun.[47] This makes little sense. After the death of Eadwig in 959, Edgar took on all the traditional trappings of an Anglo-Saxon ruler. England needed stability and denying the traditional coronation rites of a king would compromise this. More likely the 973 ceremony was a reaffirmation of Edgar's power and status, much as later medieval kings would be involved in a formal crown-wearing ritual to affirm and confirm their position. It is believed that a formal delegation had made its way from Edgar's court to Germany shortly before and its reports of some of the ceremonies witnessed there may have inspired the king.

The setting of a former imperial city like Bath could not have been more appropriate. Bath and its massive ruins had made a profound impression on the Anglo-Saxon psyche. A famous surviving poem from the period is believed to have been referring to it with its 'snapped rooftrees, towers fallen, the work of the Giants'.[48] Edgar further emphasised his power and his intentions to rule as a strong monarch with well-developed centralised control by introducing a uniform coinage across England. It was also probably no coincidence that Edgar had reached the age of thirty, the traditional age for ordaining a bishop and also the age at which Christ had left home and set out on his evangelizing mission. It was as if the king was putting himself in a position as a spiritual as well as a secular figurehead of his fledgling nation.

The most significant event of his reign in symbolic terms was when Edgar met six (or eight, depending on which version is to be believed) Scottish and Welsh kings in Chester. In the more romantic versions of this event, he was rowed along the Dee by the other kings in recognition of his authority over them whilst he took the helm of the boat as if symbolically steering the ship of state.[49] Writing just a couple of decades later, Byrhtferth of Ramsey wrote unequivocally that Edgar subdued 'the ferocious and foolish kings of the Scots and Welsh'. A twelfth-century account from Durham tells how Earl Oslac of York, a man of Scandinavian stock, and Eadwulf of Bamburgh escorted Cinead (Kenneth) II of Scotland to meet Edgar. In return for acknowledging Edgar's supremacy Cinead was given Lothian, a fiercely contested border territory for centuries. If this is correct, then not only was Edgar's reign giving shape to England – it was also contributing to the formation of Scotland, too.

Some charters from Edgar's reign include several witnesses with Scandinavian names.[50] Edgar came to the throne of a united kingdom with the strong support of the leading men of Mercia and Northumbria. In these regions there was of course a long-established Scandinavian presence. This has led some historians to suggest that the support of these Viking-derived elements came at a price that was extracted from Edgar in return. In 1976, Niels Lund suggested that Edgar might have allowed them to act with a certain degree of autonomy under his rule; this might explain an enigmatic comment in the *ASC* that '[Edgar] had bad, foreign habits, and brought heathen customs too fast into this land and attracted the alien here, and introduced a damaging people to this country'.[51]

This is a strange comment in some ways. The chronicler, who is writing after the event (his comments are retrospective but were included under the year 959, right at the beginning of Edgar's rule of a unified kingdom), clearly was unhappy at the king's accommodating approach towards foreign elements. It seems nonsensical to accuse Edgar of introducing a 'damaging people' to his country; Scandinavians had been regular visitors to England for over 150 years and Viking settlements went back eighty years at least. But perhaps Edgar was introducing a new Viking element, possibly in the form of mercenaries to help protect his throne.

This is speculative of course. What is not, though, is a reference in the laws known as 'IV Edgar':

> I will that such good laws be enforced among the Danes as they best prefer, and I have always granted them (this), and will grant (it) as long as my life endures, for your obedience which you have ever manifested to me.[52]

There is little ambiguity in this. It appears to be giving the 'Danes' a degree of autonomy in return for services rendered. It is also noteworthy that this is not a chronicler's interpretation of what was said or done but a law, devoid of sugar-coating or bias.

Whilst the Vikings may not have been actively raiding during Edgar's reign, their impact was undeniable. One major motivation for Æthelwold's reform programme was to rebuild after their past depredations. The *ASC* for 963 note that he approached Edgar and 'asked him that he would give him all the monasteries the heathen men had broken up earlier, because he wanted to restore it [the monastic life]; and the king happily granted it'. A charter granted to Malmesbury Abbey sheds further light on this issue, stating that Edgar was driven to repair the damage done previously with the thought that 'I should renew all the sacred monasteries in my kingdom. Not only are they visibly destroyed down to their wall tops with moss-cornered tiles and rotten roof beams, but also and more importantly, their insides have become almost completely neglected and emptied of worship of God.'[53]

Edgar also played a key role in developing a navy according to some sources. 'Florence' (or John) of Worcester quotes some highly suspect figures in his work, claiming that Edgar assembled a fleet of '3,600 stout ships' and that every year after Easter he would send three squadrons of 1,200 vessels each on a ceremonial procession along the west, east and north coasts respectively. There was therefore an annual circumnavigation of Britain reminding everyone that Edgar was in charge. Florence suggests that this took the form of a military exercise to ensure that England and its fleet stayed on a war footing. Whilst some of these comments should be taken with a very large pinch of salt, it is nevertheless plausible that the establishment of a strong fleet (even if the numbers seem very exaggerated) would have a powerful deterrent effect on any would-be raiders.[54]

Surviving records for Edgar's reign are sparse. There is perhaps one major reason for this, and that is that this was a period of tranquillity. With no major battles or controversies, to chroniclers it is almost as if there 'is nothing to see here'. Yet there was much to observe. This was a period when the dream of a country called England came to fruition. It seemed like the disturbances of yesteryear were confined to the past. In truth, they were anything but. Later chroniclers would view Edgar's reign as a golden age. Nearly two centuries later, William of Malmesbury would say that 'the transactions of his reign are celebrated with peculiar splendour even in our times'; and this after a complete regime change following the Norman triumph at Hastings.[55] In reality, it was an Indian summer for the dynasty of which Edgar was a paragon. If he had brought calm to his kingdom, it was very much a calm before the storm.[56] Chroniclers in times much closer to Edgar's than our own recognised as much, William of Malmesbury acknowledging that 'after his departure, the state and the hopes of the English met with a melancholy reverse'.[57]

There is an alternative view of Edgar's reign which has been put forward. The famous twentieth-century historian of the Anglo-Saxon period Sir Frank Stenton commented that it was a time largely devoid of incident. This view is supported by the description of Edgar as 'the Peaceable' or 'the Pacific'. But there are also suggestions that he could be ruthless. A reference by Lantfred of Winchester in about 975 to a law which meted out draconian mutilation to those found guilty of theft suggests that he was a strong, even severe king. The punishment to be meted out is gruesome in the extreme: the culprit would 'be tortured at length, by having his eyes put out, his hands cut off, his ears torn off, his nostrils carved open and his feet removed; and finally, with the skin and hair of his head shaved off, he would be abandoned in the open fields dead in respect of nearly all his limbs, to be devoured by wild beasts and birds and hounds of the night'.[58] This sounds like a king who ruled with a rod of iron, crushing dissent. If so, it is conceivable that once his strong hand had been removed, years of pent-up frustration would explode. His reign epitomised strength, but it may well have disguised an underlying fragility.

The storm was not long in coming after Edgar's premature and sudden death on 8 July 975 at just thirty-two years of age. The unexpected passing of Edgar led to an unusually philosophical entry in the *ASC*: 'Here Edgar, king of the English, ended earthly pleasures; he chose another light, radiant and happy, and abandoned this poor, this transitory, life.'[59]

Edgar was buried at Glastonbury, an unsurprising choice given its links with Dunstan, whose fortunes had been so closely linked to those of the late king. It was also the last resting place of Edmund, Edgar's father. This burial marked the rising power of Glastonbury in the English church too – after Dunstan's death in 988, the next six archbishops of Canterbury all had links to the abbey.[60] When Edgar's tomb was reopened in 1052 his body was found to be incorrupt, as befitted a man of his supposed piety and religious devotion.

Edgar had built up powerful support around him. Yet as always in such a situation there are losers as well as winners. His support for the reform movement had no doubt alienated those churchmen who lost out as a result, as well as their secular supporters. Edgar left behind two sons, both young. It was ultimately the elder, Edward, who took his place, even though it would seem he was not Edgar's choice. The stability of the realm quickly started to unravel. The problems appear to have started in Mercia, where ealdorman Ælfhere led a pushback against the reform movement, starting to undo some of the reforms instituted by Æthelwold there. There was then serious disruption in the north. Earl Oslac fled, leading some to speculate that he had been closely associated with Edgar (which may have been controversial as he was probably of Scandinavian stock). Perhaps this event is also linked to those enigmatic comments about Edgar's overreliance on foreign elements.[61] Byrhtferth is unequivocal in his comments on this period, suggesting that the kingdom was shaken, the bishops thrown into confusion, the ealdormen angry, the monks fearful and the people terrified, though the clerics were happy at the turn of events.[62] He paints an uncertain and disturbing picture which did not augur well (though he was writing in hindsight, so he may just have been wise after the event).

The impression is that of an inexperienced, youthful king struggling to keep on top of things. In fairness, Edward's youth meant that any criticism should be reserved more for his councillors, who were probably in charge of the day-to-day running of the kingdom. And in the background, there was a disappointed and ambitious stepmother who thought that her son should be king. Two distinct factions emerged. One, headed by Archbishop Dunstan and Ealdorman Æthelwold, supported Edward whilst the other, with adherents including Bishop Æthelwold and Ealdorman Ælfhere (connected by blood to Ælfthryth/Elfrida), backed the claims of Æthelred. The latter was not yet in his teens so there would need to be a regency in place until he reached adulthood should he become king. Despite this – or perhaps because of it – Æthelred attracted powerful supporters. Ironically given his later canonisation, King Edward had some outspoken near-contemporary critics. The writer of the *Life of St Oswald* reported that Edward 'inspired in all not only fear but even terror, for [he scourged the people] not only with words but truly with dire blows, and especially his own men dwelling with him'.[63] As always, this might not be literally the case – there is insufficient corroborating evidence to form a conclusion – but might just as likely reflect the factionalism that was threatening the stability of the country.

It took a year for Edward to be crowned. This was not unique in Anglo-Saxon history but may nevertheless suggest a great deal of dissension and manoeuvring. To add to the general sense of gloom there were several signs that even otherworldly powers were far from impressed at the state of affairs. One indicator, so beloved of contemporary chroniclers, was a comet in the sky. Another more unusual omen was observed at a council meeting at Calne in Wiltshire in 978. Discussions were in full flow on the upper floor of a building when suddenly it collapsed beneath the attendees. As if by a miracle, Dunstan was standing on a plank which stood firm, but many others were less fortunate. A number of the leading men of the kingdom, many supporters of Edward, were killed or badly injured. Yet another bad portent was a crop failure followed by famine.

On 18 March 978, Edward visited his stepmother at her home in Corfe, Dorset. This was a much humbler residence than the gaunt Norman ruin that stands there today, though it may have been at the top of the same hill, which is in a magnificent natural defensive position guarding a pass between two extensive ridges. The story of what happened next appears to have been considerably embellished over time. In the earliest account, that in the 'A' (Winchester) version of the *ASC*, the barest details are given, stating matter-of-factly that Edward was murdered. This early account does not even say where the momentous event took place, though slightly later versions say that it was at 'Corfe passage'.

Another, slightly later account in the *Life of St Oswald* gives more detail, describing an impromptu attack by an opportunistic group of political opponents, supporters of what might be called the 'Æthelred party'. Later versions would accrete additional details until the blame was put squarely on the shoulders of Edward's stepmother. Certainly it was her son who stood to gain the most.

It was an ominous start to Æthelred's reign, for he would duly become Edward's successor. Edward would soon be seen as a martyr and miracles were associated with his earthly remains which, after an initial humble and disrespectful interment at Wareham, were later transferred to a more appropriate resting place in the nunnery that Alfred had founded at Shaftesbury. Only with hindsight would the awful timing of these events become apparent. Just as England was starting to fall apart, a powerful new force was rising in Denmark, one which would in effect sign the death warrant of Alfred's dynasty and the Anglo-Saxon nation that it had forged.

9

Ragnarök

Alas, bright cup! Alas, burnished fighter! Alas, proud prince! How that
time has passed, dark under night's helm, as though it had never been!
'The Wanderer', Anglo-Saxon poem

The Road to Maldon – and Beyond

Æthelred was the last surviving male member of the line of direct
descent from Alfred, and he duly became king. The only remaining
male in the bloodline other than him was the chronicler Æthelweard,
who was a very distant descendant of Alfred's elder brother Æthelred
I, who had died over a century before. Yet the new king was a child
at a time when being governed by a child ruler could have disastrous
repercussions. The sighting of a comet in 978, 'which was sometimes
the colour of blood and other times fiery', added to the sense of
foreboding.[1] The killing of an anointed monarch, the event that led to
Æthelred's succession, was a heinous crime in the context of the times.
A papal pronouncement of 786 spoke in dire terms of the fate of those
responsible for such an act: 'Let no one dare to conspire to kill a king,
for he is the lord's anointed, and if anyone take part in such a crime ...
let him be expelled, everyone who has consented to such sacrilege shall
perish in the eternal fetters of anathema.'[2] If individuals were implicated
in such terrible acts and were subject to exemplary punishment as a
result, might not nations too be subject to divine retribution for
vicarious involvement in such awful events?

Signs of such a development were not long in coming. The Vikings seem
to have been in receipt of political intelligence which kept them informed

of developments that weakened the fabric of countries and regions that might make them more vulnerable to raids and attacks. The fragmentation of England after the death of Edgar seems to have happened at an alarming rate, and potential raiders were wise to this. During the reign of 'the Peaceable' there are very few signs of Viking attacks but in 980 a raid on an old target, Southampton, was recorded, and some accounts suggest that most of the citizens were either massacred or taken into captivity.[3] It was followed by others. A raid on St Petroc's monastery at Padstow in 981 was followed by others along the south coast of England, including at Portland (982) and Watchet (988). The latter led to the deaths of prominent local Anglo-Saxon thegns Goda and Strenwold. Despite these losses, the raiders apparently suffered more, and the defenders were victorious.[4] This suggests that the local *fyrd* had had some warning of the attack and had managed to assemble in time to fight it off.

These were initially small-scale raids, more like pirate attacks than anything else (seven ships were mentioned as being involved in the raid on Southampton, and only three on Portland).[5] In the wider political context they were more of an irritant than a major threat and many of them were concentrated in the period 980–982. The location of the raids suggest that the attacks were launched from one or more of now well-established Viking ports in Ireland. However, there was about to be a change in direction and a massive increase in scale.

Despite the very negative image of Æthelred that later developed, his actions in the early part of his reign were often sensible. In 991, Pope John XV negotiated a treaty between Æthelred and Duke Richard of Normandy. This was a wise move. Since the establishment of a Viking fiefdom in Normandy under Duke Rollo in the early tenth century, a new and highly dangerous power had emerged in the shape of the Normans. Their Viking roots made Normandy a perfect spot from which to launch raids on the nearby coasts including England's south-east. It was sensible to try and neutralise this threat as much as possible by depriving Viking raiders of Norman ports.

But the agreement with Normandy did little to deter more attacks, wherever they originated. An alarming fork in the road was reached in 991 when over ninety ships launched a major assault, setting up a base at Sandwich in Kent (which over the next two decades would reveal itself as a weak point in England's defences) and then moving up the coast of East Anglia to attack Ipswich. There were several thousand men in this force, posing a threat on a par with that presented by the Great Heathen Army in 865.

East Anglian defensive arrangements were in the hands of Ealdorman Byrhtnoth, and when the Viking fleet took up position in the Blackwater

Estuary the scene was set for one of the epic battles of the Anglo-Saxon era. The fight which followed at Maldon ratcheted up the pressure on Æthelred, now ruling in his own right having come of age and having effectively put his dominant mother into domestic exile soon after. But perhaps even more than this it led to the writing of what has become one of the iconic poems of the Anglo-Saxon period in the form of an extensive surviving fragment known as 'The Battle of Maldon'.

As well as being hauntingly evocative, the poem fragment tells us something about battles between Anglo-Saxons and Vikings, a rare ray of light on a subject generally obscured from view. Some of the details may owe something to poetic licence but it would be unwise to reject everything in it given the paucity of detail we have from other sources. The Vikings on their Northey Island base were separated from the East Anglian army that came up to meet them by a causeway. The Anglo-Saxon force was in a dominant position; it was virtually impossible for the enemy to cross the causeway given its narrowness. Several tried, but they were quickly cut down. The leader of the Viking host shouted across the waters, asking Byrhtnoth to let his men cross over and have a fair fight.

In what many considered a rash move, the ealdorman agreed to do so. Perhaps the elderly warrior believed in outmoded concepts of fair play or was simply complacent ('overswayed by his heart's arrogance' as the poet put it). An alternative explanation which is kinder to Byrhtnoth is that his force might quickly disintegrate if no battle was forthcoming and he might not get a better chance to face up to the enemy again in the near future. The Vikings moved across, formed their shield wall, and prepared for the fight. Byrhtnoth had already urged his men on in a rousing speech, telling them to dismount: 'Then he bade his men let go bridles, drive far the horses and fare forward.'

He reminded them of tactics, perhaps necessary for what was in effect a militia, not a professional army:

> Then Byrhtnoth dressed his band of warriors,
> from horseback told each man his task,
> where he should stand, how keep his station.
> he bade them brace their linden-boards [shields] aright,
> fast in finger-grip, and to fear not.
> Then when his folk was fairly ranked
> Byrhtnoth alighted where he loved best to be
> and was held most at heart – among hearth-companions.

The events that followed are described in some poetic detail, a battle of thrusting spears and slashing swords. Then Byrhtnoth was struck by a spear. A young warrior next to him, Wulfmær, pulled the spear out and reused it: 'In a flash he plucked from its place the blood-black point; again it flew. Home sank the steel, stretched on the plain him who had so late pierced the Prince [i.e. ealdorman] so grievously.' A Viking moved in nevertheless, intending to strip the fallen Byrhtnoth of his armour, his armbands and his ornate sword. The desperately wounded ealdorman did his best to fight back but it was useless, as we are told in graphic detail: 'One of the spoilers cut short the blow, his swing unstringing the Earl's sword-arm.'

Even as he lay dying, in true heroic fashion Byrhtnoth urged his men forward; but then reality breaks in on the poem. Dismayed, 'the lack-willed left the battlefield'. Some of these inglorious men are named: Godric, Godwine, Godwiy, brothers 'who had no gust for fighting'. They 'wheeled from the war to the wood's fastness, sought shelter and saved their lives'. Their lives may have been safe, but clearly their reputations were not. And so the battle was won and lost, a bitter blow for King Æthelred but a triumph for the Viking leader, Óláfr Tryggvason, who would later become king of Norway.[6]

Yet it was not Óláfr who would be the greatest threat to England in the long term. Events were taking place in Denmark which sowed the seeds of the Anglo-Saxon dynasty's ultimate destruction. Whilst events towards the creation of a Danish state had been experimented with since the turn of the ninth century, it was only in the tenth that they led to something more permanent in the reign of Gorm the Old (r. 936–958). He would be better remembered and celebrated if he had not been a convinced pagan of the old school. It was in the reign of his son and successor, Harald Bluetooth, that Denmark officially became a Christian nation. This helped cement Harald's rule and the status of his kingdom.

These events did not result in total stability. Harald's powerful and ambitious son Sweyn 'Forkbeard' conspired against his father, ultimately leading to civil war. In 987, Harald was fatally wounded in battle. Sweyn, however, did not immediately succeed him. In the fallout that followed these events King Erik of Sweden seized Denmark, provoking Sweyn to embark on a period of extensive raiding which echoed past glories – and England was right in the firing line. It is even possible that Sweyn and his men took part in the Maldon campaign, and though there is not much evidence of this, soon after the widow of a man named Æthelric is on record as appealing to clear her late husband's name. In a tantalising glimpse of distant treachery, Æthelric had been accused of conspiring to help Sweyn to invade England.[7]

After Maldon, Æthelred made the first of a number of payments for which he has become infamous. He would be castigated for this by writers who were being wise many centuries after the event. There was a gradual ratcheting up of the sums involved: £10,000 in 991, £16,000 in 994, £24,000 in 1002, £36,000 in 1006 and £21,000 in 1014. This 'Danegeld inflation' has been offered up as evidence that the policy was spectacularly unsuccessful (though at the time the term 'Danegeld' was not in use – such payments were called *gafol* or tribute). But some evidence should be offered up in Æthelred's defence. He was not the first English king to make such payments: as we have seen, Alfred, that kingly paragon, had done the same.

There is also an alternative way of looking at this. It is very possible that at least some of the payments were in fact made to hire Viking warriors as mercenaries. Charles the Bald, the ninth-century Frankish emperor, had done so. It is also possible that Edgar employed similar tactics, though the evidence for this is scanty. The payment in 994 is particularly interesting. In that year, Óláfr Tryggvason was baptised at Andover and paid off. There had been a series of raids on the south coast earlier that year, and Óláfr was encamped with his men outside Southampton before being escorted to Andover. After his baptism he returned to Norway where he fought a successful campaign to become king. Whether or not this was the result of some kind of pact with Æthelred is unclear, but it does not really matter. For the next six years, Óláfr was involved in a bitter conflict with Sweyn Forkbeard which kept the latter distracted as far as England was concerned (though it did not stop raids altogether). Rather than the work of a weak man, Æthelred's machinations here look politically astute.[8] Even so, it is undeniable that the onerous taxes levied to fund these payments would have made the king unpopular with his people.

As Æthelred began to rule in his own right, the charters he issued suggest some resentment on his part concerning what he had been persuaded to do in the previous decade. In particular he righted some perceived wrongs done to Abingdon Abbey that he blamed on the greed of Wulfgar, bishop of Ramsbury, and Ealdorman Ælfric of Hampshire. Ælfric's brother Edwin had then been made abbot of Abingdon and proceeded to dole out lands under the abbey's control to family members. In 993, Ælfric's son Ælfgar was blinded on the king's orders, marking a change in the relationship. All was not well between Æthelred and some of his councillors, and this disunity would manifest itself repeatedly in the years ahead.

Æthelred performed one part of his role to the full. It was important that a king (and of course his consort) produced a good number of heirs. It may seem odd to think of these as assets as opposed to human beings, but in the Anglo-Saxon political context they certainly were. Perhaps ten children were born to Æthelred and his first consort in only a dozen or so years (there were six sons and an unknown number of daughters). This consort is not named in early records, but it was later suggested that she was Æthelgifu of York. Tradition would assert that she was the daughter of Thored, earl of Northumbria, a man whose name hints strongly at Scandinavian links. Perhaps this is another example of the political utility of marital alliances to deal with potentially problematic situations.[9] The names of these children reveal the importance of dynastic considerations to Æthelred: Æthelstan, Ecgbert, Edmund, Eadred, Eadwig and Edgar. Amongst the daughters were names that echoed those of illustrious ancestors too, including Edith and Ælfgifu. Of these children, Edmund in particular would make a name for himself in the years to come.

A Viking attack on the symbolically important royal estate at Æthelingadene (East and West Dean in Sussex) in 1001 was a powerful reminder that the Viking threat had not gone away. The usefully distracting war in Norway between Óláfr Tryggvason and Sweyn Forkbeard had come to an end in 1000 when the former suffered a decisive defeat in a sea battle at Svöld off the coast of Scandinavia. Óláfr was dead (unless there is truth to hagiographical tales of the now firmly Christian ruler surviving and making pilgrimage to Jerusalem). The distraction had in truth been far from total. There were raids on Bamburgh (993), London and Southampton (994) and a number in the West Country in 997, including Watchet in Somerset and Lydford and Tavistock in Devon (the latter particularly associated with the family of Ælfthryth, Æthelred's mother).

A ravaging of Dorset in 998 also saw the raiders establish the Isle of Wight as a base, marking a strategy that they would repeat in the future. Kent, and in particular Rochester, suffered in 999. The relocation of mints to hill forts at this time may reflect a move to seek greater security. That at Wilton was transferred to Old Sarum, that at Ilchester to South Cadbury and the one at Chichester to Cissbury. In the other direction, the duchy of Normandy, home to many of the raiders, may have been subject to an English raid in 1000. Cumbria, Strathclyde and the Isle of Man were also attacked by the English, arguing against the perception of a useless and inept ruler that would later define Æthelred. Such attacks are indicative of a king who wants to emphasise his imperial ambition, a trait that was further highlighted in a charter of 1001 which stated that Æthelred was 'king of the whole island'.[10] This is evidence of a king who wants to emulate the reflected greatness of ancestors like Æthelstan and Edgar. But these actions did not stop further Viking attacks. In 1001 Devon suffered heavily, with a bloody battle fought at Pinhoe near Exeter and Kingsteignton burned.

This upping of the ante led to some dramatic developments. One was Æthelred's marriage to Emma of Normandy, the great granddaughter of Rollo, the first Viking ruler of the duchy, who arrived in England in 1002. Emma, who formally became Æthelred's queen, took the very traditional English name Ælfgifu on her arrival, suggesting a desire for dynastic continuity (though potentially confusing for historians as his first consort had the same name). She would prove herself a formidable political operator and a born survivor. She was given a generous allocation of land in Winchester as part of her marriage portion including Godbegot House, echoes of which can still be found in the city. The marriage was an astute political move which should have made it less likely that the dukes of Normandy would offer a base to their Viking cousins from which they could raid England. Yet at the same time, unbeknownst to Æthelred, it would have fatal consequences by introducing a potential claim to the English throne from an entirely new direction. It was also a complete change of emphasis in marriage politics. Throughout the tenth century Anglo-Saxon kings had normally selected wives from the West Saxon or Mercian nobility. There had not been a move like this since King Æthelwulf had married Judith of Francia 150 years before.

The marriage to Emma was a positive move despite these later consequences. The same could not be said of the other great drama of 1002. What may have precipitated it was the desertion of Æthelred in the previous year by a prominent man named Pallig. He was according to some accounts married to Sweyn Forkbeard's sister, but Æthelred thought that he had bought Pallig's loyalty with gifts in the form of land, gold and silver. Pallig took part in the devastating raid on Devon, after which the raiders returned to the Isle of Wight. It would be understandable if Pallig's defection rankled, though the raiders were paid off in 1002.[11] Some might have thought that was the end of the problem. It was anything but.

When the blow fell it was like a thundercloud blotting out the sun. An order was given that was chilling in its import: 'The king ordered all the Danish men who were among the English race to be killed on Brice's Day 13 November 1002, because it was made known to the king that they wanted to ensnare his life – and afterwards all his councillors – and have his kingdom afterwards.'[12] The chroniclers had a field day with this terrible story. William of Malmesbury, who manages to set these events about a decade later than they should have been, says that amongst the dead was Gunnhild, the wife of Pallig and sister to Sweyn Forkbeard. Incensed at her cruel treatment, Sweyn was inspired to invade and ultimately conquer England. According to William, Gunnhild was forced to watch whilst her husband was killed and her son transfixed with four spears. She was then beheaded.[13] Roger of Wendover tells a similar tale, adding the detail that Gunnhild had 'mediated a peace between the Danes and English and had given herself, with her husband and only son, as a hostage to king Ethelred [*sic*] for its security'.[14] This paints a picture of a deceitful king who broke the conventions of decent Christian behaviour without a second thought.

Henry of Huntingdon writes of secret orders being sent across the country so that a coordinated dawn raid could be launched, with instructions that the Danes be killed by the sword or burned alive.[15] Florence of Worcester says that the intention was that all Danes of every age and every sex should die.[16] Whilst these accounts add lurid detail and should be treated with caution, this cannot be said of a charter of 1004 which made restitution to the church of St Frideswide's in Oxford for damage done when it had been burned down. Inside were a party of Danish men fleeing in vain for their lives. The angry mob had set the building ablaze with them inside. The charter, issued in Æthelred's name, states that 'a decree was sent out by me with the counsel of my leading men and magnates, to the effect that all the Danes who had sprung up in this island, sprouting like cockle amongst the wheat, were to be destroyed by a most just extermination, and this decree was to be put into effect even as far as death'. This source, which we might expect to be a mundane administrative document, describes how the Danes broke into the church by force even though it was locked at the time and resolved to make a refuge for themselves inside it. When the mob saw what they had done, they set fire to the structure and burnt it along with its ornaments and books.[17]

Modern excavations on the site in Oxford revealed the shattered remains of thirty-eight men. They had been almost literally hacked to pieces. Twenty of the skeletons bore puncture marks to vertebrae or pelvic bones and twenty-seven had broken or cracked skulls. When the bones were analysed, the results revealed that the victims had lived off a diet dominated by seafood. This suggests that they were traders or raiders rather than resident Danes who had settled permanently in England. Further finds in Dorset, stumbled upon when a bypass was being constructed across the South Dorset Ridgeway near Weymouth, uncovered fifty-four skeletons, all of whom appeared to be male. They had been beheaded in what was clearly a ritual execution, some of them meeting their end at the hands of executioners who were clearly amateurs. Although this cannot be definitively proved to be as a result of the massacre, and the number of men suggests a shipload of raiders who had perhaps run aground, the bones have been dated to the approximate period of the massacre.[18]

It is difficult to believe that these orders encompassed all Danes living in England, many of whom had been in the country for several generations and lived in the Danelaw, where one assumes that they would have been relatively safe. Rather the depredations may have been targeted either at traders south of Watling Street who had attracted the opprobrium of the Anglo-Saxons or mercenaries who had proved unreliable in the recent Viking wars. But in these events, with their description in chronicles and charters as well as conclusive archaeological evidence, we have a clear sign of hatred for a group of people who for whatever reason were seen as something 'other'. And in a modern world which has its own Srebrenicas and Rwandan genocides to face, not to mention the horrors of the Holocaust and even more contemporary events in Ukraine, we are painfully aware of how xenophobic hatred can lead to some terrible atrocities even in a supposedly more 'civilised' global environment.

Into Exile

Whilst it is tempting to attribute a subsequent upswing in Viking activities to the massacre, further attacks on England were always likely given the forcefulness and ambition of Sweyn Forkbeard. With his triumph over Óláfr Tryggvason in Norway, he was free to devote his attentions elsewhere. There were several notable incidents in 1003. Exeter was taken by a Viking army, allegedly with the connivance of a 'Frenchman' inside the walls. Sweyn later departed with his men laden with booty after levelling the walls 'from the eastern to the western gate'.[19] It was convenient for the chroniclers to be able to blame a foreigner, one who had been introduced to the country through Emma's actions. A Norman influence was already being introduced into England. This was followed by another notable attack on Wilton. The nunnery there was associated with St Edith, the king's half-sister, and as such these events would have been personally upsetting to Æthelred. His mood would not have been improved when he heard that the local *fyrd* had failed to intervene. It was led by Ælfric, the ealdorman of eastern Wessex. Rather than fight, the ealdorman lost his nerve, allegedly feigning sickness, and ran, his men following his example. Ælfric had been one of Æthelred's first appointments and as such his cowardice reflected badly on the king. It was appointments such as this that would earn him the punning nickname Æthelred Unræd, which literally translates to 'noble counsel [Æthelred] poor counsel [unræd]'. It was the start of an awful decade for England.

In 1004, there was another significant Viking attack led by Sweyn, this time in the east of England. The local defence was led by Ulfcytel, who although a senior figure was probably a thegn rather than an ealdorman. Norwich was burned and Thetford too was plundered by the raiders. The first reaction of the local officials was to try to buy off the Viking force because their army was not gathered in sufficient strength to fight them off. But Sweyn clearly sensed weakness in his opponents and pushed on to Hertford. Ulfcytel was a man of character and went on the attack after instructing the locals to burn the Viking ships that had been left behind, a command that unfortunately went unheeded. There was a violent confrontation in which both sides suffered heavy losses. However, the disparity in numbers told and the Vikings held the field whilst many of the leading men of East Anglia lay dead. But Ulfcytel and his men had fought a valiant fight and the chronicler suggested that even the raiders said that they had never been up against a more determined enemy.[20]

Æthelred was in many ways a conventional king of his time. An ardent collector of relics, he probably fully believed that the Vikings were a scourge sent from God to punish his people for their sins. The preamble to a charter of 1005 suggests as much:

> And since in our days we suffer the fires of war and the plundering of our riches, and from the cruel depredations of barbarian enemies engaged in ravaging our country and from the manifold sufferings inflicted on us by pagan races threatening us with extermination we perceive that we live in perilous times.[21]

There were no attacks in 1005. This was something of a mixed blessing, for the raiders only left because there was a great famine in England, one grimmer than any in living memory. It was a prelude to a truly awful period that began the following year. It started with some internal turbulence, and for once the *ASC* goes into detail. A prominent noble called Wulfgeat was deprived of his territory, Ealdorman Ælfhelm of Northumbria was killed and his two sons, Wulfheah and Ufegeat, were blinded. This has been offered as strong evidence of what has been called a palace revolution.[22] Certainly it suggests that the state of England was deteriorating and that Æthelred was struggling to keep control. The situation was not helped by his promotion of Eadric Streona, the son of a minor noble, who would soon become ealdorman of Mercia. Henry of Huntingdon later wrote that '[Eadric] surpassed all his contemporaries in malice and perfidy, as well as in pride and cruelty'.[23] Eadric was to become one of the most vilified characters in English history and, whilst his turpitude may have been much exaggerated, it is difficult to avoid the conclusion that this was one of Æthelred's gravest errors of judgement.

Viking leaders sometimes seemed to have acute political antennae, and possibly Sweyn had an inkling of the divisions which were starting to split England. In the second half of 1006, he and his army were back with a vengeance. They took up residence on the Isle of Wight, perfectly placed to launch attacks across the length and breadth of southern England. In an act which was designed to deliberately underscore the country's weakness they marched up to Scutchamer Knob in Berkshire (since transferred to Oxfordshire), leaving a pitiful trail of burning villages in their wake. The significance of this was that Scutchamer Knob was an old barrow where an early West Saxon king, Cwichelm, was said to have been buried. Tradition stated that no army could march this far inland without being defeated, and Sweyn now proved the falseness of such claims. A force that tried to stop him marching back to the coast was swatted aside on the Kennet. His army then marched past the walls of Winchester while the citizens cowered behind them, powerless or too terrified to intervene. It was a shocking contrast to the times of Alfred, Edward the Elder or Æthelstan.

But then there was a lull. This may have been because a huge payment of £30,000 was paid to Sweyn to persuade him to leave. It bought some time, though quite how much remained to be seen. In the absence of further attacks, Æthelred sought to renew his alliance with a very powerful ally: God. In 1008 a meeting of great significance was held at Enham in Hampshire. Its name (in Old English Eanham) means 'the place of the lambs', an animal closely associated with Christ, in Latin sometimes designated *Agnus Dei*, 'the lamb of God'. The timing was auspicious too as it was Pentecost, when tongues of fire descended from Heaven and filled Christ's followers with the Holy Spirit. These were troubled years in a spiritual as well as a political sense. Something sinister was stirring in England, a sense of fear and foreboding. The following year Wulfstan, archbishop of York (not to be confused with his predecessor of the same name who had died in 956), devised a new law which prescribed a number of penitential acts to be performed by the English people such as processing to church barefoot through the streets, an act of humiliation and humility designed to seek God's mercy.

Wulfstan was an Anglo-Saxon preacher of the fire-and-brimstone variety. One of his works, *Sermo Lupi ad Anglos*, or 'the Sermon of the Wolf to the English', argued that the attacks of the Vikings were a just punishment from God for English adherence to the ways of the Devil. Wulfstan had preached at Enham, and it is not difficult to imagine that a coruscating blast was aimed at his audience – he was no respecter of rank. At around the same time, a very unusual penny was issued. Usually coins would show the king's head on one side and a cross on the other. This one bore the image of a lamb on one side and a dove on the other in an obvious appeal for divine assistance. Only twenty-one surviving coins of this type remain, and the fact that sixteen of them were found in Scandinavia and the Baltic region, presumably carried there by Vikings, suggests that the appeal went largely unheard by the Almighty.

The events of the following years are laid on thickly in the *ASC*, by which we can conclude one of two things: either the situation was truly dire, or the author has a particular axe to grind against the king. They started with an event which provided the perfect metaphor for Æthelred's England. The king had not been idle during the period of relative calm, and a considerable amount of money had been spent assembling a fleet to fight back against the longships and their crews. The king then ordered that they should take up station at Sandwich, a place which had become a particularly vulnerable point of ingress for Viking raiders. This was all very sensible strategically, but what happened next made such measures completely superfluous. There was a major fight in the Anglo-Saxon camp between Beorhtric, the brother of ealdorman Eadric Streona ('the Acquisitor' on account of his alleged rapaciousness) on the one hand and Wulfnoth, a prominent South Saxon, on the other. Eadric accused Wulfnoth of being a traitor to the king, and Wulfnoth reacted by sailing away with twenty ships to burn and raid along the coast. Beorhtric chased after him with eighty ships, but they could not catch up. Worse still, those ships were caught up in a vicious storm and scattered along the coast. Seeing this, Wulfnoth descended on the stranded ships and burned them. The rest of the fleet simply disintegrated. The fleet had gone up in smoke. One can only imagine the feelings of those who had been compelled to pay the tax.

To rub salt in the wound, a Viking army arrived soon after and, with painful irony, sailed unchallenged into Sandwich. They then marauded across the country in what is described as a long litany of death and destruction. For once there is so much detail in the *ASC* that it is best to summarise what happened. They raided first in Kent and then moved on to Essex before attacking London, which they did not take. Then it was through the Chilterns and on to Oxford, which they burned. They came to East Anglia, specifically Ipswich, where the East Anglian army led by Ulfcytel fled. The *fyrd* from Cambridge did at least stand its ground for a while, but its men were overwhelmed at Ringmere and many prominent

Anglo-Saxons including Æthelstan, son-in-law of King Æthelred, lost their lives. The Vikings then travelled around the east of England, burning Northampton, Thetford and Cambridge amongst many other places. Even the 'wild fens' of the region did not provide protection against the raiders. In the other direction, Surrey, Berkshire, Hampshire and much of Wiltshire did not escape their depredations.

The head of this Viking army was not Sweyn but a larger-than-life figure known as Thorkell (or Thurcytel) 'Mare's Head'. He would be a giant of the next decade, ultimately proving a formidable opponent even for Sweyn himself. Covering the events of 1009 to 1011, the chronicler wrote in despair of what was happening. He said that 'when they [the Vikings] were in the east, then the army was kept in the west: and when they were in the south, then our army was in the north. Then all the councillors were ordered to the king, and they had then to decide how this country should be defended. But whatever was then decided, it did not stand for even one month. In the end there was no head man who wanted to gather an army, but each fled as best as he could; nor even in the end would one shire help another.'

This revealed an unaddressed weakness in Anglo-Saxon England: it was extremely difficult to keep a national army in the field for any length of time. Traditionally, defence had been built around local militias who did not want to travel far from home for any length of time and would probably in most cases have wanted to avoid travelling outside the immediate vicinity of their shire at all. The defensive structures of Anglo-Saxon England were being pulled apart and were in danger of being overwhelmed.

The chronicler goes on to summarise the events of these times in the entry in the *ASC* for the year 1011. He paints a frightening picture:

> Here in this year the king and his councillors sent to the raiding-army, and begged peace, and promised them tax and provisions on condition that they leave off their raiding. They had then overrun East Anglia and Essex and Middlesex and Oxfordshire and Cambridgeshire and Hertfordshire and Buckinghamshire and Bedfordshire and half Huntingdonshire, and to the south of the Thames all the Kentish and South Saxons and the Hastings district and Surrey and Berkshire and Hampshire and much in Wiltshire.
>
> All these misfortunes befell us through lack of decision, in that they were not offered tax in time; but when they had done great evil, then a truce and peace was made with them. And nonetheless for all this truce and peace and tax, they travelled about everywhere in bands and raided and roped up and killed our wretched people.

In other words, when protection money was offered to the Vikings it came too late, after the damage had already been done. To make matters worse, the raiders had no intention of honouring any commitments which they might have made in the process.[24]

It has become fashionable in recent years for historians to suggest that the awfulness of Æthelred as a king has been much exaggerated.[25] And it is certainly true that for much of his reign he managed to hold his own in the face of extraordinarily difficult circumstances. Maybe the chroniclers who wrote up their accounts later were biased against him. But we should not let the pendulum swing too far the other way. In the latter years of Æthelred's reign matters deteriorated alarmingly. Not only were there increasingly heavy Viking attacks to cope with, there was also further evidence of domestic strife. The years between 1009 and 1011 were certainly awful. But things were about to get dramatically worse.

In September 1011, a Viking force laid siege to Canterbury having dug trenches around the city. The place was both prestigious and wealthy due to its status as the headquarters of the English church. Eventually the Vikings broke in. The *ASC* suggest that this was through treachery, because an abbot named Ælfmær, whose life Archbishop Ælfheah had earlier saved, let them inside.[26] Florence of Worcester adds the detail that after this treachery a quarter of the city was set ablaze, and the army was able to break in. Some of the townsfolk were put to the sword, some died in the flames, some were thrown headlong from the walls, and some were hung by their private parts till they expired. Women were dragged by their hair through the streets of the city and then thrown into the fire and burnt. Infants torn from their mothers' breasts were impaled on spears or crushed beneath the wheels of waggons.[27]

In addition to these horrific events, several important clerics were made prisoner. Christ Church in Canterbury was plundered and burnt and many of the male population were killed after a brutal process of decimation where, out of every ten captives, nine were butchered. Florence tells of hundreds of people killed. Whilst these events may be exaggerated, as some of them appear to be quite formulaic descriptions of alleged brutality, they paint a deeply disturbing picture. When the Vikings eventually left Canterbury, they took the archbishop with them as a hostage. They then moved up to the south bank of the Thames, perhaps to Southwark or Greenwich. One evening, as the mead was flowing, the archbishop was brought out in front of the Viking army. Some of their number demanded that he raised a ransom to purchase his release, but he refused to cooperate. Their senses inflamed by too much drink, they started to shower him with stones, bones and the skulls of oxen. Eventually one of them, a man called Thrum who had recently been confirmed as a Christian, split open his head with an axe.[28]

There was a palpable sense of shock at the brutal murder of the head of the English church. What made matters worse was that just across the river, on the northern bank of the Thames, the English council was in residence. The fact that Ælfheah had been killed within just a few miles of them emphasised their impotence. The archbishop's body was recovered the next day – by what means we are not told – and buried in Old St Paul's in London. This was an event which burned itself into the English psyche and would stay there for a long time to come. A few centuries later, in December 1170, Thomas Becket gave his very last sermon at Canterbury. He remarked to the cross-bearer attending him that Canterbury had one martyr already in the shape of Ælfheah and would soon have another to accompany him.[29]

Deeply disturbing though this event was, it did lead to some more positive developments. Soon after, Thorkell changed sides. Perhaps this was a sign that he believed that a line had been crossed with the cold-blooded killing of the archbishop. More likely, the £48,000 that Æthelred paid him was the main attraction. His help would be much needed. In 1013, Sweyn reappeared on the scene. This time he approached England with a huge army. He first made his way to Sandwich but did not stay there long before moving north, sailing up the Humber and encamping at Gainsborough. He preceded to stamp his authority over much of the north of England, with Earl Uhtred and many of the Northumbrians submitting to him. Some historians believed that this was because he found a favourable reception there; many of the people had Scandinavian antecedents, after all. However, some likely felt that there was no point in resisting given that the main English defences were in the south and precious little help would be coming their way.

Whilst in the north, Sweyn acted with moderation. However, once he crossed Watling Street and moved south the gloves well and truly came off. A blitzkrieg followed. Some of the major cities in Wessex, places both politically and symbolically important such as Winchester and Bath, surrendered. Æthelmær, son of the now deceased chronicler Æthelweard and the ealdorman of western Wessex, was one of those who submitted. However, the main power base in England had by now started to shift to London and here Sweyn was faced with a more determined defence. In one failed attack, many of his men were drowned when trying to cross the Thames without the help of a bridge. However, those inside the walls began to lose hope. London was now in danger of becoming the last bastion. Isolated and increasingly desperate, the Londoners approached Sweyn seeking terms. The end, it seemed, was nigh.

What did this all mean for Æthelred? It became obvious, to him at least, that further resistance was hopeless. Thorkell was still stationed at Greenwich and offering some protection, but Æthelred felt that he had no option but to escape. Initially he made his way to the Isle of Wight, ironically a place from which several Viking attacks had been launched over the years. He stayed there for a short while before crossing the Channel to Normandy. Here he sought and was granted refuge by Duke Richard, his brother-in-law. His sons Alfred and Edward went with him. The marriage alliance with Emma of Normandy had borne dividends, but surely not in a way that he had hoped for.

The End Days

Everything seemed to be settled. Æthelred had fled to Normandy in humiliating ignominy, Sweyn was triumphant, and England was his 'and the whole nation had him as full king'.[30] And then fate – or the Hand of God – intervened. Without warning, Sweyn was taken ill and died at the beginning of February 1014, before he had been formally consecrated as the ruler of England. It was said by some that he met his end at the hands of the East Anglian martyr king Edmund, who had been subjected to a dreadful death by Viking raiders in the past. Sweyn had treated the abbey dedicated to the dead king at Bury St Edmunds with disdain, and it was said that the shade of King Edmund strode into Sweyn's presence, unseen by anyone save the Viking warlord, and ran him through with a spear.[31]

These events took place around Gainsborough. With Sweyn was his young son Cnut, little more than a youth at this stage. Those with him proclaimed Cnut king but further south, especially in London, this proclamation was ignored. Instead, Æthelred was invited to take back his throne, albeit with conditions attached. He must rule this time as a 'good' king, respectful of his people and their interests; in their words, he would be allowed back 'if he would govern them more justly than he did before'. In return he promised that he 'would improve each of the things which they all hated'.[32] This may have felt like an empty gesture, for England seemingly was no longer theirs to give. Sweyn's formidable army was still in the field, having enjoyed the collaboration of the people of Lindsey who had given them horses and offered to raid with them. But Æthelred, showing a determination and vigour that contrasts with his image as being 'Unready', launched a lightning attack on the Viking camp at Gainsborough. Cnut, showing his inexperience, was caught by surprise. His army was overwhelmed and he himself barely escaped.

The Anglo-Saxons extracted full vengeance on the region as 'all human kind that could be got at were raided and burned and killed'.[33]

Cnut sailed back to Denmark, then ruled by his brother Harald. He made a brief stopover at Sandwich to leave behind some important Anglo-Saxon hostages he had with him, minus their ears and noses – and according to William of Malmesbury for some unfortunates amongst this group of 'young men of great nobility and elegance ... even their manhood'.[34] Æthelred in the meantime paid over a further £21,000 to Thorkell to buy his continued support and protection. With the immediate Viking threat removed, Anglo-Saxon England was soon divided once more by factionalism. Eadric Streona was at the heart of this according to the Anglo-Saxon chroniclers, who make something of a pantomime villain of him. After Æthelred had retaken his throne, a council meeting was held at Oxford where the attendees included Sigeferth and Morcar, two prominent nobles from the Five Boroughs in the Danelaw. They had changed sides to support Sweyn, and presumably hoped that some kind of amnesty would now protect them. They were wrong. Whilst at Oxford they were taken and killed, apparently in Eadric's chamber.

These were rich and powerful men, and Sigeferth left behind him a widow who potentially gave access to some important lands. The king ordered that she should be taken to Malmesbury for safekeeping but his son Edmund had other ideas, abducting the widow and marrying her. Soon after he moved into the lands of Sigeferth and Morcar, whose people came over to his side. Edmund's actions had very little to do with protecting England's interests; it was much more about advancing his own. Then to make matters worse war broke out again, this time not against a Viking army but between two English factions. Eadric and Edmund were neighbours and rivals in Mercia, and they now sought to conquer each other. England was still not fully formed. The immaturity of the fledgling country was highlighted by its propensity to split itself apart even when danger was on the doorstep.

This was highlighted in alarming fashion when, at around the same time that Edmund was staking his claim, Cnut returned to English shores. After a brief stop at Sandwich, he sailed west along the coast of Wessex. Moving into the large anchorage of Poole Harbour, he reached the mouth of the Frome and then proceeded to raid Dorset, Wiltshire and Somerset. Cnut's timing was perfect. An ageing Æthelred was lying ill at Cosham, at the head of Portsmouth Harbour. Eadric and Edmund superficially sank their differences to stand against the interloper, but their display of harmony was a charade. There was a falling-out soon after and the army withdrew, leaving Cnut a clear field. Eadric then deserted with forty ships and went over to Cnut. The people of Wessex, left unprotected, submitted to the raiders, handing over hostages and horses. The Viking army would remain in Wessex until midwinter.[35]

Cnut then copied the tactics employed by Guthrum well over a century before. He launched a strike during the Christmas period, hitting Cricklade before moving further into Mercia and raiding Warwickshire early in January 1016. This was moving close to Edmund's territory, and he gathered an army to meet the threat. However, initially this resistance came to nothing. For whatever reason, his father's name still held prestige and Edmund's army melted away when the ailing king did not arrive to lead it. Eventually Æthelred summoned enough energy to make his way up from London. This was enough to encourage some men to his side, but these efforts were wasted. The army apparently was too scared to fight and the king soon after returned south.

Perhaps realising that his father was by now a spent force, Edmund raised another army in consort with his brother-in-law Earl Uhtred of Northumbria. The expectation was that this force would go on the offensive against Cnut. However, England's true weakness now revealed itself again as this army ignored the Viking threat and moved against the lands of Eadric Streona. This was not a war of national salvation; it was a grubby power struggle. Staffordshire, Shrewsbury and Chester came under attack. But Cnut, who may well have been in alliance with Eadric, launched a counterstrike. He moved north-east, behind Edmund and Uhtred's army, and up towards York, the latter's main base. It was a move that Uhtred could not ignore. He withdrew, taking his men with him. He submitted to Cnut, handing over hostages. It did not save him. Soon after he attended a meeting where he was ambushed and killed whilst unarmed. His death led to a remarkable inter-family blood feud which would last for over half a century, the last bloody act only being played out in the winter of 1073/4.[36]

London was a key target for Cnut, but a major change came before he could reach it. On St George's Day 1016, King Æthelred II breathed his last. The witan in London elected Edmund as his successor, but how long he would rule was a moot point. The Viking fleet anchored at Greenwich. London Bridge was a major potential obstacle which they sidestepped by hauling their ships overland and then relaunching them to the west of it. They then laid siege to London, hemming it in with earthen ramparts. Regular attacks were launched on the city, but they were stoically resisted.

Edmund was not there. He had previously moved into Wessex where he was involved in a battle at Penselwood near the royal manor of Gillingham in Dorset. At Sherston in Wiltshire there was another fight, this time with Cnut present. So too were Anglo-Saxon collaborators in the almost inevitable form of Eadric Streona and another prominent noble, Ælfmær Darling. While these hard-fought battles were indecisive, Edmund gained an important benefit as he was able to move to the relief of London. A Viking counterattack was driven off at Brentford, though the victory was marred by the loss of many Englishmen who were 'drowned through their own carelessness when they travelled in front of the army and wanted to seize loot'.[37]

London's reprieve was short lived. When Edmund returned to Wessex to raise more men, the Vikings attacked the city again. The fate of the war still hung in the balance. With London still holding out, Cnut and his army went on the rampage again. Moving their ships into the Orwell in Essex, they marched into Mercia 'and killed and burned whatsoever they came across, as was their custom, and provided themselves which supplies, and they drove both the ships and their herds to the Medway'.[38] Edmund once more led an army to London's relief, crossing the Thames at Brentford and moving into Kent. The raiding army fled before him, taking their horses into Sheppey, and for a time things seemed to have turned the way of the Anglo Saxons. Indeed, Ealdorman Eadric even decided to turn coat once more and re-joined the king at Aylesford. Ominously, the chronicler noted that 'there was no more unwise decision than this was'.[39]

Once more, the Viking army moved on Mercia. The Anglo-Saxons chased after them and eventually the two armies came face to face at Ashingdon (Assundun) in Essex. The fight that followed was violent but decisive. Matters started to go badly wrong for the Anglo-Saxon side when Eadric once more betrayed the cause, flying from the battle with his people. Deprived of these troops, the English army started to crumble and eventually broke. There was a long roll call of English dead. They included Eadnoth, bishop of Dorchester, Abbot Wulfsige of Ramsey, Ealdorman Ælfric of Hampshire, Ealdorman Godwine from Lindsey, Ulfcytel from East Anglia, Æthelweard, son of Ealdorman Æthelsige of East Anglia, and many other notable men. But there was one notable escapee: King Edmund.

The beleaguered king made his way west, eventually arriving in Gloucestershire. Cnut came after him but Eadric Streona this time acted as intermediary. The two rivals for the English throne, Edmund and Cnut, met on 'Ola's Island' in the Severn. They came to terms, having perhaps fought each other to a standstill. Edmund, who would earn the moniker of 'Ironside', had fought with great determination, as had Cnut, and a recovery period would have been welcomed by both men. Having said that, a payment was involved to buy off the Vikings so that had not changed with the replacement of Æthelred. The chronicler noted without being particularly convincing that they 'there affirmed their friendship, both with pledge and with oath'. A division of the kingdom was agreed, with Edmund given Wessex and Cnut Mercia.

This unlikely arrangement was probably always doomed to fail. Even so, the speed at which it dissolved may have been a shock. In typical laconic style, the *ASC* state that 'on St Andrew's Day 30 November 1016 Edmund the king passed away and is buried with his grandfather Edgar in Glastonbury'.[40] Unsurprisingly, strong rumours of foul play quickly started to circulate.

Embers

Emma's young sons Alfred and Edward were at least safely in exile in Normandy, but the death of Edmund Ironside seemed to remove the last realistic hope of Alfred's dynasty. There was a *fin-de-siècle* feel to the times. Fifty years before the Norman Conquest the course of English history had changed massively, though this fact is often lost in the shadow of that greater event. Cnut took up the reins of government in England, establishing an Anglo-Danish as opposed to an Anglo-Saxon ruling regime. He became 'the Great' in his own right, ruling over Denmark and England and for a time part of Norway, a veritable North Sea Empire. He not only took Æthelred's kingdom; he also married his widow Emma (much as with other Anglo-Saxon kings, having a previous consort still living did not prove to be an insurmountable problem even, though Cnut became a staunch supporter of the Christian church).

Cnut's marriage to Emma effectively pushed her sons from Æthelred further down the pecking order. Perhaps the arrangement was good for Emma, and even for Normandy and England, but it did not help her exiled sons very much apart from possibly reducing the worth of killing them. Certainly any closeness between mother and sons that had been there to begin with would dissipate over the years. But it is easy to overlook that the children from Emma's marriage to Æthelred (as well as the sons there was also a daughter, Godgifu) did not have just Anglo-Saxon blood flowing through their veins, there were Viking elements in them too, passed down through their mother. Godgifu was quickly married off, but the two sons remained as bachelors and were educated in the ducal court.[41]

When Cnut died in 1035, the throne passed to his son Harold 'Harefoot'. The accession was not unopposed, but in a revealing twist the opposition came not from an Anglo-Saxon but from Harold's brother Harthacnut. These were indeed different times. This was evidenced when Edward, the son of Æthelred and Emma, returned from Normandy.

His brother Alfred returned in a separate enterprise to stake a claim for the throne, ending in disaster when he was captured and blinded so cruelly that he died soon after. Earl Godwin, who had risen to prominence in the reign of Cnut, was heavily implicated in these violent events, presaging later difficulties between him and Edward. Some Norman accounts suggest that Edward won a victory near Southampton but proved unable to capitalise on it and returned to Normandy. Shortly after, Emma too fled from England. She was not the mother of Harold, who was Cnut's son from a previous relationship, and she had opposed his succession, preferring that her natural son Harthacnut should take over. Her power base in England was dwindling.

But then came another twist. Harold, still a young man, suddenly died, leaving the throne vacant. It was Harthacnut who stepped in to fill the breach. He had already made himself king of Denmark and was keen to add England to his domains. He sailed over from the continent with sixty ships. One of his first acts was to have the body of his late half-brother Harold dug up and thrown into a swamp. Soon after, for reasons which are still unclear, Harthacnut invited Edward to return to England. Explanations that this was all down to brotherly love or fear of God's punishment for the poor treatment of a kinsman, as put forward by some medieval chroniclers, fail to convince. More likely both half-brothers saw some mutual advantage in the arrangement. If not quite the last man standing as far as Alfred's dynasty was concerned, Edward still had limited prospects. Harthacnut was in his twenties, and if he married and had sons this would effectively consign Alfred's dynasty to obscurity and irrelevance. But then, yet another twist. Whilst drinking at a wedding, Harthacnut suddenly collapsed and died. Apparently from out of nowhere, Edward, son of the much maligned Æthelred, was next in line to be king.

The succession disputes of recent times ensured that there was no guarantee Edward would inherit the throne, but he did. Sweyn, Harthacnut's cousin, arguably had a strong claim but he was back in Denmark and in a poor position to affect the outcome of any succession debate. As the senior noble in England, Earl Godwin's support was critical. Given his alleged involvement in the death of Edward's brother, Alfred, he was in an awkward position. Having decided that Edward was the best bet, or at least the likely winner in any dispute, he quickly sought to ingratiate himself with the prospective new king. He presented a splendid gift to Edward, 'a loaded ship, its slender lines raked up in double row, lay anchored on the Thames, with many rowing benches side by side, the towering mast amidships looking down, equipped with six score fearsome warriors. A golden lion crowns the stern. A winged and golden dragon at the prow affrights the sea, and belches fire with triple tongue.' Godwin's magnificent offering was clearly designed to build bridges with Edward and hopefully persuade the king to forget any past indiscretions on the noble's part. For a time, this worked. Godwin was richly rewarded, though their relationship would break down in the years to come.[42]

Despite the saintly reputation of the man who would be known as 'the Confessor', Edward was no pushover. One of his first acts on becoming king was to deprive his mother, Emma, of her treasure. The information that we have for relations between mother and son, scant though it is, hints very strongly that Emma often put the children from her second marriage to Cnut ahead of those from her first to Æthelred. Certainly, very little warmth is apparent between Emma and Edward in the later years of her life.

Edward was crowned at Winchester on Easter Day 1043. Both the timing and the location were auspicious. His immediate predecessors, Cnut and Harthacnut, were buried in the city and it had also been the powerhouse of the tenth-century religious reform programme. Both archbishops, Eadsige of Canterbury and Ælfric of York, were present. As part of the ceremony, prayers were offered up that Edward would be blessed with children – something that would come to have an ironic ring about it. In the coronation feast that followed, ambassadors from countries such as Denmark, Germany and Francia presented themselves to the new king and offered up gifts, reflecting an internationalism far removed from what would have been the case during crowning ceremonies in earlier centuries.[43]

Soon after, Edward was married to Edith, the daughter of Earl Godwin. There was probably a twenty-year age gap between the married couple, though as a bride in her early twenties Edith was quite old by the mores of the time.[44] In a practice that was becoming more common, she was also crowned as queen. From the fragmentary evidence that remains, especially *The Life of King Edward*, which was written more for Edith than her husband, she was a sophisticated woman from a well-to-do Anglo-Danish family (Earl Godwin's wife Gytha was probably Cnut's sister-in-law). This contrasted with her husband, considered by some to be slightly rustic in comparison.

As the years passed and Edward grew into the role of king, it was perhaps inevitable that sooner or later he would clash with his father-in-law. The Godwin family had become immensely powerful, but the earl had problems within his own family unit. One of his sons, Sweyn, developed a well-deserved reputation for causing trouble. He fled into exile after abducting an abbess, this after he had also suggested that

Godwin was not his father at all but that he was the son of no less a person than the late, great Cnut. This hints strongly that he saw himself as Cnut's heir, which would have alarmed Edward as much as Godwin. When Sweyn was later allowed back to England, he showed his gratitude by first kidnapping and then murdering his cousin Beorn, who was the brother of Sweyn Estridsson, king of Denmark. The two men were leading a fleet to head off a Viking raid from Ireland on the West Country when Beorn was killed at Dartmouth. He was subsequently buried with great honour in Cnut's mausoleum at Winchester. Despite this and his subsequent flight to Flanders, Sweyn was allowed to return to England once more, having enlisted the support of Bishop Ealdred of Worcester as his sponsor.

These intra-family tensions may well have been exploited by Edward to remind Godwin of his rightful place. Whilst there were two other long-lived earls of note, Leofric of Mercia and the Dane Siward of Northumbria, it was undoubtedly Godwin who increasingly dominated.[45] When the archbishopric of Canterbury was vacated in 1050, the king upset his right-hand man and the priests there by overriding their candidate and appointing Robert of Jumièges, a bitter critic of Godwin. Events from around this time saw a story emerge (thanks to the later and possibly biased point of view of William of Poitiers) that Edward, then lacking an heir, nominated William, the young duke of Normandy, as his successor. This would have profound historical consequences if it were true.[46]

Matters reached a head in 1051 when Eustace, count of Boulogne, visited England.[47] On his way home, there was a brawl at Dover which quickly got out of hand. Lives were lost both amongst Eustace's party and the citizens of Dover. Eustace sought redress from Edward, who ordered Godwin to punish Dover as he was responsible for Kent. The earl did not wish to do so, and matters soon went from bad to worse. Around Godwin there developed a faction promoting the idea that the king was too much in thrall to his French advisers. Robert of Jumièges countered by accusing Godwin of plotting to kill the king. Both sides assembled significant bodies of men, and an out-and-out conflict loomed.

War did not follow. Godwin's power had alienated some powerful elements in the country and support for his cause started to fall away. Summoned to answer charges at a trial, Godwin refused to do so without a safe-conduct. Edward would not grant one, at one stage apparently suggesting that he would only award one to the earl if he could restore his murdered brother Alfred to him. Seeing that his position was deteriorating, Godwin decided to flee the country. His sons also sailed into exile, some making for Flanders (Tostig was married to Judith, daughter of Baldwin IV of Flanders), others for Ireland. Edward's wife, Godwin's daughter Edith, was put to one side for the time being, consigned to a nunnery, possibly at Wilton or Wherwell. It seemed to be very much a time for the changing of the guard, and this perception was reinforced by two other events. The first was the death of the queen mother, Emma, in 1052. She was buried at Winchester, near her second husband Cnut and son Harthacnut. The second event was the visit, mentioned in some accounts, of the young Duke William of Normandy to England, further cementing suggestions of links between England and Normandy, where Edward had spent many of his earlier years.

Yet it was one thing to drive Godwin and his clan out of England, and quite another to keep him there. It was never likely that Godwin would accept this sequence of events as a *fait accompli* and before long he was plotting his return. Several moves on England were made in 1052, coming from different directions. There were raids in the west led by Godwin's sons Harold and Leofwine. Ironically, they were launched with the aid of the Irish, more than likely on ships manned with crews from the Hiberno-Norse settlement at Dublin. They landed at Porlock – another irony as this had been a frequent target for Viking raids in the past – and were driven off, albeit at some cost. However, the brothers simply moved further up the English Channel after sailing around Land's End.

Godwin himself led another move on England in June, landing in Kent to a warm welcome. If William of Normandy had indeed visited England and had been given such a warm welcome by the king, it may have generated support for the Godwins from disaffected Englishmen who did not look kindly on the prospect of foreign rule. Edward sent an army to face up to the threat, but for various reasons no immediate confrontation followed. In August Godwin was reunited with Harold and Leofwine somewhere further west in the English Channel, possibly at Portland. One person was missing, however. Sweyn had gone on pilgrimage to Jerusalem in atonement for a misspent life. He died of exposure whilst walking barefoot through the mountains of Asia Minor, which probably came as a relief to his despairing family.

Having received significant support, Godwin felt sufficiently empowered to move on London. Before long, the armies of Edward and Godwin faced each other across the Thames. Negotiations followed, with Leofric of Mercia and Siward of Northumbria apparently reluctant to take the fight to Godwin. At the end of these discussions, Godwin was restored to his former position. Some of Edward's French advisers fled the scene rather than face Godwin, who may well have been in a vengeful mood. The crisis was over. It was further cooled when just a few months later Godwin died, probably from a stroke. He was buried at Winchester near Cnut, to whom he had effectively been a right-hand man. His son, Harold, became earl of Wessex in his stead. When Siward of Northumbria died in 1055, the year after defeating the Scottish king in battle, Harold's brother Tostig was made earl. Another sibling, Gyrth, was given a shire in East Anglia (he would later be given the whole of it). The Godwin star was on the rise.

Events during the rest of Edward's reign are largely obscure. In the face of a shortage of evidence, it is hard to get a definitive picture of Edward's character and what made him tick. In the words of one modern biographer, it may be concluded that 'he was, like many of his rank and time, a mediocrity. Nearly all his characteristics are commonplace.'[48] What comes across is a sense of enjoyment from hunting and even warfare. Although he was not personally involved in many military confrontations during his reign he was clearly a survivor, amply demonstrated by the fact that he had managed to live through his years in exile and come out the other side to be king. His reign on the whole was not marred by the excessive violence that had scarred his father's reign and for this perhaps it came to be remembered as a period of tranquillity and calm. However, it might also be said that by the time his reign came to an end the conditions had been set for a crisis of terminal proportions for the Anglo-Saxon kingdom.

During those later years, the sons of Godwin became more prominent in England, particularly Harold and Tostig, the latter of whom grew powerful in the north, always the least integrated part in the young country of England. There are also hints, especially in the *Life of King Edward*, that their sister Edith, by now returned to her position alongside the king, also played an important role. Frenchmen started to become more prominent as royal advisors again – interestingly enough, so did men with Scandinavian names. The court appears to have become more cosmopolitan. Edward came to be associated with the biblical super-king Solomon, at that time more renowned for his association with peace than with wisdom.[49] Edward seems to have basked in the reflected glory of his court, which became known for its elegance and style even though he himself did not shine particularly brightly in such company. In the end, the sons of Godwin were acting as Edward's local governors across nearly all of England; not just Harold and Tostig but also Gyrth in East Anglia and Leofwine in south-east England. They were certainly the dominant power in the land, but in the end it was their own rivalries that would destroy the Godwin dynasty and, in the process, lead to the demise of Anglo-Saxon England.

As time went on, and Edward and Edith remained childless, the problem of the succession became more urgent. There were far too many succession disputes in Anglo-Saxon history to be blasé about the issue. There were still direct living descendants of Æthelred II, though none lived in England. Two sons of Edmund Ironside had made their way to Hungary after their father died (they were infants at the time) and one of them, Edward, had done well at the royal court there. He had married Agatha, a niece of Emperor Henry II, and they had three children. There were two daughters, Margaret and Christina, and a son, Edgar (known as 'the ætheling'). Margaret would eventually play a key role in the perpetuation of the dynasty, whilst Christina would become abbess of the important nunnery at Wilton.

Hoping to attract a potential heir back to England, a delegation was sent by the king to Hungary in 1054. The response was not immediate – after all, the younger Edward had spent nearly all his life outside England and probably did not even speak the language. Nevertheless, shortly afterwards he made his way to England. His sojourn in the country was tragically brief: he died shortly after arriving, breathing his last on 19 April 1057. This left his only son, Edgar, as virtually the last man (or more accurately boy) standing.[50]

One of the great imponderables of this period of history is whether or not Edward planned for William of Normandy to become king after his death. Much of the evidence in support of this, not least Harold Godwinsson's alleged oath to the duke to support his claim (which he subsequently reneged on), is based on potentially heavily biased Norman propagandists with a rather large axe to grind. It is difficult to have any confidence about what truly happened.

Then in 1065, Harold Godwinsson was involved in conflict in the south of Wales. This was not particularly unusual as there had been flare-ups fairly regularly involving the Welsh and the Anglo-Saxons. Just a couple of years previously one of the greatest of all Welsh medieval kings, Gruffydd ap Llywelyn, had finally been brought down after years of plotting and intriguing on his part had come to a head. For many years he had allied himself to Ælfgar, earl of Mercia. In many ways, Ælfgar was the odd man out. He was not a Godwin, and perhaps it was natural that he cooperated with his Welsh neighbour as a counterbalance to their power, an alliance sealed by the marriage of Ælfgar's daughter Ealdgyth to Gruffydd. But when Ælfgar died, Gruffydd raided across the border. Harold and Tostig led a counterattack which ended with the Welsh king being killed by his own men. Harold delivered two trophies to Edward as a mark of his triumph: the prow of Gruffydd's ship and the Welsh king's head. Harold also took the late king's widow as his wife.

In 1065 there was an ominous development with the outbreak of rebellion in Northumbria, allegedly due to the harsh rule of Earl Tostig.

Amongst other things Tostig was accused of murder and extortion. There can be little doubt as to his unpopularity. He had antagonised the Northumbrian aristocracy, a dangerous development in a place that was still to some extent a region apart. Amongst the accusations levelled at him were claims that he been responsible for the deaths in cold blood of several prominent nobles and that he had levied extortionate levels of taxation. He had also spent much of his time away in the south, a combination that was unlikely to please those answerable to him in the north. The dissatisfied aristocrats received support from two Mercian brothers, the sons of Ælfgar, Earl Edwin and Morcar, the latter of whom was nominated to succeed Tostig by the rebels. It was said that the rebels also received encouragement from no less a person than Harold Godwinsson, Tostig's brother, though this is doubtful.

The rebellion quickly gained momentum. Tostig lost some of his men and a Northumbrian army pushed south as far as Oxford. In the end, a negotiated settlement was agreed in which Tostig was undoubtedly the loser. This was a rebellion aimed at removing him, not the king. Tostig went into exile at the court of his father-in-law in Flanders as a bitter, angry man. His resentment festered and mutated, gnawing away at him until dark demons took over and he found himself hatching a plot through which he hoped to elevate his fallen fortunes. These developments were a shattering blow to Edward. Contemporary accounts suggest that he tried to summon an army to put the rebels back in their place but his call to arms was largely met with a deafening silence. Possibly he was ill too, and he may have suffered a stroke at Britford in Wiltshire.[51]

The Christmas celebrations for 1065 were held at Westminster but they were sombre for it was clear that the ailing king was close to the end. His death came sometime on 4/5 January 1066, probably due to a cerebral haemorrhage. Edward's funeral service took place on 6 January, and he was buried in the new church he had sponsored at Westminster. It was a symbolically perfect location. Edward had taken an obscure abbey and built it up into something new and magnificent (or rather, ironically, this would happen after he was dead), a place that continues to play a critical role in the affairs of the English nation a thousand years later. Edward's death closed the book on the Anglo-Saxon era and marked the dawn of a new epoch. He would achieve greatness but, like his contemporary Óláfr of Norway, it would be found in his death rather than his life.

It was not long before Edward's hagiographers were reporting miracles at his tomb. One man in particular, a man called Osbert of Clare who was once prior of the abbey, wrote a life of the king. Plentiful documents of doubtful validity were produced to prove Edward's supposed benefactions to the church. Various new miracles were added to the story of his life. Osbert, who was active in the first half of the twelfth century, was determined to bolster the reputation – and, being cynical, the revenues – of Westminster and did not particularly care how he did it. The 'fact' that the king had deliberately remained a virgin despite his married status was emphasised as an example of his extreme piety. A letter from Pope Alexander III, written at Anagni and dated 7 February 1161, formally recognised Edward as a saint. Two years later his earthly remains were translated to a more prominent spot in the abbey in the presence of Henry II and the current archbishop of Canterbury, a certain Thomas Becket; by the end of the conference these two would fall out in spectacular fashion. Edward ultimately became a sanctified and mythologized role model for English kings to follow, no less than eight subsequent monarchs of England bearing his name – this is something of an irony given the airbrushing of Anglo-Saxon Edwards from the regnal numbering model adopted by later historians.

What happened immediately after Edward's death is well known. 1066 was the year of three kings: Edward 'the Confessor', Harold Godwinsson and the Norman William 'the Conqueror'. Harold was crowned on the day of Edward's funeral in the very same church. This was also the year of three battles: Fulford, Stamford Bridge and Hastings. It saw the end of an old world and the start of a new one. Anglo-Saxon England would disappear, suffering beneath the tyranny of a Norman yoke. A world had died, and with it great dynasties. The Anglo-Danish Godwins were effectively if not literally wiped out at Stamford Bridge, where Tostig fell, and Hastings, where Harold, Gyrth and Leofwine followed him. Edward's death effectively brought to an end the line of the great dynasty which had, piece by painful piece, created a country called England from the patchwork of smaller kingdoms that had preceded it.[52] The greatness of this achievement cannot be underestimated. The dynasty may have ended, but the country it created lives on.

The Dynasty Lives On

When the Normans conquered England, they did not have to build a country for they found a ready-made one already there. They would make their own contribution, of course, but many of the organisational structures necessary to run an effective modern country were already in place. It is true that in metaphorical terms they lopped off the head of the structure and replaced it with their own ruling caste, but the essential administrative and bureaucratic machinery was already there.

By 1066, England was unrecognisable from the disparate patchwork it had been two centuries before. Rulers had evolved, as if from a chrysalis, from warlords to kings; and a region that was highly fragmented had become something akin to a unified nation state. There would be many more challenges to face over the succeeding centuries: civil wars, international conflicts, great epidemics and huge social upheaval. Even in the twenty-first century the future state of Britain is as unclear as it has been for a hundred years and more since Ireland went its own separate way and the British Empire began to evaporate. Yet for all that, England, and the concept of Englishness, remains – though for some there is a kind of unease about what it stands for sometimes. Whatever else happens, it is hard to imagine that this underlying reality is going anywhere anytime soon. None of this would have been possible without the contribution of perhaps Britain's greatest ever dynasty, though it is largely forgotten. It is well past time that their story should be told again, for their achievements saw their culture survive, and a nation was born that would eventually, for good or ill, have a profound impact not just on a small, insignificant island off the coast of Europe but across the entire world.

In a literal sense, the dynasty did not end with Edward. Edgar 'the ætheling' survived and was a viable candidate to be king. Indeed, Edgar was elected king after Hastings but lacked the support to defend his claim against those of the Norman William, who either decided to treat him kindly or simply didn't view him as a threat. In this case, might most certainly was right and Edgar eventually left for Scotland. His position was never strong anyway. He was only in his mid-teens in 1066, his experience was limited and he had spent the first half of his short life abroad; little to compare with a ruthless conqueror approaching the peak of his powers and prestige. Even so, many of William's potential subjects had little time for conquerors. The early years of his reign were characterised by violent upheavals, one of which led to the brutal campaign of repression known as 'the Harrowing of the North', which left much of the region a wasteland for decades.

This looked like the last contribution of Alfred's dynasty to the English royal bloodline, but not so. Edgar's sister Margaret, known as Margaret of Wessex, married Malcolm III, king of Scotland. Edgar himself went on to lead an adventurous life, albeit one lived largely outside of England. Historic labelling is always a dangerously simplistic concept, but what was loosely the Viking Age was morphing into the equally loosely categorised Age of the Crusades. The so-called First Crusade (actually a series of separate expeditions) set out to reconquer Jerusalem for Christendom in 1095. En route it faced a major obstacle at Antioch. When matters seemed to be in the balance, the pendulum swung the Crusaders' way when a fleet sailed into the nearby port of St Symeon. At its head was Edgar, who had joined it in Constantinople. He did not join the final successful push to Jerusalem, but he made a valuable contribution towards its ultimate outcome. He is last recorded in 1106 in the *ASC* as being captured in what was effectively a civil war in Normandy between Henry I, king of England and his brother Robert. Edgar had switched allegiances from Henry to Robert, a poor decision as the latter was defeated and spent the rest of his natural life in captivity in England. Edgar had greater fortune, and was 'afterwards let go unmolested'. No doubt it helped that his niece was married to the victor.[1]

Matilda (originally christened Edith, a revered Anglo-Saxon name), the daughter of Malcolm and Margaret and the great-great-granddaughter of Æthelred II, married Henry I in 1100 after spending some time in the nunnery at Wilton, very much a pillar of Anglo-Saxon culture (King Harold's daughter Gunnhild also became a nun there).[2] Henry, an unlikely claimant to the crown as there were older brothers ahead of him in the pecking order, no doubt saw the match as a way of strengthening his legitimacy.

It is also easy to overlook that Matilda perhaps saw marriage to Henry as a way of re-establishing what she almost certainly would have seen as the legitimate ruling dynasty.[3] The *ASC* certainly saw it this way, noting that the bride was 'of the rightful royal family of England'.[4] When Matilda died, she was buried next to Edward 'the Confessor' in Westminster Abbey, which soon became a national royal mausoleum and an essential symbol of 'Englishness'. Henry and Matilda had a daughter, also named Matilda, who became an empress and was the mother of Henry II, the first Plantagenet king of England. And so the bloodline of Alfred was reintroduced to the English ruling dynasty. Nine hundred years later, however much diluted by the passing of time, it flows there still.

Notes

Prologue: The Forgotten Dynasty

1. Although not widely used in modern works, the term Southumbria was often given to the lands south of the Humber in the past.

1 Beginnings

1. Both the Hwicce who lived in what we would now call the West Midlands and the nearby Magonsaetan whose lands bordered on Wales have names which suggest a British rather than Anglo-Saxon origin. Their absorption into Mercia can be seen in the downgrading of their rulers over time from kings to sub-kings and finally to mere earls. See Peers 36. The term heptarchy was first used by the twelfth-century historian Henry of Huntingdon.
2. Bede 38
3. Peers 26
4. Myres 14 suggests that 'Vortigern' is a title meaning something like 'proud tyrant' rather than a personal name.
5. Myres 47. Old Saxony is not the same as Saxony in modern Germany, a landlocked state in the east. Old Saxony is located on the North Sea coast and includes parts of the modern states of Lower Saxony and Westphalia amongst others. Orosius, the early fifth-century Roman writer, described the Saxons as 'a people of the Ocean settled in pathless swamps and on the sea shore' (in Myres 51).
6. The arguments are well-summarised in Peers 29–32
7. See e.g. Myres 85–87. See also map in Myres 88.
8. A heroic tradition still apparent in the tenth-century epic poem 'The Battle of Maldon' though it also shows commendable realism by describing supporters running away when faced with defeat rather than lose their lives as well as men fighting and dying heroically.
9. Bede 58

10. Unfortunately, there is no conclusive evidence of when precisely Gildas did write. The majority view is that it was in around 540 but some historians argue that it was several decades before this. Given the decisive nature of these early events as far as the longer-term formation of England is concerned this uncertainty is very regrettable.
11. Major 9
12. Myres 6 in summary suggests that we could do worse than follow the 'salutary scepticism' of the Venerable Bede and accept that there is so little chance of dating much with confidence that we should not worry too much about trying to do so in anything except very general terms.
13. Gildas 32
14. Ibid 13
15. Finberg 24
16. Marsden 62
17. This first amongst equals amongst the Anglo-Saxon kings was known as the *Bretwalda*. The provenance of this word is unclear. One version suggests it means 'wide ruler', another that it is 'Britain ruler'.
18. John 14–17 discusses the role of the *Bretwalda* in some detail.
19. See Author's Note.
20. In Marsden 101. Hatfield was claimed by the sixteenth-century writer to be at a site near Doncaster but there is in fact no convincing evidence for this. Peers 68 suggests that it may have been at Edwinstowe in Sherwood Forest, as does Zaluckyj.[30]
21. Oswald and Oswiu were not members of Edwin's bloodline which was decimated at Hatfield but of his predecessor Æthelfrith, the man who had attempted to dispose of Edwin when he was still a child.
22. Discussed further in Zaluckyj 31–32. An alternative suggestion for the siting of the battle is near Wigan.
23. Marsden 147
24. Yorke 19
25. Although rebuilt and added to on several occasions during the later Middle Ages and Renaissance, it stands on the site of the hostel – the *Schola Saxonum* – constructed by the West Saxon King Ine for visiting pilgrims in around 727.
26. Finberg 45
27. Peers 61
28. Although Charlemagne did not become emperor until 800, for ease of reference he will be given his imperial title throughout this book.
29. Peers 38
30. Peers 26, 38–39
31. See e.g. Yorke 10–11. A hide is often stated to be the area of land needed to feed a family for one year. The provenance and purpose of the *Tribal Hidage* is problematic. Some historians think it is Mercian, others Northumbrian. Some argue that it is a list that was used as the basis of calculating the tribute due to one particular kingdom from the others. There is a great deal of uncertainty about all of this. See also Wood 82–83.

32. Zaluckyj 17
33. See e.g. Peers 136–140
34. The Carolingian influence on Offa's thinking should not be overplayed. A recent biographer of Charlemagne suggests that it was not until the mid-790s, i.e. around the time of Offa's death, that Aachen became the royal palace of the future Holy Roman Emperor. See Nelson.[23]
35. Wood 88
36. See Nelson 26
37. Alcuin 57–58
38. Peers 147
39. Henry of Huntingdon 139
40. Myres 127
41. Myres 138
42. The exception was Essex whose kings claimed decent from Seaxnet who, although now little known, was still being honoured by continental Saxons in the eighth century. See Finberg 17, Yorke.[15]
43. Holland 21
44. Cerdic is certainly a British name and there was a king called this in Elmet, a late-remaining British enclave in Yorkshire in the early seventh century. This creates some question marks about whether the earlier 'Saxon' king with this name was actually Saxon at all.
45. Yorke 4
46. Clarkson *Æthelflæd* 21
47. Finberg 31
48. A thegn was a senior member of society, the next rank down from an ealdorman. Those from lower down the Anglo-Saxon social structure were known as ceorls, with slaves at the very bottom of the pile.
49. Whitehead 92
50. Or so says the Peterborough version of the *ASC*; the Winchester version calls them 'Danish men' as does the chronicler Æthelweard. Given the precise moment in history when this first raid took place, Hordaland, which is the region around Bergen, appears the more likely point of origin.
51. Æthelweard 27

2 Ecgberht and Æthelwulf

1. Æthelweard 28
2. Venning 109. Note that some modern historians dismiss the marriage to Redburga as a more recent fiction.
3. See Sarah Bowden, *Charlemagne's Unspeakable Sin,* https://tvof.ac.uk/blog/charlemagnes-unspeakable-sin, first published 10 June 2019, retrieved 13 July 2021.
4. Yorke 115
5. Venning 109
6. Zaluckyj 37
7. Ibid 153
8. Hindley 103

9. Venning 107. Henry of Huntingdon 142 suggests that Eadbert and Ecgberht were kinsmen though corroborating evidence of this is lacking.
10. Alcuin 10
11. Yorke 21
12. Henry of Huntingdon 141
13. *Brut Y Tywysogion* 11
14. Ibid
15. Venning 118
16. Stenton 231
17. Henry of Huntingdon 141
18. Details published in the *Daily Mail* of 31 January 2020.
19. As recorded in an account written at Reichenau in Germany; see Hadley and Richards 34.
20. Henry of Huntingdon 143
21. Ibid 144
22. *ASC* 60
23. Henry of Huntingdon 146
24. Whitehead 115, Zaluckyj 237
25. See Michel Rouche in Fossier 396
26. Charter from Wiglaf to archbishop Wulfred, granting land at Botwell, Middlesex, dated 831. In Sawyer 119.
27. The situation in ninth-century Denmark is somewhat confused. There were powerful kings such as Horic I during the period but how wide their rule was is unclear. Certainly, later in the century whatever unity there was unravelled and not until the time of Gorm in the tenth century did this situation change back again.
28. Price 305
29. Stenton 243 footnote 1 estimates that a Viking ship in 877 carried about thirty-seven fighting men.
30. Henry of Huntingdon 142
31. See Price 284
32. Reported as per the BBC at https://www.bbc.co.uk/news/uk-england-wiltshire-58028670 retrieved 7 August 2021. I am grateful to Robert Powell for pointing me in the direction of this interesting discovery.
33. Huscroft 41
34. Ibid 44
35. Note that some versions of the *ASC* say that Æthelstan was Æthelwulf's son, others that he was his brother. The majority view amongst historians seems to be that he was his son.
36. Huscroft 44
37. *Annals of St Bertin* year 839
38. Huscroft 98
39. Hinton 14
40. Ibid 66
41. Æthelweard 30
42. Ibid
43. *Annals of St Bertin* year 844

44. 'Long port' is an ominously familiar title, for chroniclers of the time referred to Viking bases as *longphuirt* (singular *longphort*) which means 'ship harbour'.
45. *ASC* year 848
46. *ASC* 64 note 5
47. Simeon of Durham 52
48. Henry of Huntingdon 150
49. *ASC* entry for 853
50. Simeon of Durham 53
51. Huscroft 46
52. Bartlett *Vikings* 114–115
53. Davies 81
54. See Hadley and Richards 51–53
55. Asser 69
56. Ibid
57. *ASC* for 855. The documents by which the king handed over his land to the Church are known evocatively as the Decimation Charters.
58. Asser 70. For a doubter's view, see Smyth 15.
59. A mancus was a gold coin, equivalent in value to thirty silver pence.
60. Sheila Sharp in Higham and Hill 80
61. The *Annals of St Bertin* record the events affecting Francia in the period in much the same way as the *ASC* did for England. St Bertin was a monastery on the north-west coast of Francia opposite Kent. However, the *Annals* were not written there but get their name because the only surviving copy of them was kept there. Note that Charles was not emperor at the time – he was king of West Francia – and would not become so for several decades, and then only briefly.
62. Huscroft 50–51. The two ealdormen in Kent reflected the situation in earlier periods when the kingdom often had two kings, one in the east, the other in the west. Rather than being joint kings with equal powers, quite often one – often in the west – would be junior to the other.
63. The arguments for and against forgery can be found in Smyth, chapters XI and XII, and Whitelock's *The Genuine Asser* respectively.
64. *Annals of St Bertin* 84

3 The Sons of Æthelwulf

1. Asser 73
2. *Annals of St Bertin* 97
3. Details in *Anglo-Saxon Charters* 151
4. See the entries for 860 in both the *ASC* and the *Annals of St Bertin*.
5. Asser 74
6. Asser 74, *ASC* for 865, Æthelweard 35
7. See Price 178
8. See Smyth, *Scandinavian Kings...* chapter IX. Some accounts have suggested that Ivarr and Óláfr were brothers but Smyth states that this hypothesis is in error.
9. *Historia de Sancto Cuthberto* 51

10. See Waggoner, Introduction x
11. *The Tale of Ragnar's Sons* and *The Saga of Ragnar Lodbrok and his Sons* are both translated in Waggoner.
12. For the diaspora, see Price chapter 13.
13. Price 302. Price's book cogently argues for a cocktail of factors that resulted in both 'push' and 'pull' elements that together combined to fuel motivations for Viking activity.
14. For the story of Harald's attempts to woo Gyda, see *Heimskringla* 52
15. Æthelweard 35
16. *ASC* for 866
17. Æthelweard 36
18. Hadley and Richards 202
19. Simeon of Durham 56
20. Price 92
21. *Annals of St Bertin*, 60, Footnote 1
22. See Smyth *Scandinavian Kings...* chapter IV.
23. *The Saga of Ragnar Lodbrok and his Sons* 27–31
24. Smyth *Scandinavian Kings...* 220
25. *The Saga of Ragnar Lodbrok and his Sons* 32–36. However there is various evidence to suggest that some of the brothers stayed in England with Ivarr.
26. *Fragmentary Annals* 348
27. Smyth *Scandinavian Kings...* 192
28. *The Tale of Ragnar's Sons* 68–70
29. Saxo Grammaticus 264–265
30. See especially Smyth, *Scandinavian Kings...* chapter I
31. In Smyth, *Scandinavian Kings...* 5
32. Zaluckyj 242
33. Asser 77
34. Whitehead 124. Who exactly the Gaini were is unclear but presumably they were one of the smaller regional groups who were eventually subsumed within Mercia of which the best-known example is probably the Hwicce. There were several men called Mucel attesting charters in Mercia between 814 and 866. See Keynes and Lapidge in Asser 240, Footnote 57. Clarkson *Æthelflæd* 24 suggests that there may be an echo of them in the name of the town of Gainsborough in Lincolnshire.
35. Abbo 22
36. *ASC* for 869
37. See Smyth *Scandinavian Kings*
38. Abbo 22
39. Swanton *ASC* 70 Footnote 2
40. Æthelweard 36
41. Asser 78
42. Abbo 33–34
43. Ibid 43–44
44. Ibid 48
45. William of Malmesbury *Bishops of England* 123

46. Hadley and Richards 227
47. Griffith 94. *Fragmentary Annals* year 870
48. Hill *Viking Wars* 38

4 On the Edge of a Precipice

1. Asser 78. Note that some historians are not at all convinced that Alfred was born in Wantage, which had only recently become part of Wessex and according to some might not even have been part of the kingdom at all at the time. See Smyth 5–7.
2. Æthelweard 37
3. See Hill *Viking Wars* 49 for an alternative suggestion that it was at Marten, 20 miles north of Wilton.
4. Smyth *Alfred...*385 As well as the references in the *ASC* details of the campaign in 871 can be found in Asser 78–81 and Æthelweard 37–40
5. Æthelweard 39
6. Hadley and Richards 74–78
7. Whitehead 125–126
8. From Kipling's poem 'Dane-geld' first published in 1911.
9. Chapter 4 in Hadley and Richards is devoted to the excavations at Torksey.
10. *ASC* for 873
11. Leahy 161–188
12. Hadley and Richards 115
13. Price 220
14. Details of the archaeology and its interpretation can be found at http://archaeology.co.uk/articles/features/resolving-repton.htm dated June 6 2019, retrieved June 14 2021.
15. Hill *Viking Wars* 60
16. Smyth 55
17. Whitehead 127
18. Hadley and Richards 233
19. *History of the Church of Durham* 655–656
20. Hadley and Richards 136
21. Æthelweard 41
22. Asser mentions the river Tarrant and not the Piddle. The Tarrant is a river further north in Dorset which flows into the Stour, which is some miles off from Wareham, so the biographer's geography here seems inaccurate.
23. Hinton 8
24. Æthelweard 41
25. See Asser 83, *ASC* for 876 and footnote 3
26. Wood 85
27. See Hill *Viking Wars* 71–73
28. *ASC* for 878
29. See Smyth 41–47 and Stenton *Abingdon* 30–32
30. Kelly 58–59

31. Details from Asser 83–84, the *ASC* for 878 and Æthelweard 42–43. Accounts of Viking casualties vary. Æthelweard says 800, the *ASC* 800 plus 40 of Ubba's personal warband, Asser 1,200.
32. See Smyth *Scandinavian Kings* appendix II
33. For a discussion of various possible locations for Ecgberht's Stone see Kelly, chapter 6.
34. Price 206
35. Bartlett, *Vikings* 85, quoting the words of Notker, a contemporary Frankish chronicler.
36. *Annals of St Bertin* year 876

5 Alfred the Great

1. *ASC* for 884 and 885, Æthelweard 44–45
2. Hadley and Richards 28–29
3. *Art, Word, War* 30
4. *Asser* 183
5. Huscroft 98–99
6. Ibid 100
7. Though not by Alfred Smyth (546–547) who takes issue with the views of many historians about various aspects of the king's reign.
8. See Keynes and Lapidge in the Introduction to Asser 27. Fulco's letter is reproduced in Asser 182–186
9. Asser 93, 103
10. Ibid 105
11. Ibid 94
12. According to William of Malmesbury he was working on the remaining psalms at the time of his death in 899.
13. Boethius xi
14. Asser 108
15. Extracts from the laws of Alfred are included in Asser 163–170
16. In *Asser* 188
17. Boethius in Asser 132
18. In Lavelle 20
19. Asser 102
20. Figures from the *Burghal Hidage* reproduced in Lavelle 21.
21. Asser 105
22. See Charter S1628 in Sawyer.
23. The dating can be worked out by a reference in Asser 101. He says here that Alfred was now in his forty-fifth year and elsewhere that he was born in 849. Not everyone is convinced that this birthdate is completely accurate but that is irrelevant to Asser's calculations.
24. Asser 270 footnote 220.
25. Ibid 41-42
26. *ASC* for 892
27. Æthelweard 49–50. These events involving Edward are not mentioned in the *ASC*.
28. Ibid 50

29. *History of the Church of Durham* 664–665
30. Hadley and Richards 131
31. Ibid 180–188
32. These names are unlikely to be exactly accurate; they sound far more Anglo-Saxon than Frisian.
33. The information included here is mostly from the *ASC* which were, as noted, far more detailed for these years than many others. Possibly this was because this was around the time that the great work was first written up at Winchester and these events were therefore fresh in the mind.
34. *Beowulf* 81
35. Huscroft 49–50
36. *History of the Church of Durham* 659
37. The *Life of St Neot* is translated in Asser 197–202 which also includes references to the later embellishments of the basic storyline which accreted themselves over time.
38. Asser 44–45
39. In Huscroft 73
40. The outline of the Old Minster can still partly be traced on the ground next to the later cathedral where it is marked out in brick.
41. Horspool 212–215
42. Details of the Alfred Jewel can be found in *Asser* 203–206

6 Edward and Æthelflæd

1. Asser 90
2. Barbara Yorke in Higham and Hill 27
3. Higham and Hill 32
4. Barbara Yorke in Higham and Hill 32. There is some disagreement amongst historians concerning when the new *ordo* was first used. Foot 18, quoting Nelson, suggests that it was called into use on the crowning of Æthelstan in 925. However, the innovation within it for the crowning of a queen as well as a king seems to make more sense in the context of Edward rather than Æthelstan. The latter did not have a queen.
5. In the previous version of the *ordo*, the king being consecrated would have a helmet rather than a crown placed on his head. In other words, this may be the first formal 'crowning' of an English monarch.
6. Norton 63
7. See Alfred's will in Asser 177
8. Barbara Yorke in Higham and Hill 31
9. Whitelock *English Historical Documents*, quoted by Alex Woolf in Higham and Hill 96
10. HH Wood, 152
11. *ASC* 92 footnote 8
12. Whitelock *EHD* 376
13. Clegg 27
14. Hadley and Richards 242, Hadley 55

15. Richard Hall in Higham and Hill 196
16. *ASC* for 903
17. Æthelweard 52
18. Higham and Hill 36
19. HH Wood 165
20. Æthelweard 52
21. William of Malmesbury 131
22. Ibid 139
23. Karras 38–45
24. Clarkson *Æthelflæd* 85
25. See Sheila Sharp in Higham and Hill 81
26. Clarkson *Æthelflæd* 85
27. The charter is translated in Whitelock 498.
28. The precise dating of this is extremely unclear and relies to some extent on some quite dubious later documentation which may include elements of fabrication. See Alexander R. Rumble in Higham and Hill 242.
29. Alexander R. Rumble in Higham and Hill 237
30. Ibid 244
31. See Keynes in Higham and Hill 50–56
32. *Fragmentary Annals* year 907
33. *Brut Y Tywysogion* year 900 although historians date the battle later, in 905; see David Griffiths in Higham and Hill 179.
34. *Fragmentary Annals* year 907
35. Ibid
36. See chapter 16 by James Graham-Campbell in Higham and Hill.
37. Æthelweard 53
38. Clarkson *Æthelflæd* 22–23
39. Ibid 39
40. Ibid 60
41. Clarkson *Æthelflæd* 118–119
42. Different versions of the *ASC* contradict each other, with the 'A' (Winchester) version saying it was Flat Holme, whilst the 'D' (Worcester) version suggests it was Steep Holme. The two islands are in fact near neighbours.
43. Swanton *ASC* 101 footnote 12 suggests this might have been at Wigmore in Herefordshire. This seems unlikely. Wigmore was very much in Mercia's sphere of influence rather than Edward's – it is unlikely therefore that Edward would have ordered a fort to be built there. In any event, all other attacks mentioned during the period were much further east of here.
44. Hadley and Richards 191–192
45. Ibid 197
46. Ibid chapter 10. They give Thetford as another good example of how a Viking Great Heathen Army camp later developed into a town.
47. Clarkson *Æthelflæd* 143–146
48. Symeon of Durham 86
49. See Hadley and Richards 261–262

50. The brief entries in the Mercian Register are reproduced in Clarkson *Æthelflæd* 179–180
51. Clarkson *Æthelflæd* 156
52. Maggie Bailey in Higham and Hill 124
53. *The Annals of Redon*
54. Michael R. Davidson in Higham and Hill 202
55. Clarkson *Strathclyde* 49
56. William of Malmesbury 131
57. See Keynes in Higham and Hill 41
58. *Prose Edda* 71–75

7 Æthelstan

1. Foot 30
2. Huscroft 115
3. Foot 17
4. William of Malmesbury 138
5. Hadley 48
6. Livingstone 10. Foot 194 suggests some doubt about whether the story about the lance is genuine or maybe an invention of William's based on an account in the *Chanson de Roland* which appeared in about the year 1100.
7. Foot 48
8. Reproduced in Whitelock 821–922. Æthelstan also founded a religious house at Muchelney in Somerset according to William of Malmesbury.
9. Bartlett *Vikings* 209
10. Foot 115–117
11. William of Malmesbury 133
12. See in the 'D' version of the *ASC* under the year 926 though it is generally accepted that these events actually took place the year after.
13. Michael R. Davidson in Higham and Hill 207
14. Symeon of Durham 88 suggests that Gothfrith was Sihtric's son.
15. Æthelweard 54
16. William of Malmesbury 133
17. Ibid
18. Ibid
19. Livingstone 10
20. Foot 97–98
21. Orme 94
22. In Foot 102
23. Reynolds 1
24. BBC documentary *King Alfred and the Anglo-Saxons*, 2013, episode 3
25. Barker and Brooks 10
26. Foot 214
27. *Heimskringla* 80–81
28. William of Malmesbury 134
29. Ibid 140
30. Simeon of Durham 88

31. Florence of Worcester 134, Simeon of Durham 88, Henry of Huntingdon 169. Many historians now believe that the history traditionally attributed to Florence of Worcester was in fact the work of John of Worcester.
32. Foot 166
33. Woolf 158
34. Foot 207
35. Another portrait of him from around the same time is known to have existed but was lost in a catastrophic fire at Ashburnham House in October 1731 when a number of priceless works were lost in one of the greatest tragedies ever to hit British antiquarianism.
36. *Simeon's History of the Church of Durham* 668–669, *Historia de Sancto Cuthberto* 65 which lists the twelve vills.
37. The charter is translated in Whitelock 505–508
38. Simeon of Durham *History of the Church of Durham* 669
39. Woolf 165
40. Simeon of Durham 88, John of Worcester 97
41. Woolf 168
42. Smyth *Scandinavian Kings* 151–152
43. *Egil's Saga* 88–91
44. See Orme 16
45. As quoted in a Wirral Archaeology press release dated 21 October 2019: retrieved from https://liverpooluniversitypress.blog/2019/10/22/the-search-for-the-battle-of-brunanburh-is-over/ on 6 December 2021.
46. See https://www.medievalists.net/2019/10/battle-brunanburh-battlefield-discovered/ retrieved 7 December 2021.
47. As suggested by Walker in Reuter 31–34
48. Quotes from the *ASC* in Livingston 39–43
49. *Egil's Saga* vii
50. Foot 188
51. William of Malmesbury 141

8 The Age of Edgar

1. Stenton 357
2. Wood 153-154
3. Simeon of Durham 89
4. *ASC* for 944.
5. Henry of Huntingdon 172
6. *ASC* 945
7. Henry of Huntingdon 172
8. See Hart. Ælfstan had witnessed a charter in Nottingham in June 934 but does not appear as a witness thereafter.
9. Dales 27
10. William of Malmesbury 143
11. *ASC* for 946
12. See under the year 952 in the *ASC*
13. See Downham *Eric Bloodaxe – Axed?*

14. William of Malmesbury 145
15. In Wood 165–167
16. *Egil's Saga* 130. Loki was the Norse trickster god who played an inglorious role in the events of Ragnarök. His daughter Hel was the loathsome goddess who ruled over the lands of the dead where those who were not chosen for Valhalla went. The 'eagle's food' is a graphic reference to the corpses of the dead who littered the fields of battle.
17. Quoted in Wood 151
18. Ibid 176
19. See Stenton in *ASC* year 952
20. Dales 38
21. See Keynes in Scragg 7
22. William of Malmesbury 145
23. See Venning 150
24. Henry of Huntingdon 173
25. Lavelle 40
26. Roger of Wendover 257
27. Dales 46
28. See *ASC* Worcester (D) version year 958
29. Dales 47
30. Keynes in Scragg 9
31. Jayakumar in Scragg 86. The Byrhthelm who became archbishop of Canterbury was soon replaced as it was felt he was not up to the task. He returned to his former position as archbishop of Wells where he stayed until his death in 973. Just to confuse matters further there was a third Bishop Byrhthelm (of Selsey) in post at around this time.
32. Dales 41
33. Simeon of Durham 91
34. Æthelweard 56
35. Roger of Wendover 259, Florence of Worcester 101, William of Malmesbury 146. As above, the work long attributed to 'Florence' of Worcester is now regarded by most historians as actually being primarily that of a fellow monk, John of Worcester.
36. Henry of Huntingdon 174
37. Jayakumar in Scragg 92–93
38. See *ASC* year 962 and footnote 2 (114).
39. Oswald would later be made a saint. He should not be confused with the seventh-century Northumbrian king and saint also called Oswald.
40. Keynes in Scragg 42
41. Keynes in Scragg 28
42. Jayakumar in Scragg 94
43. William of Malmesbury 160
44. Norton 53–55
45. Jayakumar in Scragg 98
46. Keynes in Scragg 3
47. Norton 55
48. Alexander 30

49. Florence of Worcester 105
50. Keynes in Scragg 13
51. Peterborough version year 959
52. Translation by Whitelock quoted in Abrams in Scragg 171
53. Norton 96
54. Florence of Worcester 105–106
55. William of Malmesbury 147
56. Keynes in Scragg 4
57. William of Malmesbury 162
58. Quoted in Reynolds 25
59. Winchester version year 975
60. Dales *Dunstan* 56
61. Keynes in Scragg 57
62. In Scragg 54
63. Quoted in Norton 130

9 Ragnarök

1. Florence of Worcester 107
2. In Whitehead 94
3. Florence of Worcester 107
4. Ibid 109
5. Lavelle *Aethelred* 55
6. Quotes from Alexander 114–123
7. Lavelle *Aethelred* 70
8. Ibid 78–79
9. Williams 24–25
10. Lavelle *Aethelred* 102
11. *ASC* years 1001 and 1002
12. Peterborough version year 1002
13. William of Malmesbury 185
14. Roger of Wendover 283
15. Henry of Huntingdon 184
16. Florence of Worcester 114
17. Reproduced in Whitelock *English Historical Documents* 545
18. See Bartlett *Cnut* 70–71. The Ridgeway finds are described in detail in Loe *et al.*
19. Henry of Huntingdon 114
20. Peterborough version year 1004
21. Barlow *Edward* 3
22. Lavelle *Æthelred* 117
23. Henry of Huntingdon 116
24. The details and quotes concerning these years are mainly drawn from the *ASC* for 1009–1011.
25. See e.g. Lavelle *Aethelred* chapter 10 for a justification of his actions.
26. *ASC* year 1011
27. Florence of Worcester 120
28. Ibid

29. Urry 82
30. *ASC* year 1013
31. Florence of Worcester 123
32. *ASC* year 1014
33. Ibid
34. William of Malmesbury 191
35. *ASC* year 1015
36. A story that is compellingly retold in Fletcher *Bloodfeud*.
37. *ASC* year 1016
38. Ibid
39. Ibid
40. Ibid
41. See Barlow *Edward* 40
42. *The Life of King Edward the Confessor* 13–14
43. Barlow *Edward* 63
44. Barlow *Godwins* 49
45. One consequence of Danish influence was that ealdormen increasingly came to be known as earls, similar to the Scandinavian jarl.
46. For considerable doubts about this course of events, see Barlow *Edward* 108.
47. Eustace was the second husband of Godgifu, daughter of Æthelred.
48. Barlow *Edward* 134
49. Ibid 192
50. Edgar was probably around five years old at the time. Æthelred's daughter, Godgifu, King Edward's sister, had two sons, both of whom died before 1066. One of these sons was the father of a boy, Harold, who was still alive when King Edward died so he was also in a direct line of ascent to the English throne.
51. Barlow *Edward* 240
52. Some historians argue that Harold was descended from a line that could be traced back to the chronicler Æthelweard and through him the Anglo-Saxon ruling dynasty, but this is far from certain.

Epilogue: The Dynasty Lives On

1. *ASC* Version E ('Peterborough')
2. Gunnhild's status as a nun did not stop her from being involved in some scandalous relationships which may or may not have involved marriage but certainly involved her living with several men. She later claimed in a letter to Anselm, archbishop of Canterbury, that she had never been formally consecrated as a nun. Edith/Matilda had first spent time at Romsey before transferring to Wilton when still a child.
3. Hollister 127
4. Peterborough version year 1100.

Bibliography

Primary sources

Alexander, Michael (translated): *The Earliest English Poems*, Penguin, 1970

Allott, Stephen: *Alcuin of York*, Sessions Book Trust, York, 1987

Barlow, Frank (edited): *The Life of King Edward the Confessor*, Thomas Nelson and Sons, London etc. 1962

Campbell, A (edited): *The Chronicle of Æthelweard*, Thomas Nelson and Sons, London etc., 1962

Elton, Oliver: *The Danish History – The Nine Books of the Danish History of Saxo Grammaticus*, Bravo Ebooks, undated reprint of a work published in 1905

Forest, Thomas (translated): *The Chronicle of Henry of Huntingdon – Comprising the History of England, From the Invasion of Julius Caesar to the Accession of Henry II*, London, 1853

Giles, JA (translated): *Gildas – On The Ruin of Britain (De Excidio Brittaniae)*, Serenity Publishers, Rockville, Maryland, 2009

Giles, JA (translated): *Roger of Wendover's Flowers of History Volume 1*, Henry G Bohn, 1849

Giles, JA (translated): *William of Malmesbury's Chronicle of the King of England*, Henry G Bohn, London, 1857 (republished by Forgotten Books, 2012)

Heaney, Seamus (translated): *Beowulf*, 1999

Hennessy, William Mac (translated): *Annals of Ulster*, HMSO, Dublin, 1887

Hollis, Stephanie with WR Barnes, Rebecca Hayward, Kathleen Loncar, and Michael Wright: *Writing the Wilton Women – Goscelin's Legend of Edith and Liber consortatorius*, Brepols Publishers, Turnhout, Belgium, 2004

Ibhel, The Rev. John Williams ab (edited): *Brut Y Tywysogion or the Chronicle of the Princes*, Longman, London, 1860

Keynes, Simon and Lapidge, Michael (translated): *Asser's Life of King Alfred and Other Contemporary Sources*, Penguin, London etc., 1983

Laing, S: *Snorre Sturlason (sic): Heimskringla – The Norse King Sagas*, Lightning Source UK, undated reprint, first published 1844

Lapidge, Michael (edited and translated): *Byrhtferth of Ramsey – The Lives of St Oswald and St Ecgwine*, Clarendon, Oxford, 2010

Nelson, Janet L (translated and annotated): *The Annals of St Bertin*, Manchester University Press, Manchester and New York, 1991

Preest, David (translated): *The Deeds of the Bishops of England (Gesta Pontificum Anglorum)*, Boydell Press, Woodbridge, 2002

Radice, Betty (edited): *Boethius – The Consolation of Philosophy*, Penguin, London etc., 1999

Radner, Joan Newlon (translated): *The Fragmentary Annals of Ireland*, copyright School of Celtic Studies, Dublin Institute of Advanced Studies, available online at https://celt.ucc.ie//published/T100017.html and retrieved on 10 May 2021

Sawyer, P.H: *Anglo-Saxon Charters – An Annotated List and Bibliography*, Offices of the Royal Historical Society, London, 1968

Scudder, Bernard: *Egil's Saga*, Penguin, London etc., 2004

Sherley-Price, Leo (translated): *Bede – A History of the English Church and People*, Penguin Books, Harmondsworth etc., 1979

Smith, Ted Johnson (edited): *Historia de Sancto Cuthberto*, DS Brewer, Cambridge, 2002

Stevenson, J (translated): *Simeon of Durham – A History of the Church of Durham*, Church Historians of England, 1855 (facsimile reprint, Llanerch Enterprises, 1993)

Stevenson, J (translated): *Simeon of Durham – A History of the Kings of England*, Church Historians of England, 1858 (facsimile reprint, Llanerch Enterprises, 1987)

Swanton, Michael (translated and edited): *The Anglo-Saxon Chronicles*, Orion, London, 2003

Waggoner, Ben (translated): *The Sagas of Ragnar Lodbrok*, Troth Publications, New Haven, 2009

Webb, Simon: *The Passion of Saint Edmund by Abbo of Fleury*, Langley Press, 2018 [reissue of a 1907 translation by Francis Hervey)

Whitelock, Dorothy: *English Historical Documents I c500-1042*, Eyre & Spottiswoode, London, 1955

Winterbottom, Michael and Lapidge, Michael (edited and translated): *The Early Lives of St Dunstan*, Clarendon Press, Oxford, 2011

Secondary sources

Barlow, Frank: *Edward the Confessor*, Yale University Press, New Haven & London, 1997 edition

Barlow, Frank: *The Godwins – The Rise and Fall of a Noble Dynasty*, Routledge, London and New York, 2013

Barker, Katherine with Brooks, Nicholas: *Aldhelm and Sherborne – Essays to celebrate the founding of the bishopric,* Oxbow Books, Oxford and Oakville, 2010

Bartlett, WB: *King Cnut and the Viking Conquest of England 1016,* Amberley, Stroud, 2016

Bartlett, WB: *Vikings – A History of the Northmen,* Amberley, Stroud, 2019

Breay, Claire and Story, Joanna (edited): *Anglo-Saxon Kingdoms – Art, Word, War,* British Library, 2018

Chandler, John: *A Higher Reality – The History of Shaftesbury's Royal Nunnery,* Hobnob Press, Salisbury, 2003

Clarkson, Tim: *Æthelflæd: The Lady of the Mercians,* Birlinn, Edinburgh, 2018

Clarkson, Tim: *Strathclyde and the Anglo-Saxons in the Viking Age,* Birlinn, Edinburgh, 2014

Clegg, A Lindsay: *A History of Wimborne Minster and District,* Outspoken Press, Bournemouth, 1960

Dales, Douglas: *Dunstan – Saint and Statesman,* James Clarke & Co, Cambridge, 2013

Davies, John: *A History of Wales,* Penguin Books, London etc., 1993

Downham, Clare: *Eric Bloodaxe – Axed? The Mystery of the Last Scandinavian King of York, Medieval Scandinavia 14,* 2004

Finberg, HPR: *The Formation of England 550-1042,* Paladin, St Albans 1974

Fletcher, Richard: *Bloodfeud -Murder and Revenge in Anglo-Saxon England,* Allen Lane, London etc. 2002

Foot, Sarah: *Æthelstan – The First King of England,* Yale University Press, New Haven and London, 2011

Fossier, Robert (edited)/Sondheimer, Janet (translated): *The Cambridge Illustrated History of the Middle Ages 350-950,* Cambridge University Press, Cambridge, 1989

Gneuss, Helmut: *Ælfric of Eynsham – His Life, Times, and Writings –* Old English Newsletter Subsidia 34, Medieval Institute Publications, Western Michigan University, 2009

Griffiths, Paddy: *The Viking Art of War,* Casemate, Philadelphia & Newbury, 1995

Hadley, DM: *The Vikings in England – Settlement, Society and Culture,* Manchester University Press, Manchester, 2006

Hadley, Dawn M and Richards, Julian D: *The Viking Great Army and the Making of England,* Thames and Hudson Ltd, London, 2021

Hart, Cyril: *Athelstan 'Half King' and his Family, Anglo-Saxon England 2,* 1973, 115–44. http://www.jstor.org/stable/44510619.

Haywood, John: *Dark Age Naval Power – Frankish and Anglo-Saxon Seafaring Activity,* Anglo-Saxon Books, Norfolk, 1999 (2006 reprint)

Higham, NJ and Hill, DH: *Edward the Elder 899-924,* Routledge, London and New York, 2009

Hill, Paul: *The Anglo-Saxons at War 800-1066,* Pen & Sword, Barnsley, 2016

Hill, Paul: *The Viking Wars of Alfred the Great,* Pen & Sword, Barnsley, 2008

Hindley, Geoffrey: *A Brief History of the Anglo-Saxons,* Robinson, London, 2015

Hinton, David A: *Alfred's Kingdom – Wessex and the South 800-1500,* Book Club Associates, 1977

Holland, Tom: *Athelstan – The Making of England,* Allen Lane, 2016

Hollister, C. Warren: *Henry I,* Yale University Press, 2003

Horspool, David: *Alfred the Great,* Amberley, Stroud, 2014

Huscroft, Richard: *Making England, 796-1042,* Routledge, Amazon & New York, 2019

John, Eric: *Orbis Britanniae and Other Studies,* Leicester University Press, 1966

Karras, Ruth Mazo: *Unmarriages – Women, Men, and Sexual Unions in the Middle Ages,* University of Philadelphia Press, Pennsylvania, 2012

Kelly, Dr Paul: *King Alfred: A Man on the Move,* Black Slash Publications, Weymouth, 2019

Lavelle, Ryan: *Aethelred II, King of the English:* The History Press, Stroud, 2008

Lavelle, Ryan: *Fortifications in Wessex c800-1066,* Osprey Publishing, Oxford, 2003

Lavelle, Ryan and Roffey, Simon: *Danes in Wessex – The Scandinavian Impact on Southern England c800-c1100,* Oxbow Books, Oxford & Philadelphia, 2016

Leahy, Kevin: *The Anglo-Saxon Kingdom of Lindsey,* The History Press, Sutton, 2010

Livingstone, Michael (edited): *The Battle of Brunanburh – A Casebook,* University of Exeter Press, Exeter, 2011

Loe, Louise, Boyle, Angela, Webb, Helen and Score, David: *'Given to the Ground' – A Viking Age Mass Grave on Ridgeway Hill, Weymouth:* Dorset Natural History and Archaeological Society Monograph Series: No. 22 2014

Major, Albany: *Early Wars of Wessex,* Blandford Press, Poole, 1978 (first published 1913)

Marsden, John: *Northanhymbre Saga – The History of the Anglo-Saxon Kings of Northumbria,* Kyle Cathie Ltd, London, 1992

Myres, JNL: *The English Settlements,* Oxford University Press, Oxford etc., 1986

Nelson, Janet L: *Charles the Bald,* Longman, London and New York, 1992

Nelson, Janet L: *King and Emperor – A New Life of Charlemagne,* Allen Lane, UK etc., 2019

Norton, Elizabeth: *Elfrida – The First Crowned Queen of England,* Amberley, Stroud, 2014

Orme, Nicholas: *Medieval Pilgrimage – With a Survey of Cornwall, Devon, Dorset, Somerset and Bristol,* Imprest Books Limited, Exeter, 2018

Peers, Chris: *Offa and the Mercian Wars – The Rise and Fall of the First Great English Kingdom,* Pen & Sword, Barnsley, 2017

Price, Neil: *The Children of Ash & Elm – A History of the Vikings,* Allen Lane, UK etc., 2020

Randsborg, Klavs: *The Viking Age in Denmark,* Duckworth, London, 1980

Reuter, Timothy (edited): *Warriors and Churchmen in the High Middle Ages: Essays Presented to Karl Leyser,* Hambledon Press, London, 1992

Reynolds, Andrew: *Anglo-Saxon Deviant Burial Customs,* Oxford University Press, Oxford, 2009

Scragg, Donald (edited): *Edgar – King of the English, 959-975,* The Boydell Press, Woodbridge, 2008

Smyth, Alfred P: *King Alfred the Great,* Oxford University Press, Oxford, 1995

Smyth, Alfred P: *Scandinavian Kings in the British Isles 850-880,* Oxford University Press, Oxford, 1977

Stenton, Sir Frank: *Anglo-Saxon England,* Oxford University Press, Oxford, 1988 (third edition)

Stenton, FM: *The Early History of the Abbey of Abingdon,* Paul Watkins, Stamford, 1989

Urry, William: *Thomas Becket – His Last Days,* Sutton Publishing Ltd, Stroud, 1999

Venning, Timothy: *The Kings & Queens of Anglo-Saxon England,* Amberley, Stroud, 2013

Welch, Martin: *Anglo-Saxon England,* B T Batsford, London, 1992

Whitehead, Annie: *Mercia – The Rise and Fall of a Kingdom,* Amberley, Stroud, 2020

Whitelock, Dorothy: *The Genuine Asser [The Stenton Lecture 1967,* University of Reading, 1968

Williams, Ann: *Æthelred the Unready – The Ill-Counselled King,* Hambledon and London, London and New York, 2003

Wood, Harriet Harvey: *Edward the Elder and the Making of England,* Sharpe Books, 2018

Wood, Michael: *In Search of the Dark Ages,* Book Club Associates, London, 1981

Woolf, Alex: *From Pictland to Alba,* Edinburgh University Press, 2014 edition

Yorke, Barbara: *Kings and Kingdoms of Early Anglo-Saxon England,* Routledge, London and New York, 1990

Young, Francis: *Edmund – In Search of England's Lost King,* JB Tauris, 2018

Zaluckyj, Sarah: *Mercia – The Anglo-Saxon Kingdom of Central England,* Logaston Press, Herefordshire, 2013 edition

Index